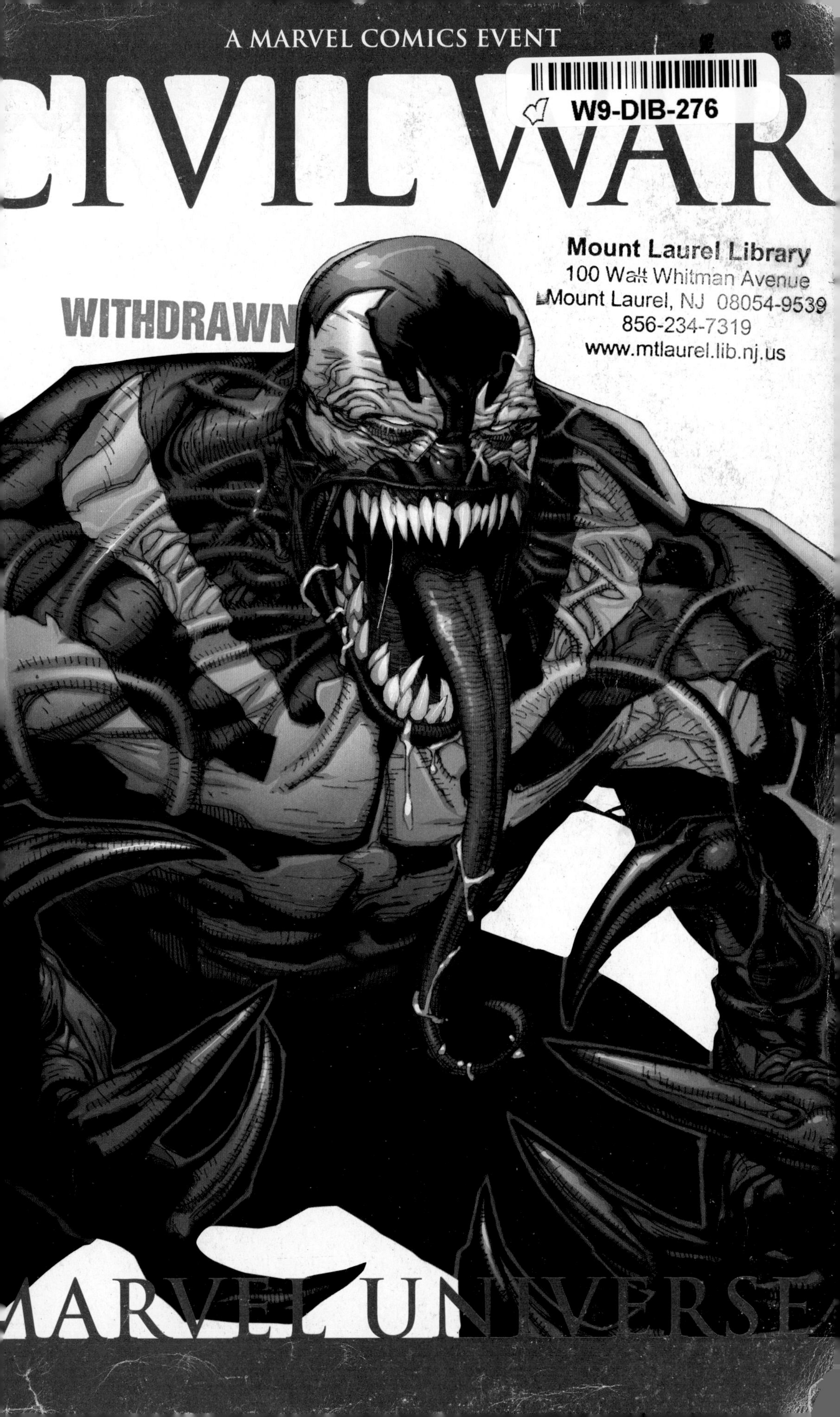
A MARVEL COMICS EVENT
CIVIL WAR
MARVEL UNIVERSE

A

MARVEL COMICS

PRESENTATION

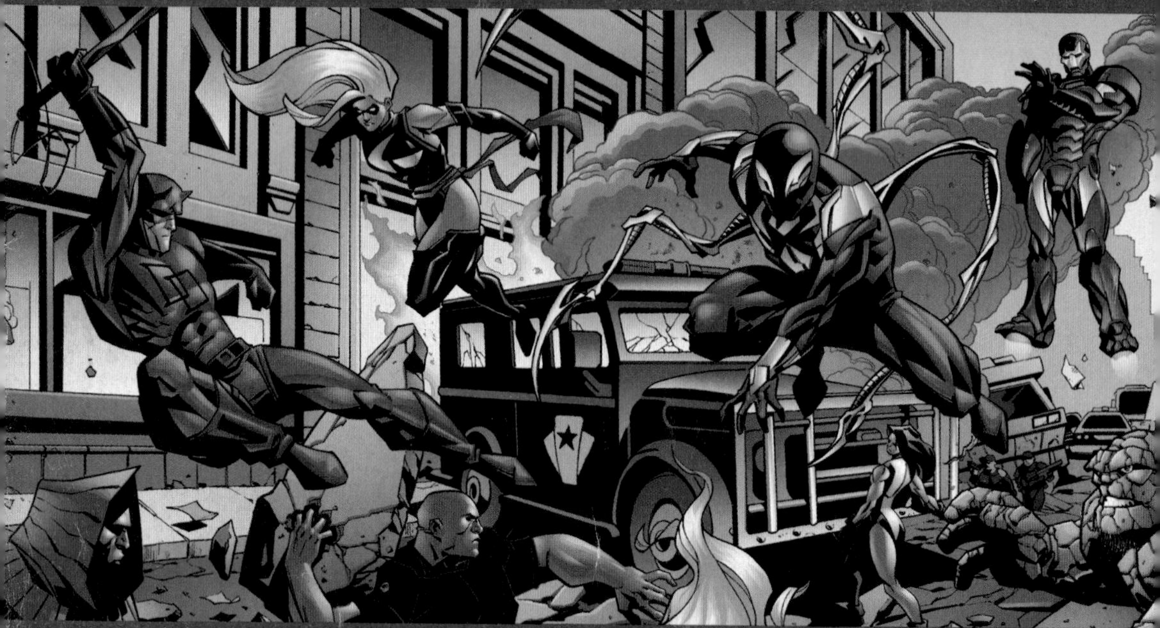

CIVIL

MA

SHE-HULK #8

WRITER
DAN SLOTT

ARTIST
PAUL SMITH

COLORIST
AVALON'S DAVE KEMP

LETTERER
DAVE SHARPE

COVER ART
GREG HORN

ASSISTANT EDITORS
MOLLY LAZER &
AUBREY SITTERSON

EDITOR
TOM BREVOORT

CIVIL WAR: THE RETURN

WRITER
PAUL JENKINS

PENCILER
TOM RANEY

INKER
SCOTT HANNA

COLORIST
GINA GOING (PAGES 1-13) &
SOTOCOLOR'S
A. CROSSLEY (PAGES 14-23)

LETTERER
DAVE SHARPE

ASSISTANT EDITORS
MOLLY LAZER & AUBREY
SITTERSON

EDITOR
STEVE WACKER

CIVIL WAR: THE INITIATIVE

WRITERS
BRIAN MICHAEL BENDIS &
WARREN ELLIS

PENCILS
MARC SILVESTRI

ART & LETTERS
TOP COW PRODUCTIONS

COLORS
FRANK D'ARMATA

ASSISTANT EDITORS
MOLLY LAZER &
AUBREY SITTERSON

EDITOR
TOM BREVOORT

CIVIL WAR: CHOOSING SIDES

WRITERS
MARC GUGGENHEIM,
ROBERT KIRKMAN,
ED BRUBAKER &
MATT FRACTION,
MICHAEL AVON OEMING
& TY TEMPLETON

ARTISTS
LEINIL YU,
PHIL HESTER &
ANDE PARKS,
DAVID AJA,
SCOTT KOLINS &
ROGER LANGRIDGE

COLORISTS
DAVE MCCAIG,
BILL CRABTREE,
MATT HOLLINGSWORTH,
BRIAN REBER &
SOTOCOLOR'S J. BROWN

LETTERERS
VIRTUAL CALLIGRAPHY'S
JOE CARAMAGNA &
DAVE LANPHEAR

EDITORS
MOLLY LAZER,
AUBREY SITTERSON,
WARREN SIMONS,
ANDY SCHMIDT &
TOM BREVOORT

WAR
VEL UNIVERSE

COLLECTION EDITOR
JENNIFER GRÜNWALD

ASSISTANT EDITORS
MICHAEL SHORT &
CORY LEVINE

ASSOCIATE EDITOR
MARK D. BEAZLEY

SENIOR EDITOR,
SPECIAL PROJECTS
JEFF YOUNGQUIST

SENIOR VICE
PRESIDENT OF SALES
DAVID GABRIEL

PRODUCTION
JERRY KALINOWSKI

BOOK DESIGNER
DAYLE CHESLER

VICE PRESIDENT
OF CREATIVE
TOM MARVELLI

EDITOR IN CHIEF
JOE QUESADA

PUBLISHER
DAN BUCKLEY

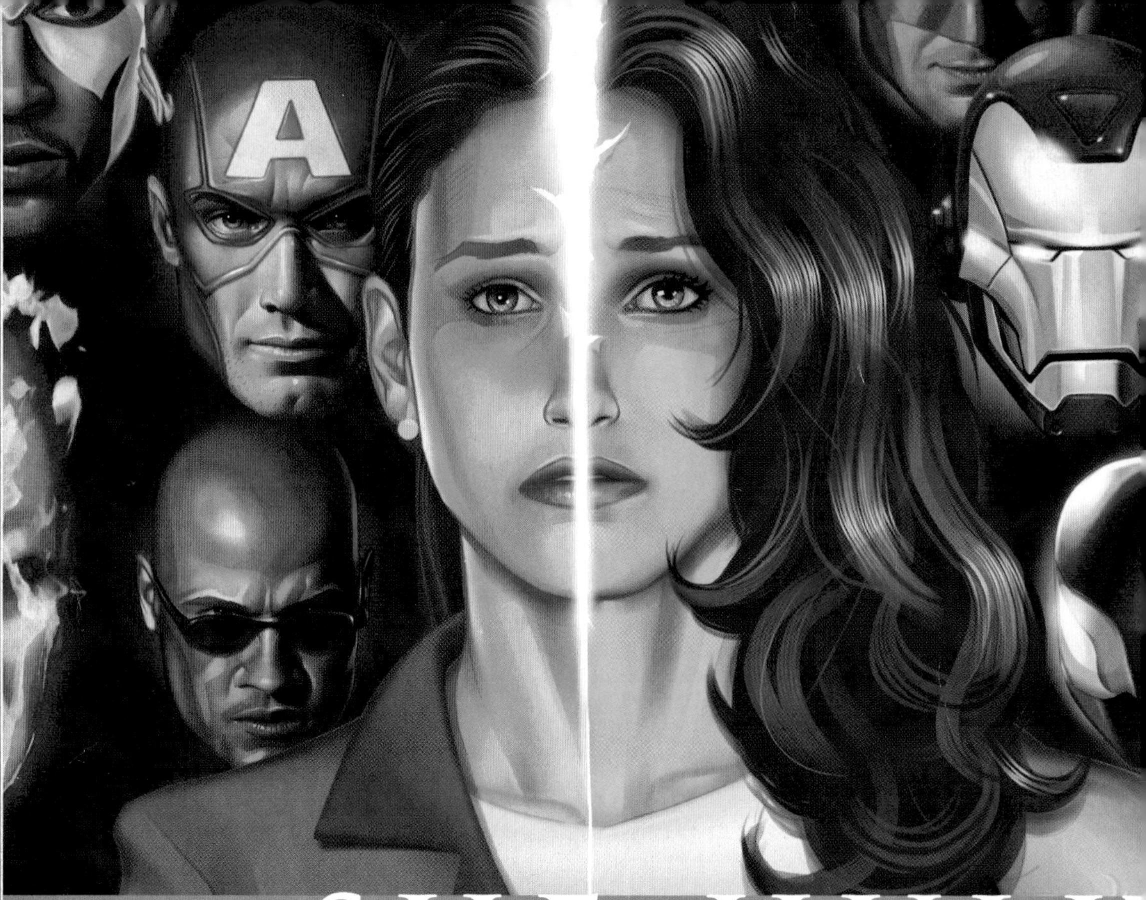

SHE-HULK

A MARVEL COMICS EVEN

CIVIL WAR

SHE-HULK #8

NIFER WALTERS HAD ALWAYS THOUGHT THAT BEING A LAWYER WAS IN HER BLOOD... UNTIL A GAMMA-IRRADIATED BLOOD TRANSFUSION GAVE HER THE ABILITY TO CHANGE INTO THE WORLD'S SEXIEST, SASSIEST, AND STRONGEST SUPER HEROINE:

PREVIOUSLY IN CIVIL WAR

Hoping to boost their ratings, four New Warriors, young super heroes and reality television stars, attempted to apprehend a quartet of villains holed up in Stamford, Connecticut. Unfortunately, when confronted, the explosive Nitro employed his self-detonation ability, blowing the New Warriors and a large chunk of Stamford to oblivion. The entire incident was caught on tape.

Casualties number in the hundreds.

As a reaction to this tragedy, public outcry calls for reform in the way super heroes conduct their affairs. On Capitol Hill, a Superhuman Registration Act is debated which would require all those possessing paranormal abilities to register with the government, divulging their true identities to the authorities and submitting to training and sanctioning in the manner of federal agents.

Some heroes, such as Iron Man, see this as a natural evolution of the role of super heroes in society, and a reasonable request. Others, embodied by Captain America, take umbrage at this assault on their civil liberties.

When Captain America is called upon to hunt down his fellow heroes who are in defiance of the Registration Act, he chooses to go AWOL, becoming a public enemy in the process.

In the wake of the tragedy in Stamford, She-Hulk appears on CNN advocating the training and licensing of super heroes...

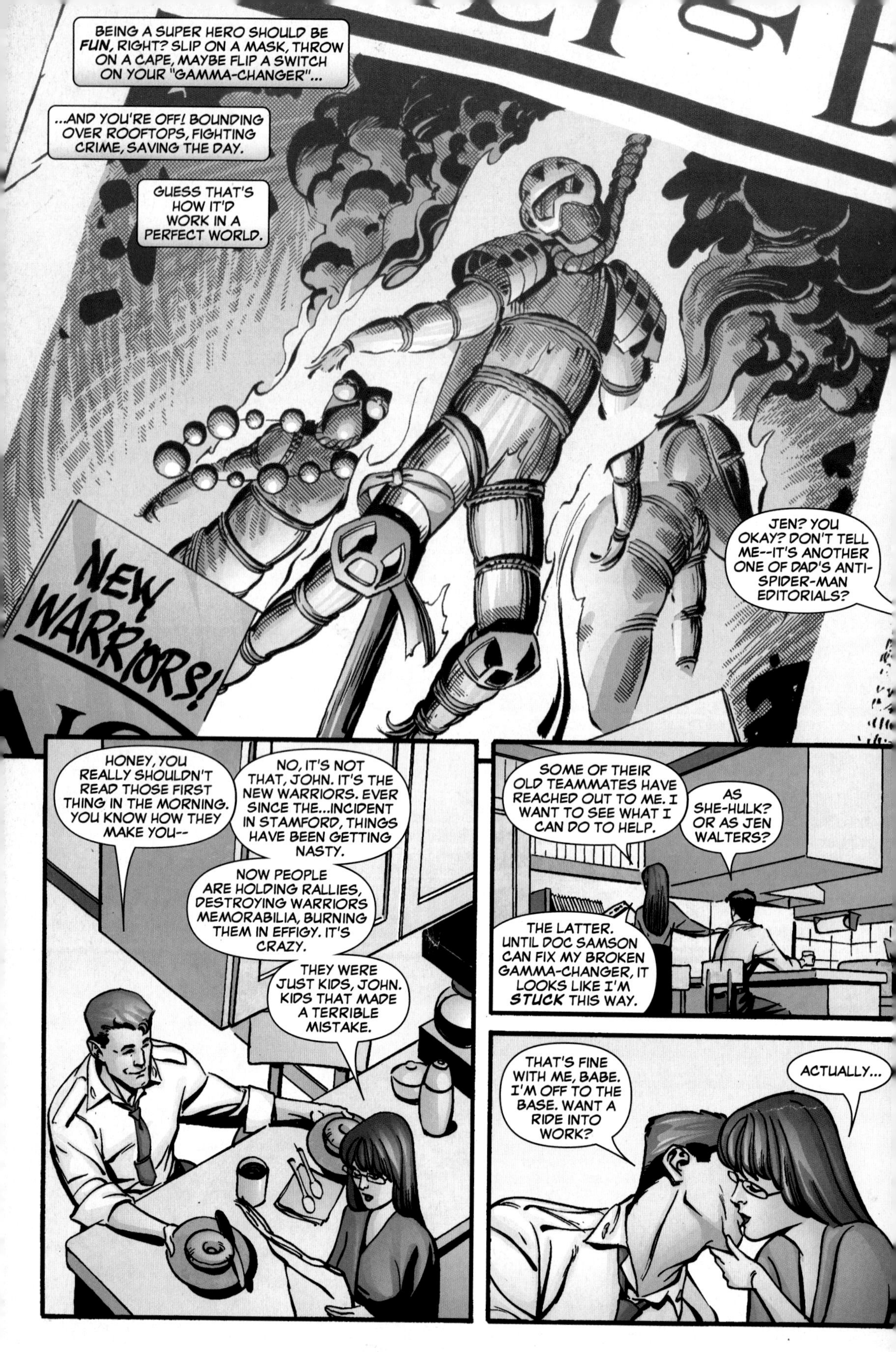
BEING A SUPER HERO SHOULD BE FUN, RIGHT? SLIP ON A MASK, THROW ON A CAPE, MAYBE FLIP A SWITCH ON YOUR "GAMMA-CHANGER"...
...AND YOU'RE OFF! BOUNDING OVER ROOFTOPS, FIGHTING CRIME, SAVING THE DAY.
GUESS THAT'S HOW IT'D WORK IN A PERFECT WORLD.
NEW WARRIORS!
JEN? YOU OKAY? DON'T TELL ME--IT'S ANOTHER ONE OF DAD'S ANTI-SPIDER-MAN EDITORIALS?
HONEY, YOU REALLY SHOULDN'T READ THOSE FIRST THING IN THE MORNING. YOU KNOW HOW THEY MAKE YOU--
NO, IT'S NOT THAT, JOHN. IT'S THE NEW WARRIORS. EVER SINCE THE...INCIDENT IN STAMFORD, THINGS HAVE BEEN GETTING NASTY.
NOW PEOPLE ARE HOLDING RALLIES, DESTROYING WARRIORS MEMORABILIA, BURNING THEM IN EFFIGY. IT'S CRAZY.
THEY WERE JUST KIDS, JOHN. KIDS THAT MADE A TERRIBLE MISTAKE.
SOME OF THEIR OLD TEAMMATES HAVE REACHED OUT TO ME. I WANT TO SEE WHAT I CAN DO TO HELP.
AS SHE-HULK? OR AS JEN WALTERS?
THE LATTER. UNTIL DOC SAMSON CAN FIX MY BROKEN GAMMA-CHANGER, IT LOOKS LIKE I'M STUCK THIS WAY.
THAT'S FINE WITH ME, BABE. I'M OFF TO THE BASE. WANT A RIDE INTO WORK?
ACTUALLY...

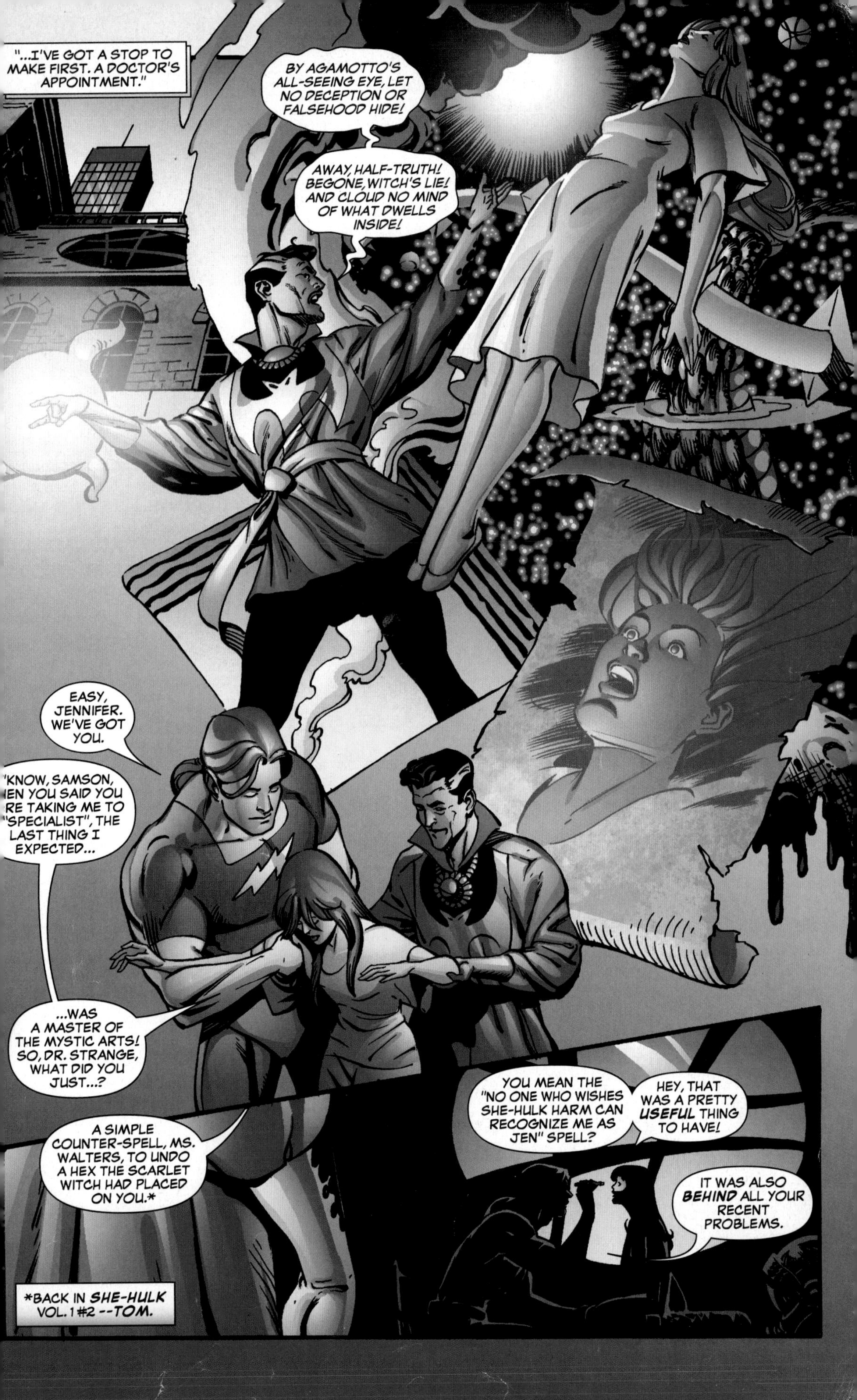
"...I'VE GOT A STOP TO MAKE FIRST. A DOCTOR'S APPOINTMENT."
BY AGAMOTTO'S ALL-SEEING EYE, LET NO DECEPTION OR FALSEHOOD HIDE!
AWAY, HALF-TRUTH! BEGONE, WITCH'S LIE! AND CLOUD NO MIND OF WHAT DWELLS INSIDE!
EASY, JENNIFER. WE'VE GOT YOU.
'KNOW, SAMSON, IEN YOU SAID YOU RE TAKING ME TO "SPECIALIST", THE LAST THING I EXPECTED...
...WAS A MASTER OF THE MYSTIC ARTS! SO, DR. STRANGE, WHAT DID YOU JUST...?
A SIMPLE COUNTER-SPELL, MS. WALTERS, TO UNDO A HEX THE SCARLET WITCH HAD PLACED ON YOU.*
YOU MEAN THE "NO ONE WHO WISHES SHE-HULK HARM CAN RECOGNIZE ME AS JEN" SPELL?
HEY, THAT WAS A PRETTY USEFUL THING TO HAVE!
IT WAS ALSO BEHIND ALL YOUR RECENT PROBLEMS.
*BACK IN SHE-HULK VOL. 1 #2 --TOM.

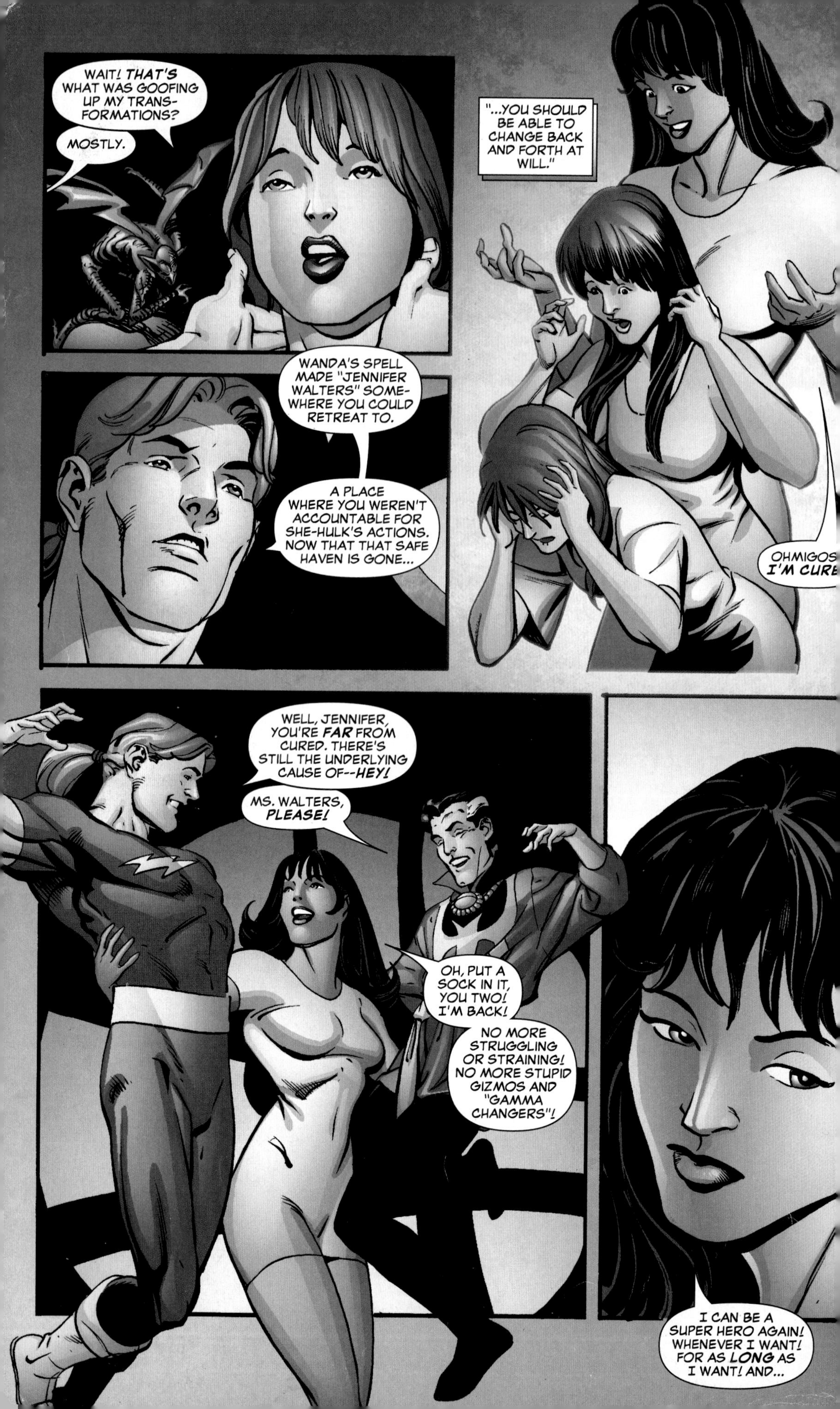
WAIT! THAT'S WHAT WAS GOOFING UP MY TRANS-FORMATIONS?
MOSTLY.
"...YOU SHOULD BE ABLE TO CHANGE BACK AND FORTH AT WILL."
WANDA'S SPELL MADE "JENNIFER WALTERS" SOME-WHERE YOU COULD RETREAT TO.
A PLACE WHERE YOU WEREN'T ACCOUNTABLE FOR SHE-HULK'S ACTIONS. NOW THAT THAT SAFE HAVEN IS GONE...
OHMIGOS
I'M CURE
WELL, JENNIFER, YOU'RE FAR FROM CURED. THERE'S STILL THE UNDERLYING CAUSE OF--HEY!
MS. WALTERS, PLEASE!
OH, PUT A SOCK IN IT, YOU TWO! I'M BACK!
NO MORE STRUGGLING OR STRAINING! NO MORE STUPID GIZMOS AND "GAMMA CHANGERS"!
I CAN BE A SUPER HERO AGAIN! WHENEVER I WANT! FOR AS LONG AS I WANT! AND...

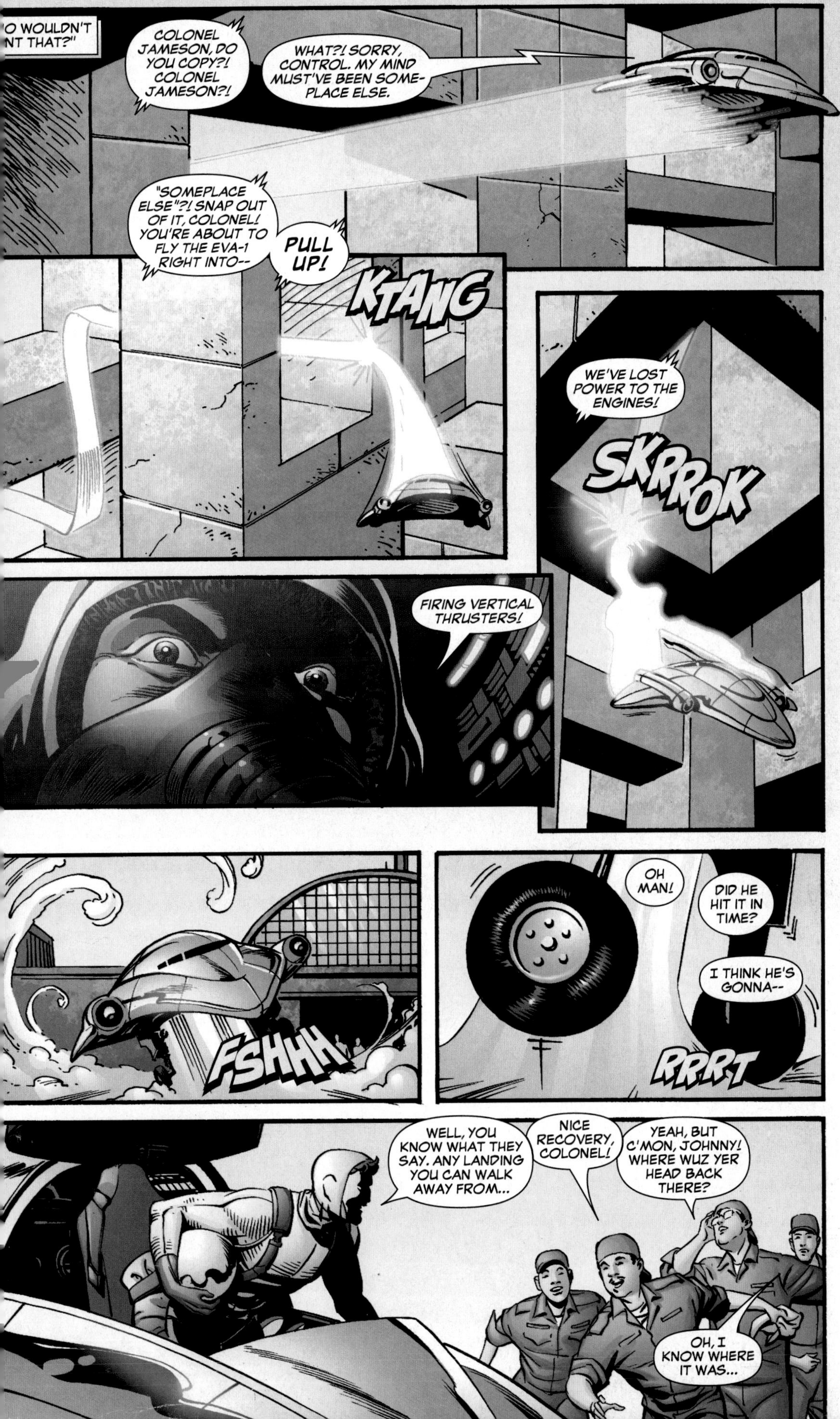

O WOULDN'T NT THAT?"
COLONEL JAMESON, DO YOU COPY?! COLONEL JAMESON?!
WHAT?! SORRY, CONTROL. MY MIND MUST'VE BEEN SOME-PLACE ELSE.
"SOMEPLACE ELSE"?! SNAP OUT OF IT, COLONEL! YOU'RE ABOUT TO FLY THE EVA-1 RIGHT INTO--
PULL UP!
KTANG
WE'VE LOST POWER TO THE ENGINES!
SKRROK
FIRING VERTICAL THRUSTERS!
FSHHH
OH MAN!
DID HE HIT IT IN TIME?
I THINK HE'S GONNA--
RRRT
WELL, YOU KNOW WHAT THEY SAY. ANY LANDING YOU CAN WALK AWAY FROM...
NICE RECOVERY, COLONEL!
YEAH, BUT C'MON, JOHNNY! WHERE WUZ YER HEAD BACK THERE?
OH, I KNOW WHERE IT WAS...

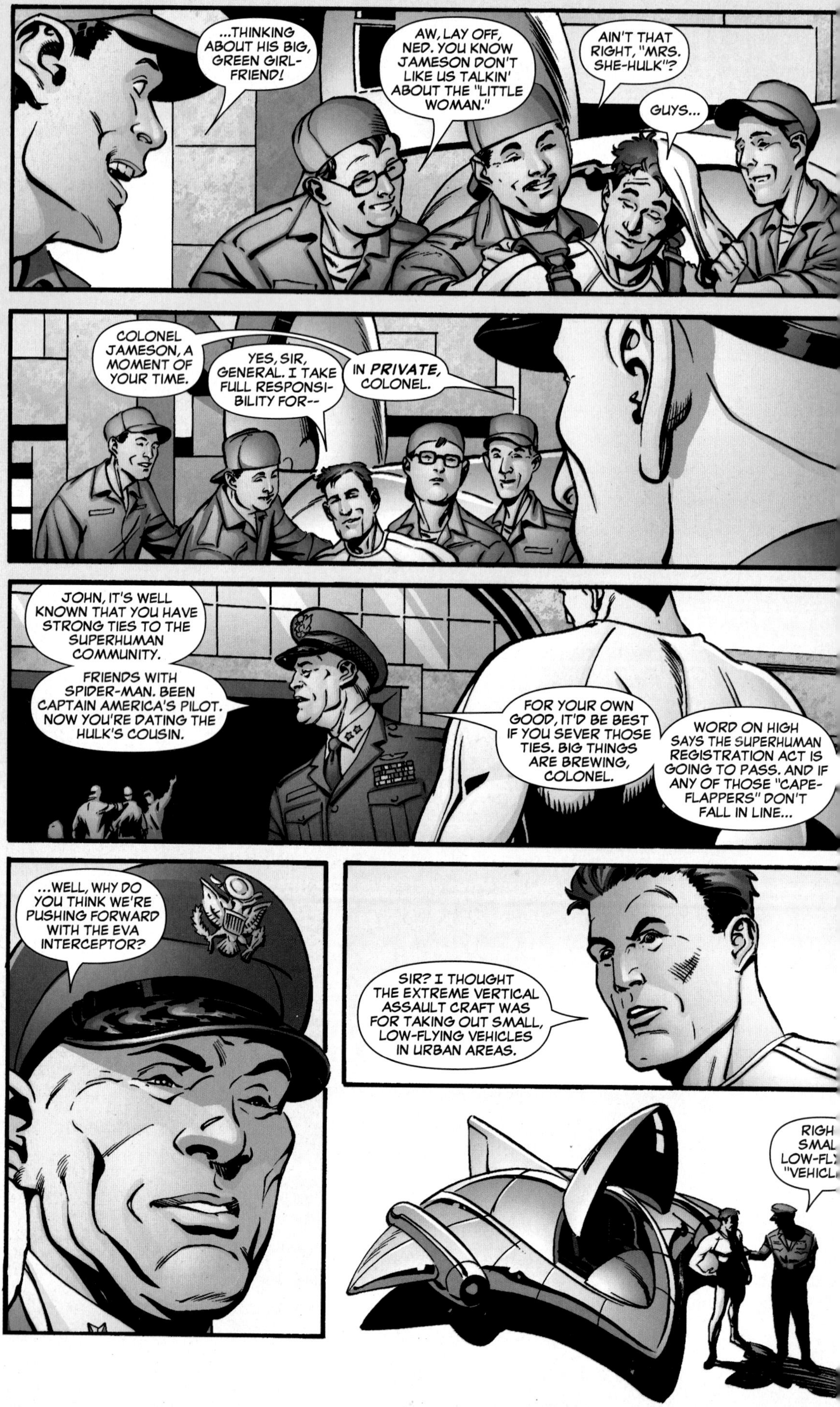
...THINKING ABOUT HIS BIG, GREEN GIRL-FRIEND!
AW, LAY OFF, NED. YOU KNOW JAMESON DON'T LIKE US TALKIN' ABOUT THE "LITTLE WOMAN."
AIN'T THAT RIGHT, "MRS. SHE-HULK"?
GUYS...
COLONEL JAMESON, A MOMENT OF YOUR TIME.
YES, SIR, GENERAL. I TAKE FULL RESPONSI-BILITY FOR--
IN *PRIVATE,* COLONEL.
JOHN, IT'S WELL KNOWN THAT YOU HAVE STRONG TIES TO THE SUPERHUMAN COMMUNITY.
FRIENDS WITH SPIDER-MAN. BEEN CAPTAIN AMERICA'S PILOT. NOW YOU'RE DATING THE HULK'S COUSIN.
FOR YOUR OWN GOOD, IT'D BE BEST IF YOU SEVER THOSE TIES. BIG THINGS ARE BREWING, COLONEL.
WORD ON HIGH SAYS THE SUPERHUMAN REGISTRATION ACT IS GOING TO PASS. AND IF ANY OF THOSE "CAPE-FLAPPERS" DON'T FALL IN LINE...
...WELL, WHY DO YOU THINK WE'RE PUSHING FORWARD WITH THE EVA INTERCEPTOR?
SIR? I THOUGHT THE EXTREME VERTICAL ASSAULT CRAFT WAS FOR TAKING OUT SMALL, LOW-FLYING VEHICLES IN URBAN AREAS.
RIGH SMAL LOW-FL "VEHICL

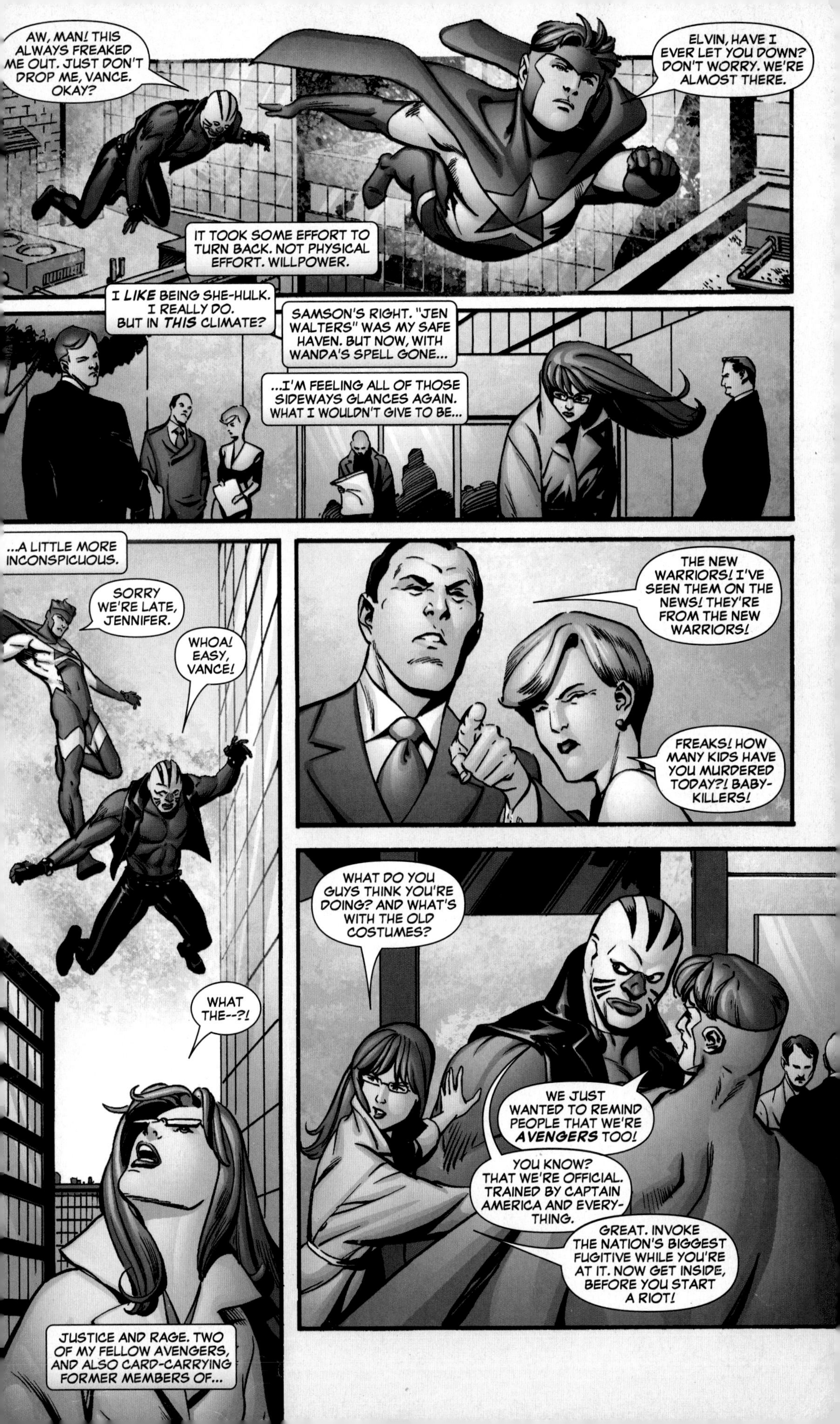
AW, MAN! THIS ALWAYS FREAKED ME OUT. JUST DON'T DROP ME, VANCE. OKAY?
ELVIN, HAVE I EVER LET YOU DOWN? DON'T WORRY. WE'RE ALMOST THERE.
IT TOOK SOME EFFORT TO TURN BACK. NOT PHYSICAL EFFORT. WILLPOWER.
I LIKE BEING SHE-HULK. I REALLY DO. BUT IN THIS CLIMATE?
SAMSON'S RIGHT. "JEN WALTERS" WAS MY SAFE HAVEN. BUT NOW, WITH WANDA'S SPELL GONE...
...I'M FEELING ALL OF THOSE SIDEWAYS GLANCES AGAIN. WHAT I WOULDN'T GIVE TO BE...
...A LITTLE MORE INCONSPICUOUS.
SORRY WE'RE LATE, JENNIFER.
WHOA! EASY, VANCE!
WHAT THE--?!
JUSTICE AND RAGE. TWO OF MY FELLOW AVENGERS, AND ALSO CARD-CARRYING FORMER MEMBERS OF...
THE NEW WARRIORS! I'VE SEEN THEM ON THE NEWS! THEY'RE FROM THE NEW WARRIORS!
FREAKS! HOW MANY KIDS HAVE YOU MURDERED TODAY?! BABY-KILLERS!
WHAT DO YOU GUYS THINK YOU'RE DOING? AND WHAT'S WITH THE OLD COSTUMES?
WE JUST WANTED TO REMIND PEOPLE THAT WE'RE AVENGERS TOO!
YOU KNOW? THAT WE'RE OFFICIAL. TRAINED BY CAPTAIN AMERICA AND EVERY-THING.
GREAT. INVOKE THE NATION'S BIGGEST FUGITIVE WHILE YOU'RE AT IT. NOW GET INSIDE, BEFORE YOU START A RIOT!

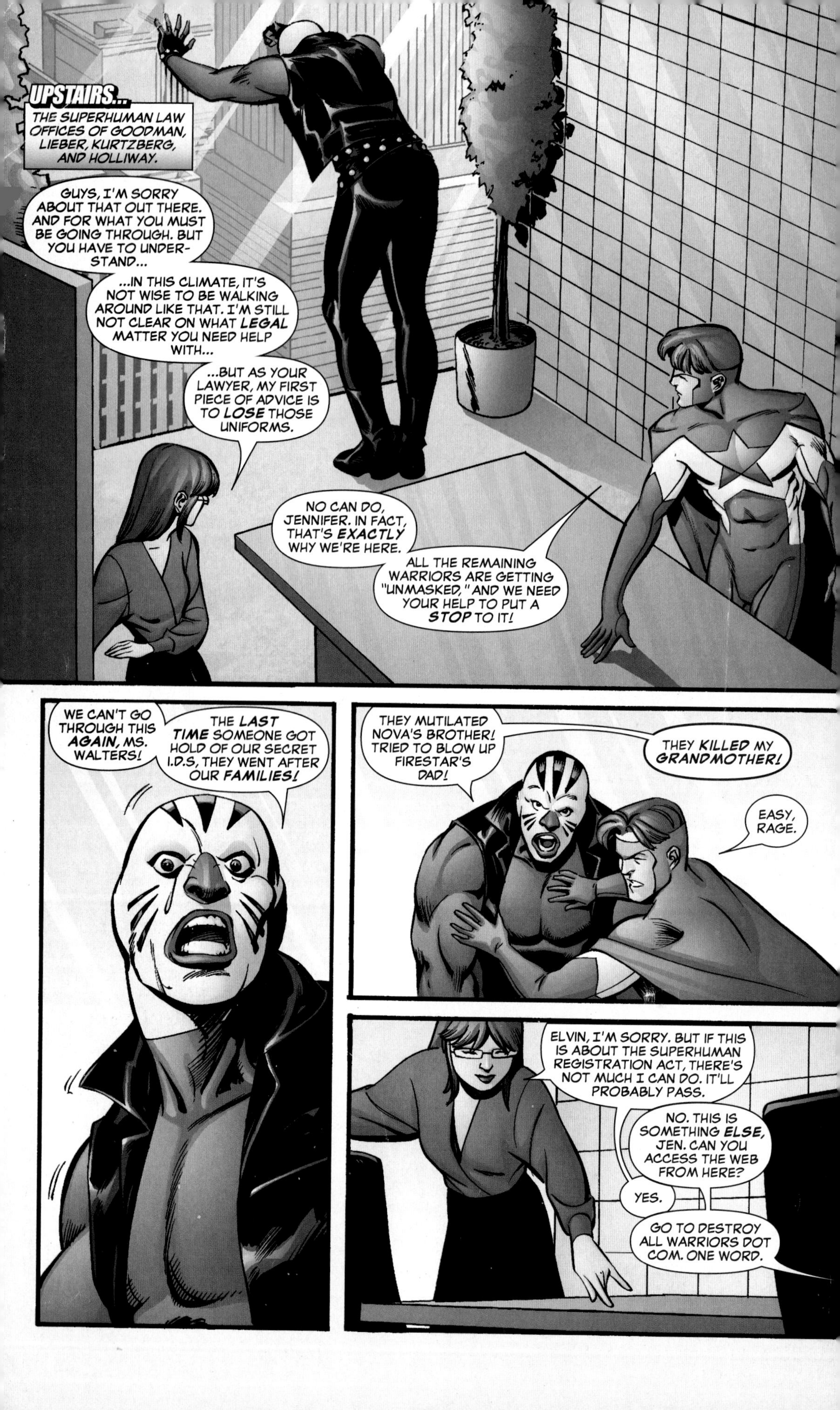
UPSTAIRS...
THE SUPERHUMAN LAW OFFICES OF GOODMAN, LIEBER, KURTZBERG, AND HOLLIWAY.
GUYS, I'M SORRY ABOUT THAT OUT THERE. AND FOR WHAT YOU MUST BE GOING THROUGH. BUT YOU HAVE TO UNDER-STAND...
...IN THIS CLIMATE, IT'S NOT WISE TO BE WALKING AROUND LIKE THAT. I'M STILL NOT CLEAR ON WHAT LEGAL MATTER YOU NEED HELP WITH...
...BUT AS YOUR LAWYER, MY FIRST PIECE OF ADVICE IS TO LOSE THOSE UNIFORMS.
NO CAN DO, JENNIFER. IN FACT, THAT'S EXACTLY WHY WE'RE HERE.
ALL THE REMAINING WARRIORS ARE GETTING "UNMASKED," AND WE NEED YOUR HELP TO PUT A STOP TO IT!
WE CAN'T GO THROUGH THIS AGAIN, MS. WALTERS!
THE LAST TIME SOMEONE GOT HOLD OF OUR SECRET I.D.S, THEY WENT AFTER OUR FAMILIES!
THEY MUTILATED NOVA'S BROTHER! TRIED TO BLOW UP FIRESTAR'S DAD!
THEY KILLED MY GRANDMOTHER!
EASY, RAGE.
ELVIN, I'M SORRY. BUT IF THIS IS ABOUT THE SUPERHUMAN REGISTRATION ACT, THERE'S NOT MUCH I CAN DO. IT'LL PROBABLY PASS.
NO. THIS IS SOMETHING ELSE, JEN. CAN YOU ACCESS THE WEB FROM HERE?
YES.
GO TO DESTROY ALL WARRIORS DOT COM. ONE WORD.

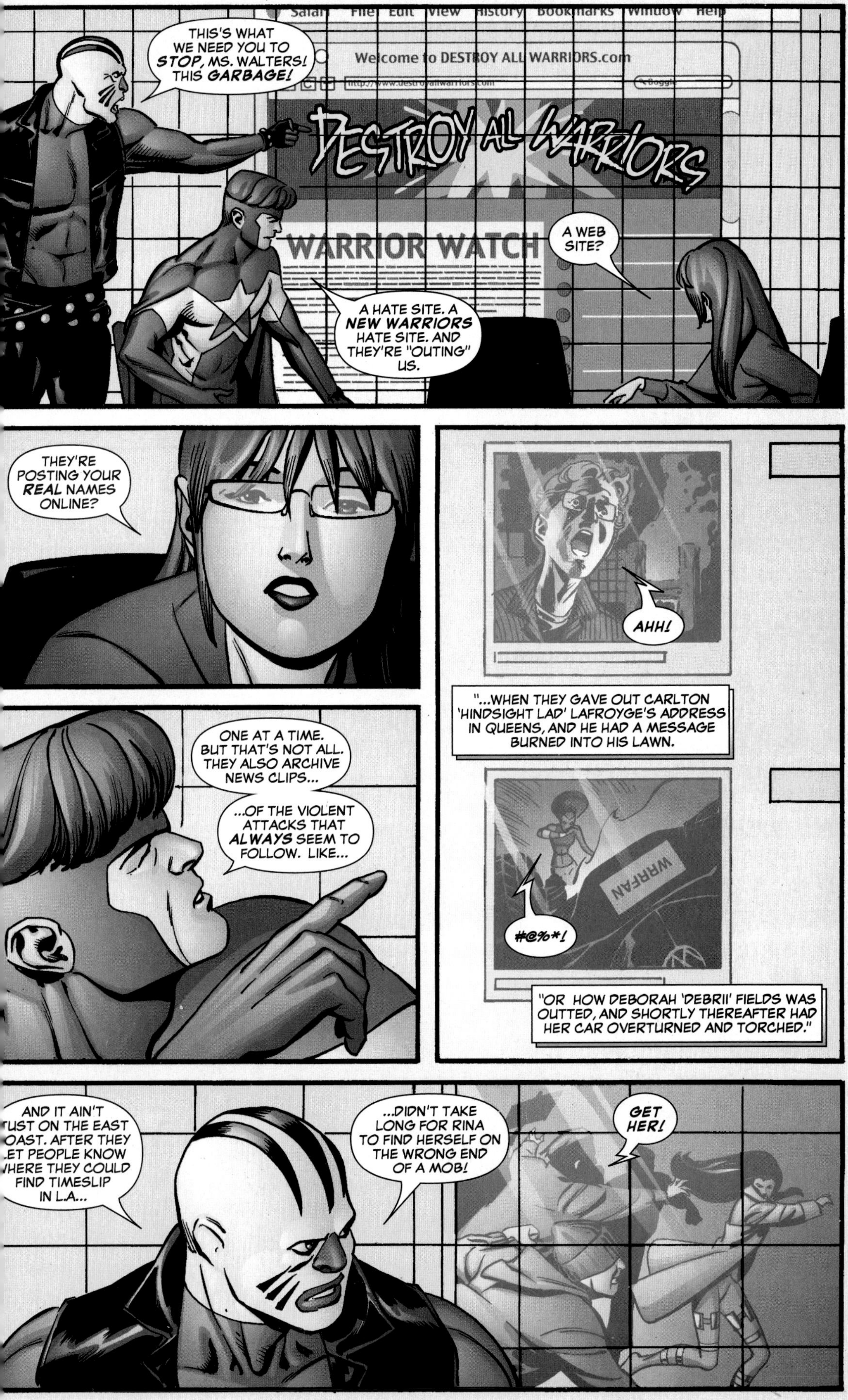
Safari File Edit View History Bookmarks Window Help
Welcome to DESTROY ALL WARRIORS.com
THIS'S WHAT WE NEED YOU TO STOP, MS. WALTERS! THIS GARBAGE!
DESTROY ALL WARRIORS
WARRIOR WATCH
A WEB SITE?
A HATE SITE. A NEW WARRIORS HATE SITE. AND THEY'RE "OUTING" US.
THEY'RE POSTING YOUR REAL NAMES ONLINE?
ONE AT A TIME. BUT THAT'S NOT ALL. THEY ALSO ARCHIVE NEWS CLIPS...
...OF THE VIOLENT ATTACKS THAT ALWAYS SEEM TO FOLLOW. LIKE...
AHH!
"...WHEN THEY GAVE OUT CARLTON 'HINDSIGHT LAD' LAFROYGE'S ADDRESS IN QUEENS, AND HE HAD A MESSAGE BURNED INTO HIS LAWN.
WARFAN
#@%*!
"OR HOW DEBORAH 'DEBRII' FIELDS WAS OUTTED, AND SHORTLY THEREAFTER HAD HER CAR OVERTURNED AND TORCHED."
AND IT AIN'T JUST ON THE EAST COAST. AFTER THEY LET PEOPLE KNOW WHERE THEY COULD FIND TIMESLIP IN L.A...
...DIDN'T TAKE LONG FOR RINA TO FIND HERSELF ON THE WRONG END OF A MOB!
GET HER!

THIS IS *DEPLORABLE.* WHATEVER PEOPLE ARE FEELING ABOUT THE STAMFORD DISASTER...

...FOR SOMEONE TO FOCUS ON IT THIS WAY, TO USE IT TO PLACE *OTHER* LIVES IN DANGER...

IT'S WORSE THAN THAT. THEY'RE GETTING OFF ON IT! LOOK!

THEY'VE GOT A DEAD POOL GOING! WAITIN' TO SEE WHICH OF US WILL GET IT NEXT!

ULTRA GIRL
SUZANNA SHERMAN
ALIVE

SPEEDBALL
ROBBIE BALDWIN
DEAD

NAMORITA
NITA PRENTISS
DEAD

MICROBE
ZACHARY SMITH
DEAD

DEAD

DEBRII
DEBORAH FIELDS
ALIVE

FIREST
COMING
ALIV

YOU HAVE TO DO SOMETHING, MS. WALTERS. THE WARRIORS DESERVE BETTER THAN GOIN' OUT LIKE THIS...

...WITH EVERYBODY THINKING OF US AS SCREW-UPS. OR VICTIMS.

YOU'RE NOT, ELVIN. YOU'RE HEROES. AND YOU'RE FAMILY.

AND TOGETHER, WE'LL BEAT THIS.

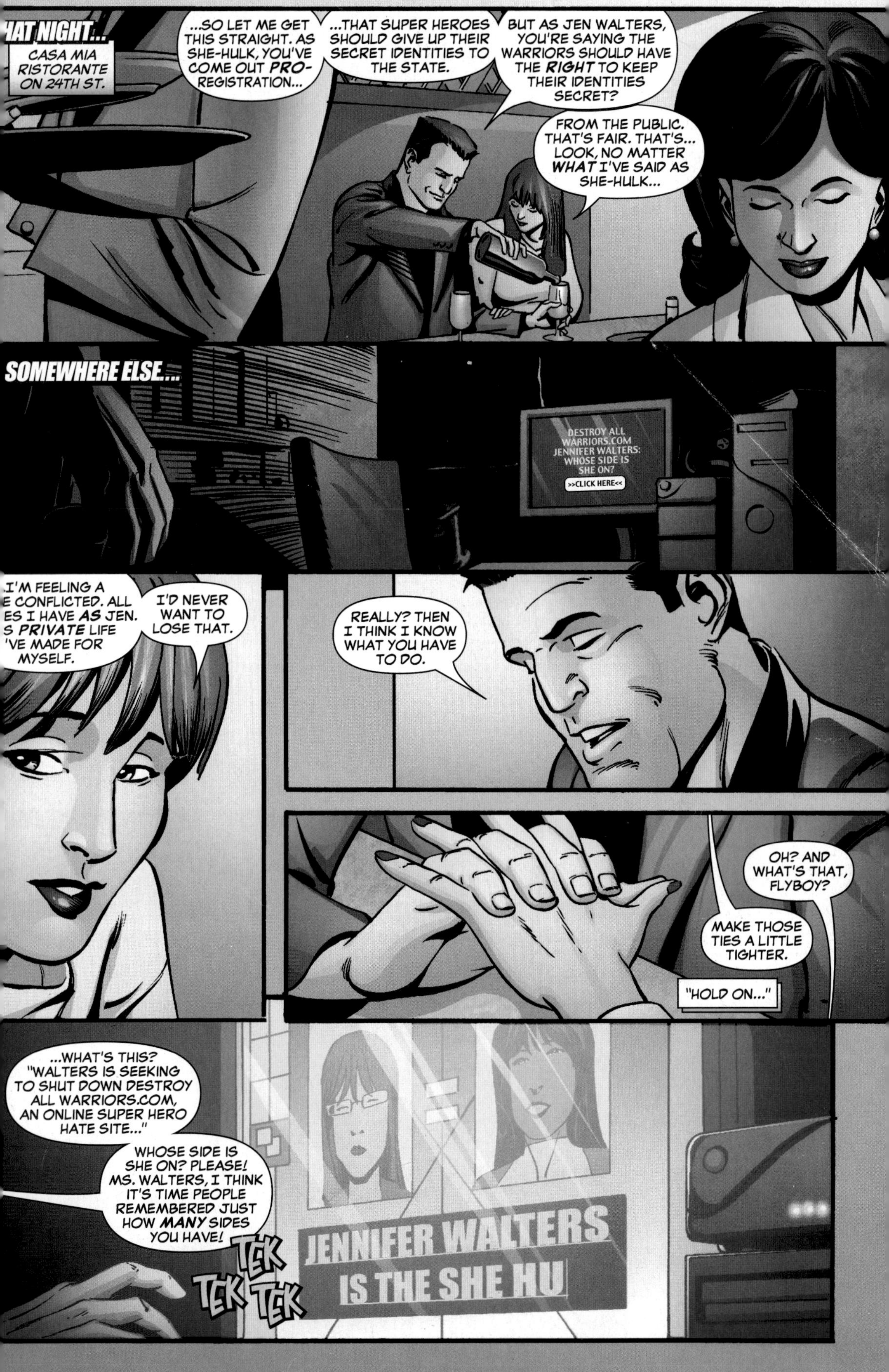

HAT NIGHT...
CASA MIA RISTORANTE ON 24TH ST.
...SO LET ME GET THIS STRAIGHT. AS SHE-HULK, YOU'VE COME OUT PRO-REGISTRATION...
...THAT SUPER HEROES SHOULD GIVE UP THEIR SECRET IDENTITIES TO THE STATE.
BUT AS JEN WALTERS, YOU'RE SAYING THE WARRIORS SHOULD HAVE THE RIGHT TO KEEP THEIR IDENTITIES SECRET?
FROM THE PUBLIC. THAT'S FAIR. THAT'S... LOOK, NO MATTER WHAT I'VE SAID AS SHE-HULK...
SOMEWHERE ELSE...
DESTROY ALL WARRIORS.COM
JENNIFER WALTERS: WHOSE SIDE IS SHE ON?
>>CLICK HERE<<
I'M FEELING A E CONFLICTED. ALL ES I HAVE AS JEN. S PRIVATE LIFE 'VE MADE FOR MYSELF.
I'D NEVER WANT TO LOSE THAT.
REALLY? THEN I THINK I KNOW WHAT YOU HAVE TO DO.
OH? AND WHAT'S THAT, FLYBOY?
MAKE THOSE TIES A LITTLE TIGHTER.
"HOLD ON..."
...WHAT'S THIS? "WALTERS IS SEEKING TO SHUT DOWN DESTROY ALL WARRIORS.COM, AN ONLINE SUPER HERO HATE SITE..."
WHOSE SIDE IS SHE ON? PLEASE! MS. WALTERS, I THINK IT'S TIME PEOPLE REMEMBERED JUST HOW MANY SIDES YOU HAVE!
TEK TEK TEK
JENNIFER WALTERS
IS THE SHE HU

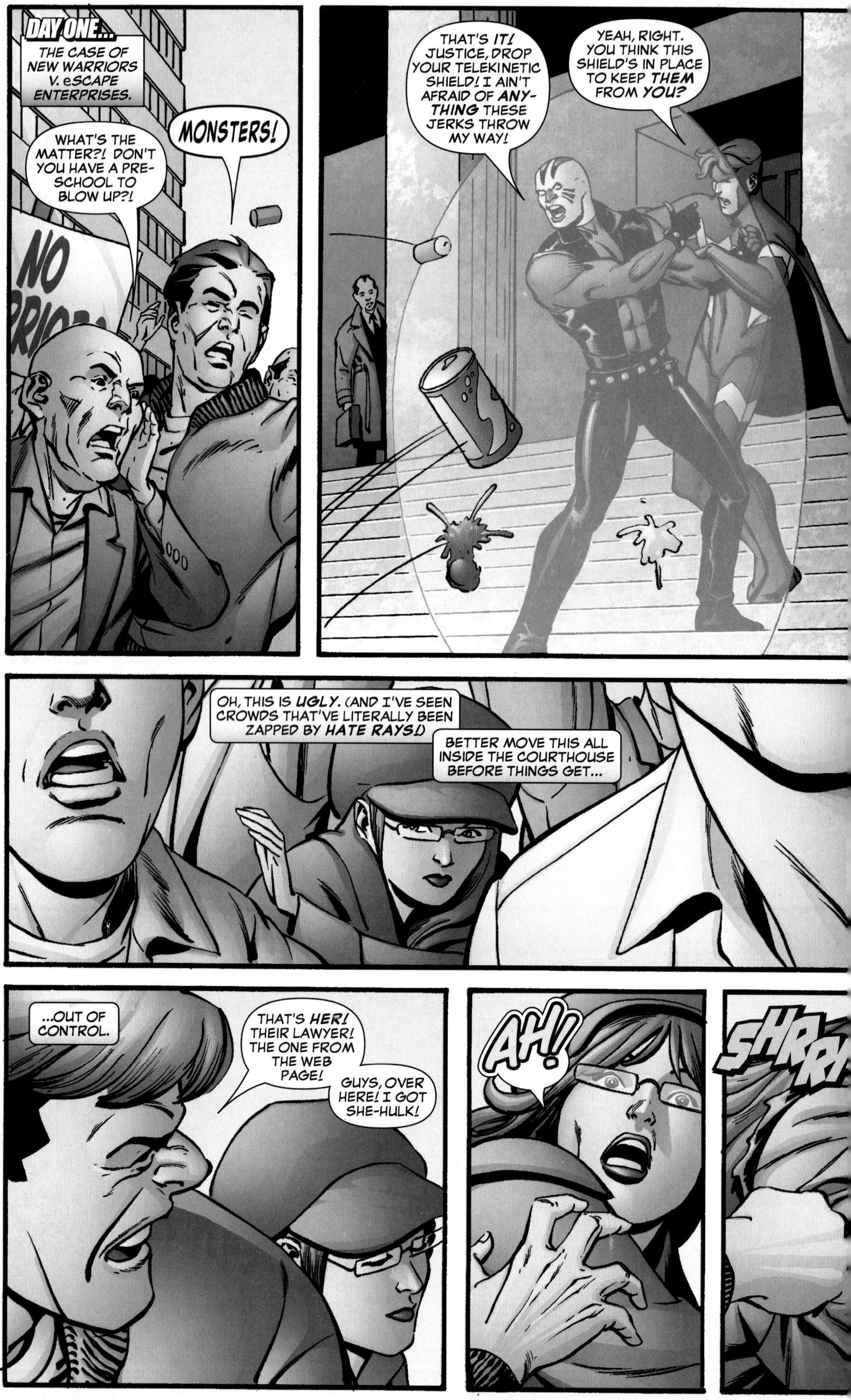
DAY ONE...
THE CASE OF NEW WARRIORS V. eSCAPE ENTERPRISES.
WHAT'S THE MATTER?! DON'T YOU HAVE A PRE-SCHOOL TO BLOW UP?!
MONSTERS!
NO
THAT'S IT! JUSTICE, DROP YOUR TELEKINETIC SHIELD! I AIN'T AFRAID OF ANYTHING THESE JERKS THROW MY WAY!
YEAH, RIGHT. YOU THINK THIS SHIELD'S IN PLACE TO KEEP THEM FROM YOU?
OH, THIS IS UGLY. (AND I'VE SEEN CROWDS THAT'VE LITERALLY BEEN ZAPPED BY HATE RAYS!)
BETTER MOVE THIS ALL INSIDE THE COURTHOUSE BEFORE THINGS GET...
...OUT OF CONTROL.
THAT'S HER! THEIR LAWYER! THE ONE FROM THE WEB PAGE!
GUYS, OVER HERE! I GOT SHE-HULK!
AH!

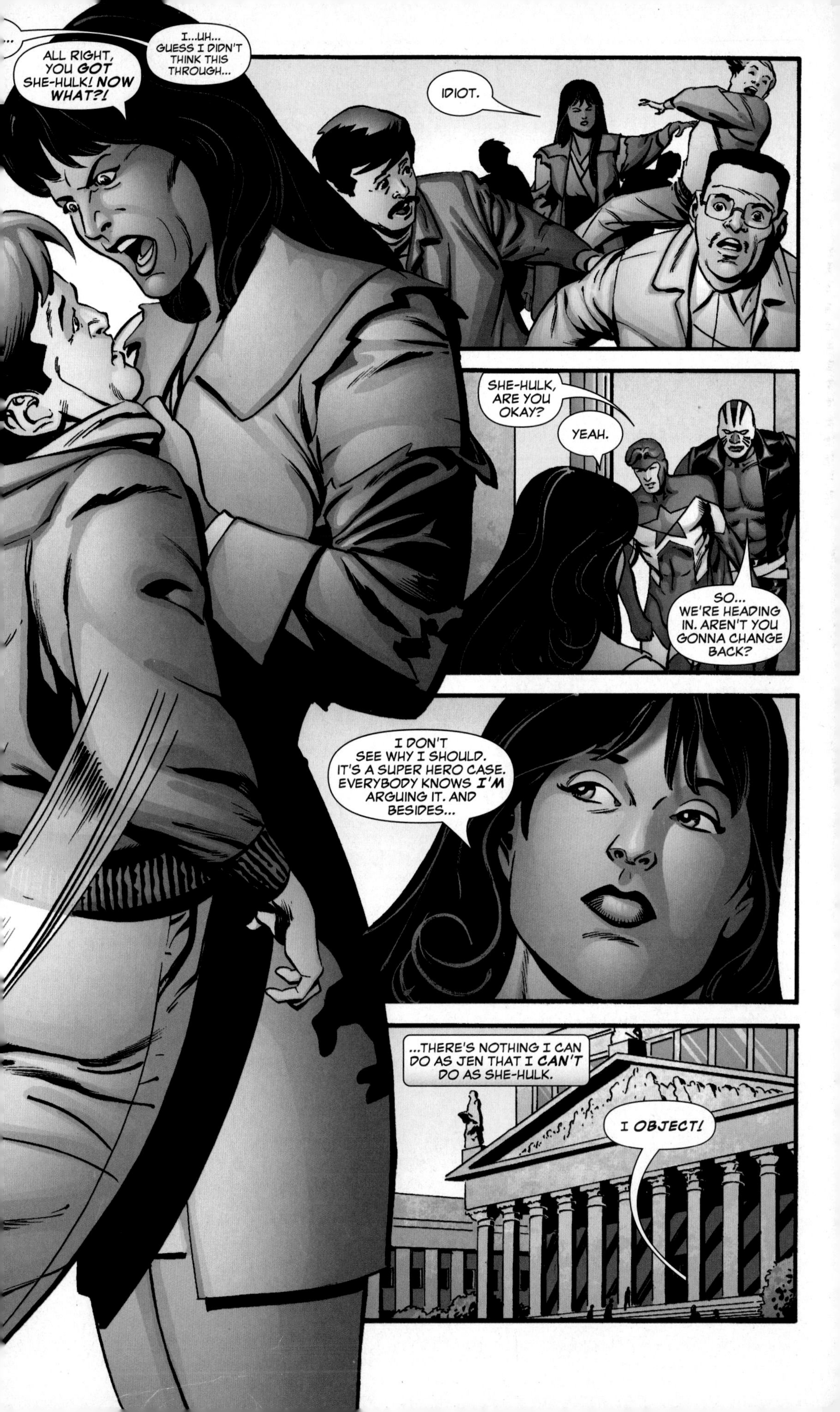
...
ALL RIGHT, YOU GOT SHE-HULK! NOW WHAT?!
I...UH... GUESS I DIDN'T THINK THIS THROUGH...
IDIOT.
SHE-HULK, ARE YOU OKAY?
YEAH.
SO... WE'RE HEADING IN. AREN'T YOU GONNA CHANGE BACK?
I DON'T SEE WHY I SHOULD. IT'S A SUPER HERO CASE. EVERYBODY KNOWS I'M ARGUING IT. AND BESIDES...
...THERE'S NOTHING I CAN DO AS JEN THAT I CAN'T DO AS SHE-HULK.
I OBJECT!

WE'RE HERE FOR A LEGAL ACTION AGAINST A *WEBSITE*. NOT TO TRY FOUR NEW WARRIORS, IN ABSENTIA...

...FOR THEIR PART IN THE STAMFORD TRAGEDY!

MY CLIENTS ARE MORE THAN JUST THE WEBSITE'S FINANCIAL BACKERS, YOUR HONOR.

THEY'RE STAMFORD *SURVIVORS*. AND THAT GOES TO THEIR MOTIVES AND THE *HEART* OF THIS CASE.

VERY WEL PROCEE

...MY TWO GRANDDAUGHTERS, BETH AND KATIE. THEY-- THEY HAD TO BE IDENTIFIED BY DENTAL RECORDS...

I WAS OUTTA TOWN AT THE STATE SCIENCE FAIR. IF I HADN'T GONE, I...I WOULD'VE...

I DON'T SLEEP MUCH ANY MORE.

WE WERE MAKING OUR FINA APPROACH WHEN SAW THAT GIANT FIREBALL. AND I JU KNEW. THEY WERE DEAD. ALL DEAD.

...AND ALL BECAUSE OF FOUR TEENAGERS PLAYING SUPER HERO. NO FURTHER QUESTIONS.

MS. WALTERS? YOU GONNA LET 'IM GET AWAY WITH THAT?

TELL 'EM 'BOUT ALL THE TIMES THE WARRIORS HAVE SAVED THE CITY, THE PLANET, HECK-- ALL OF REALITY!

RAGE HAS A POINT, JEN. WE MUST'VE SAVED EVERY- ONE *HERE* A DOZEN TIMES OVER.

NO.

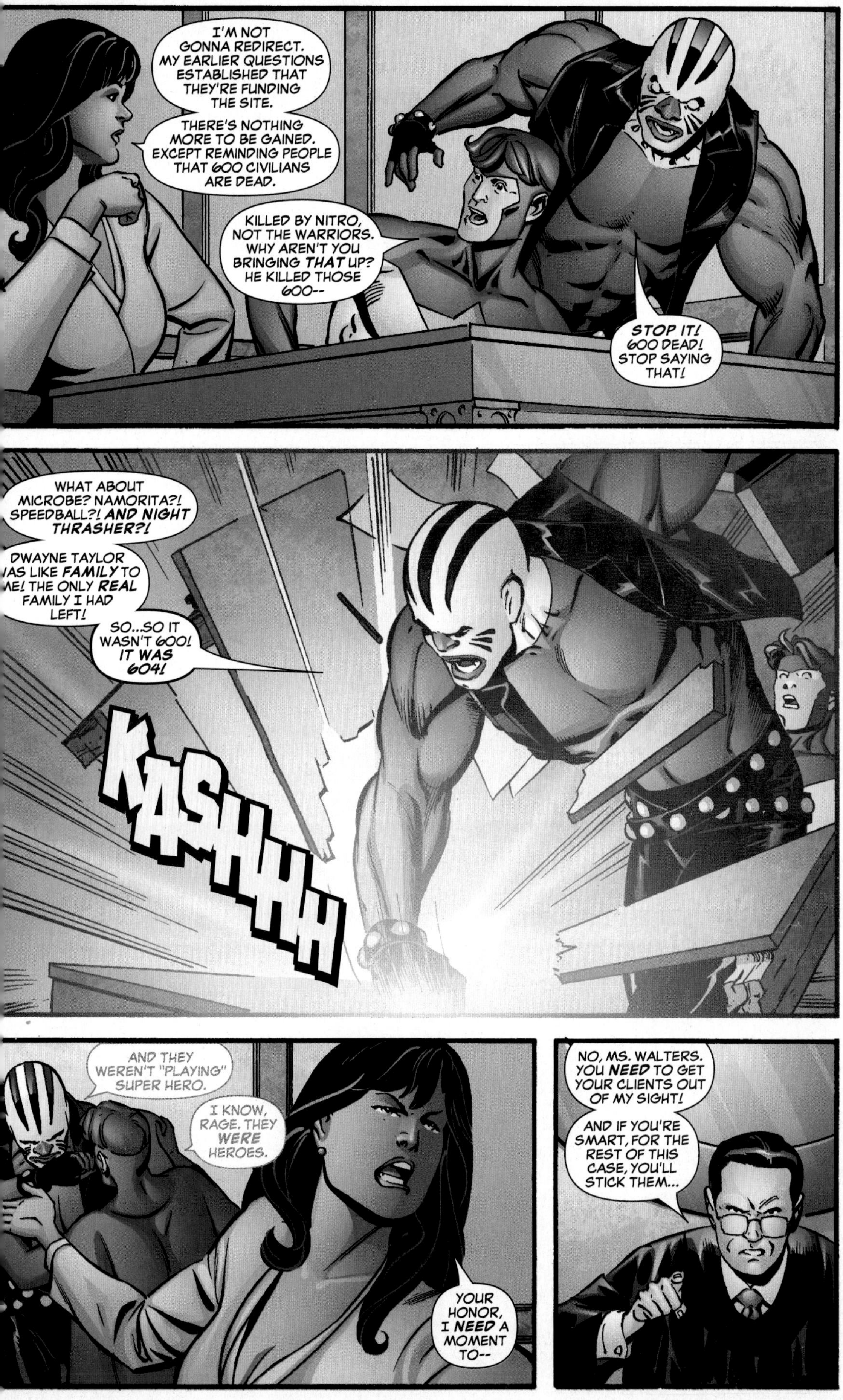

I'M NOT GONNA REDIRECT. MY EARLIER QUESTIONS ESTABLISHED THAT THEY'RE FUNDING THE SITE.
THERE'S NOTHING MORE TO BE GAINED. EXCEPT REMINDING PEOPLE THAT 600 CIVILIANS ARE DEAD.
KILLED BY NITRO, NOT THE WARRIORS. WHY AREN'T YOU BRINGING THAT UP? HE KILLED THOSE 600--
STOP IT! 600 DEAD! STOP SAYING THAT!
WHAT ABOUT MICROBE? NAMORITA?! SPEEDBALL?! AND NIGHT THRASHER?!
DWAYNE TAYLOR WAS LIKE FAMILY TO ME! THE ONLY REAL FAMILY I HAD LEFT!
SO...SO IT WASN'T 600! IT WAS 604!
KASHHHH
AND THEY WEREN'T "PLAYING" SUPER HERO.
I KNOW, RAGE. THEY WERE HEROES.
YOUR HONOR, I NEED A MOMENT TO--
NO, MS. WALTERS. YOU NEED TO GET YOUR CLIENTS OUT OF MY SIGHT!
AND IF YOU'RE SMART, FOR THE REST OF THIS CASE, YOU'LL STICK THEM...

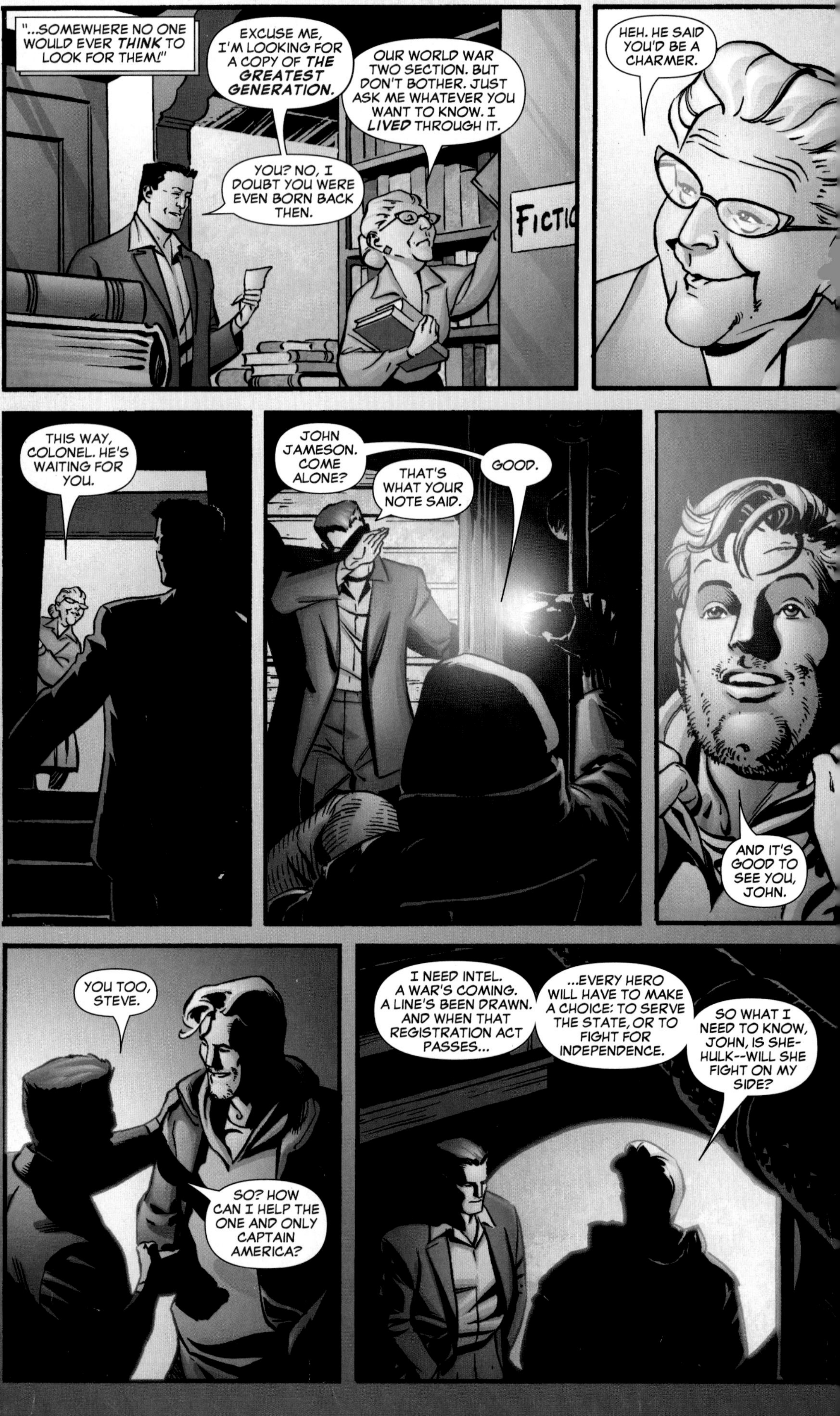
"...SOMEWHERE NO ONE WOULD EVER THINK TO LOOK FOR THEM!"
EXCUSE ME, I'M LOOKING FOR A COPY OF THE GREATEST GENERATION.
OUR WORLD WAR TWO SECTION. BUT DON'T BOTHER. JUST ASK ME WHATEVER YOU WANT TO KNOW. I LIVED THROUGH IT.
YOU? NO, I DOUBT YOU WERE EVEN BORN BACK THEN.
FICTIO
HEH. HE SAID YOU'D BE A CHARMER.
THIS WAY, COLONEL. HE'S WAITING FOR YOU.
JOHN JAMESON. COME ALONE?
THAT'S WHAT YOUR NOTE SAID.
GOOD.
AND IT'S GOOD TO SEE YOU, JOHN.
YOU TOO, STEVE.
SO? HOW CAN I HELP THE ONE AND ONLY CAPTAIN AMERICA?
I NEED INTEL. A WAR'S COMING. A LINE'S BEEN DRAWN. AND WHEN THAT REGISTRATION ACT PASSES...
...EVERY HERO WILL HAVE TO MAKE A CHOICE: TO SERVE THE STATE, OR TO FIGHT FOR INDEPENDENCE.
SO WHAT I NEED TO KNOW, JOHN, IS SHE-HULK--WILL SHE FIGHT ON MY SIDE?

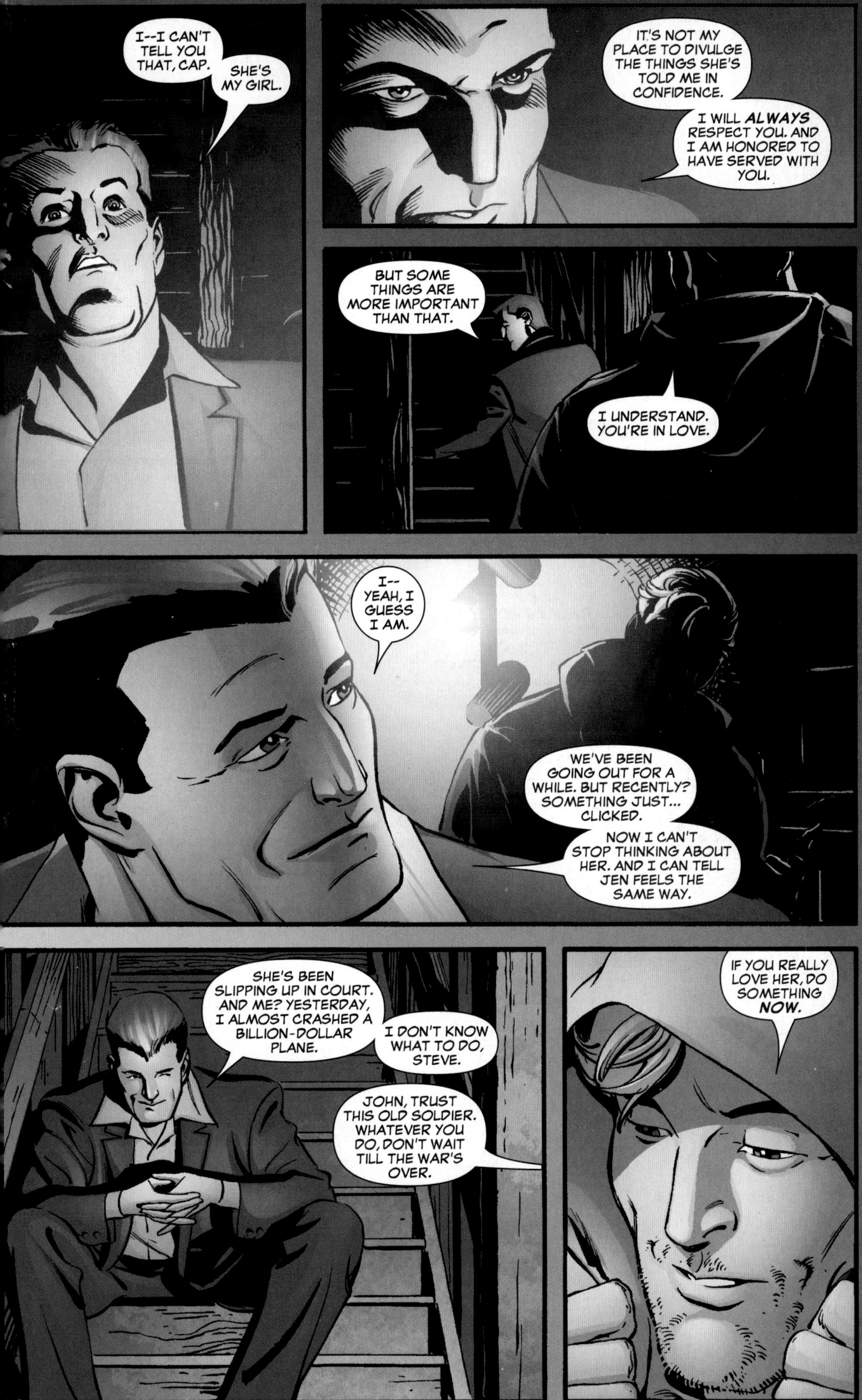
I--I CAN'T TELL YOU THAT, CAP.
SHE'S MY GIRL.
IT'S NOT MY PLACE TO DIVULGE THE THINGS SHE'S TOLD ME IN CONFIDENCE.
I WILL **ALWAYS** RESPECT YOU. AND I AM HONORED TO HAVE SERVED WITH YOU.
BUT SOME THINGS ARE MORE IMPORTANT THAN THAT.
I UNDERSTAND. YOU'RE IN LOVE.
I-- YEAH, I GUESS I AM.
WE'VE BEEN GOING OUT FOR A WHILE. BUT RECENTLY? SOMETHING JUST... CLICKED.
NOW I CAN'T STOP THINKING ABOUT HER. AND I CAN TELL JEN FEELS THE SAME WAY.
SHE'S BEEN SLIPPING UP IN COURT. AND ME? YESTERDAY, I ALMOST CRASHED A BILLION-DOLLAR PLANE.
I DON'T KNOW WHAT TO DO, STEVE.
JOHN, TRUST THIS OLD SOLDIER. WHATEVER YOU DO, DON'T WAIT TILL THE WAR'S OVER.
IF YOU REALLY LOVE HER, DO SOMETHING **NOW**.

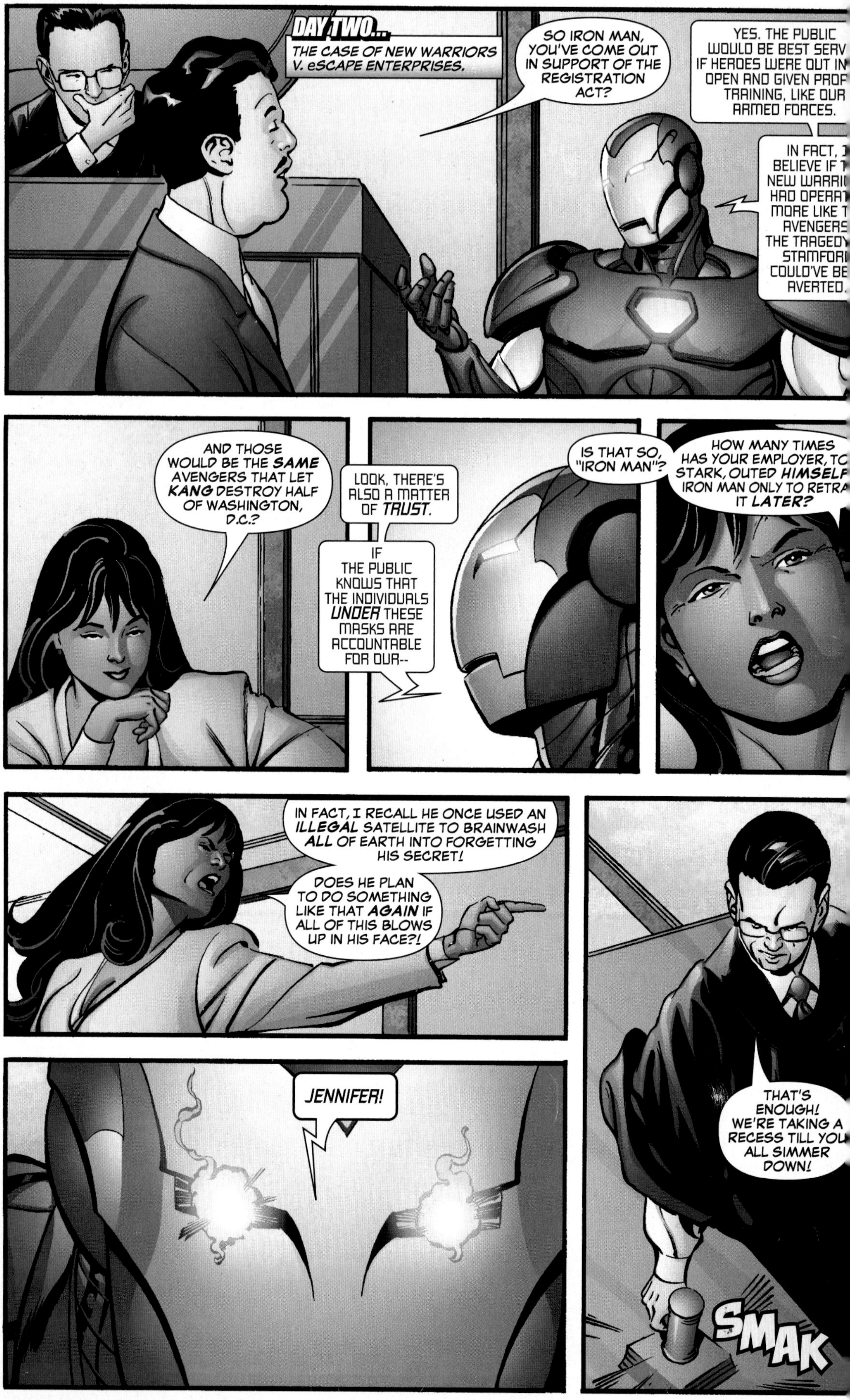
DAY TWO...
THE CASE OF NEW WARRIORS V. eSCAPE ENTERPRISES.
SO IRON MAN, YOU'VE COME OUT IN SUPPORT OF THE REGISTRATION ACT?
YES. THE PUBLIC WOULD BE BEST SERV IF HEROES WERE OUT IN OPEN AND GIVEN PROF TRAINING, LIKE OUR ARMED FORCES.
IN FACT, BELIEVE IF NEW WARRI HAD OPERA MORE LIKE AVENGERS THE TRAGED STAMFOR COULD'VE BE AVERTED.
AND THOSE WOULD BE THE SAME AVENGERS THAT LET KANG DESTROY HALF OF WASHINGTON, D.C.?
LOOK, THERE'S ALSO A MATTER OF TRUST.
IF THE PUBLIC KNOWS THAT THE INDIVIDUALS UNDER THESE MASKS ARE ACCOUNTABLE FOR OUR--
IS THAT SO, "IRON MAN"?
HOW MANY TIMES HAS YOUR EMPLOYER, TO STARK, OUTED HIMSELF IRON MAN ONLY TO RETRA IT LATER?
IN FACT, I RECALL HE ONCE USED AN ILLEGAL SATELLITE TO BRAINWASH ALL OF EARTH INTO FORGETTING HIS SECRET!
DOES HE PLAN TO DO SOMETHING LIKE THAT AGAIN IF ALL OF THIS BLOWS UP IN HIS FACE?!
JENNIFER!
THAT'S ENOUGH! WE'RE TAKING A RECESS TILL YOU ALL SIMMER DOWN!
SMAK

HOW'S IT GOING IN THERE, JEN?

I'M NOT SURE, VANCE. GIMME A SECOND.

I WANT A WORD WITH YOU, SHE-HULK.

WE'RE VERY MUCH LIKE, YOU AND I. WHEN I'M TONY STARK AND I'M CLOSING A DEAL, ALL I WANT TO DO IS WIN.

I'D EXPECT NO LESS OF YOU IN THE COURTROOM. BUT UNDERSTAND THIS...

...IT'S NO LONGER ENOUGH TO PROTECT THE PEOPLE. WE *NEED* THEM ON OUR SIDE.

AFTER YOUR COUSIN DESTROYED LAS VEGAS...

...AND YOUR FIRM HELPED STARFOX GET AWAY WITH SEXUAL ASSAULT--

WE DIDN'T--

I'M TALKING. AND NOW, WITH WHAT'S HAPPENED IN STAMFORD...

...THEY'RE NOT GOING TO TOLERATE US RUNNING AROUND LIKE LAWLESS IDIOTS ANYMORE.

HERE. TAKE THIS.

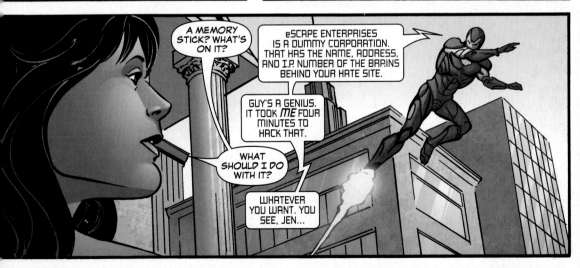

A MEMORY STICK? WHAT'S ON IT?

eSCAPE ENTERPRISES IS A DUMMY CORPORATION. THAT HAS THE NAME, ADDRESS, AND I.P. NUMBER OF THE BRAINS BEHIND YOUR HATE SITE.

GUY'S A GENIUS. IT TOOK *ME* FOUR MINUTES TO HACK THAT.

WHAT SHOULD I DO WITH IT?

WHATEVER YOU WANT. YOU SEE, JEN...

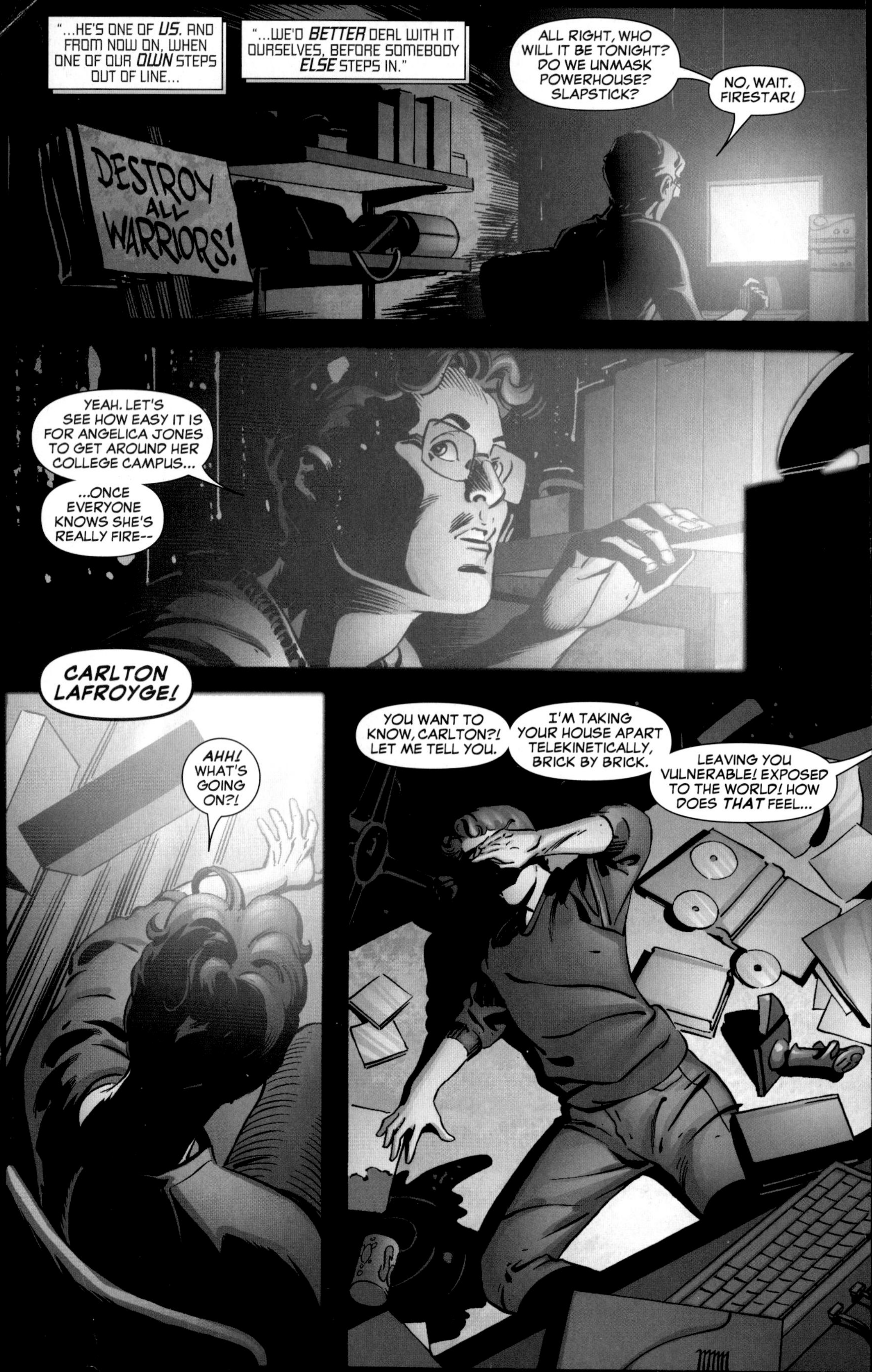
"...HE'S ONE OF US. AND FROM NOW ON, WHEN ONE OF OUR OWN STEPS OUT OF LINE...
"...WE'D BETTER DEAL WITH IT OURSELVES, BEFORE SOMEBODY ELSE STEPS IN."
ALL RIGHT, WHO WILL IT BE TONIGHT? DO WE UNMASK POWERHOUSE? SLAPSTICK?
NO, WAIT. FIRESTAR!
DESTROY ALL WARRIORS!
YEAH. LET'S SEE HOW EASY IT IS FOR ANGELICA JONES TO GET AROUND HER COLLEGE CAMPUS...
...ONCE EVERYONE KNOWS SHE'S REALLY FIRE--
CARLTON LAFROYGE!
AHH! WHAT'S GOING ON?!
YOU WANT TO KNOW, CARLTON?! LET ME TELL YOU.
I'M TAKING YOUR HOUSE APART TELEKINETICALLY, BRICK BY BRICK.
LEAVING YOU VULNERABLE! EXPOSED TO THE WORLD! HOW DOES THAT FEEL...

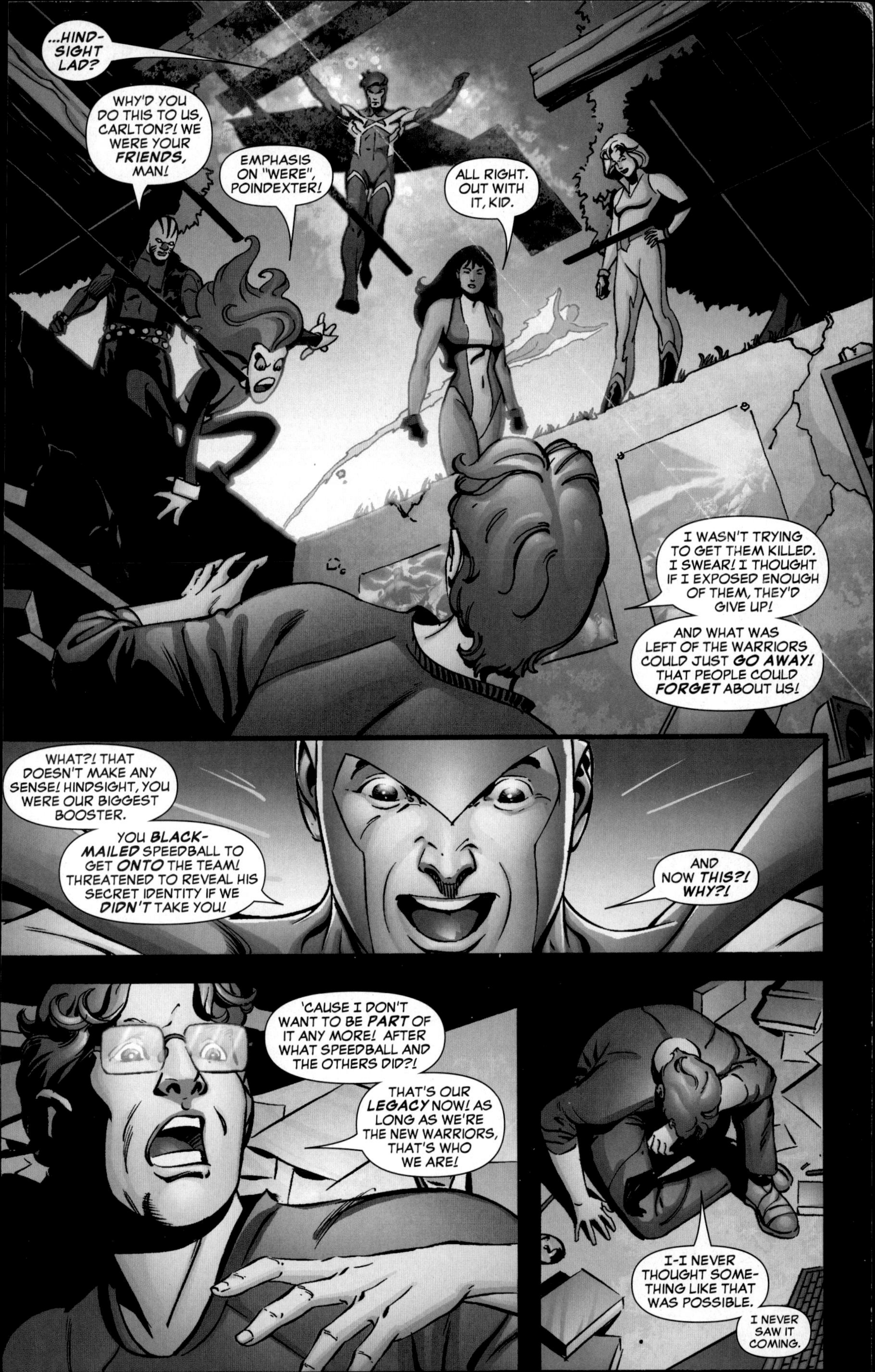
...HIND-SIGHT LAD?
WHY'D YOU DO THIS TO US, CARLTON?! WE WERE YOUR FRIENDS, MAN!
EMPHASIS ON "WERE", POINDEXTER!
ALL RIGHT. OUT WITH IT, KID.
I WASN'T TRYING TO GET THEM KILLED. I SWEAR! I THOUGHT IF I EXPOSED ENOUGH OF THEM, THEY'D GIVE UP!
AND WHAT WAS LEFT OF THE WARRIORS COULD JUST GO AWAY! THAT PEOPLE COULD FORGET ABOUT US!
WHAT?! THAT DOESN'T MAKE ANY SENSE! HINDSIGHT, YOU WERE OUR BIGGEST BOOSTER.
YOU BLACK-MAILED SPEEDBALL TO GET ONTO THE TEAM! THREATENED TO REVEAL HIS SECRET IDENTITY IF WE DIDN'T TAKE YOU!
AND NOW THIS?! WHY?!
'CAUSE I DON'T WANT TO BE PART OF IT ANY MORE! AFTER WHAT SPEEDBALL AND THE OTHERS DID?!
THAT'S OUR LEGACY NOW! AS LONG AS WE'RE THE NEW WARRIORS, THAT'S WHO WE ARE!
I-I NEVER THOUGHT SOME-THING LIKE THAT WAS POSSIBLE.
I NEVER SAW IT COMING.

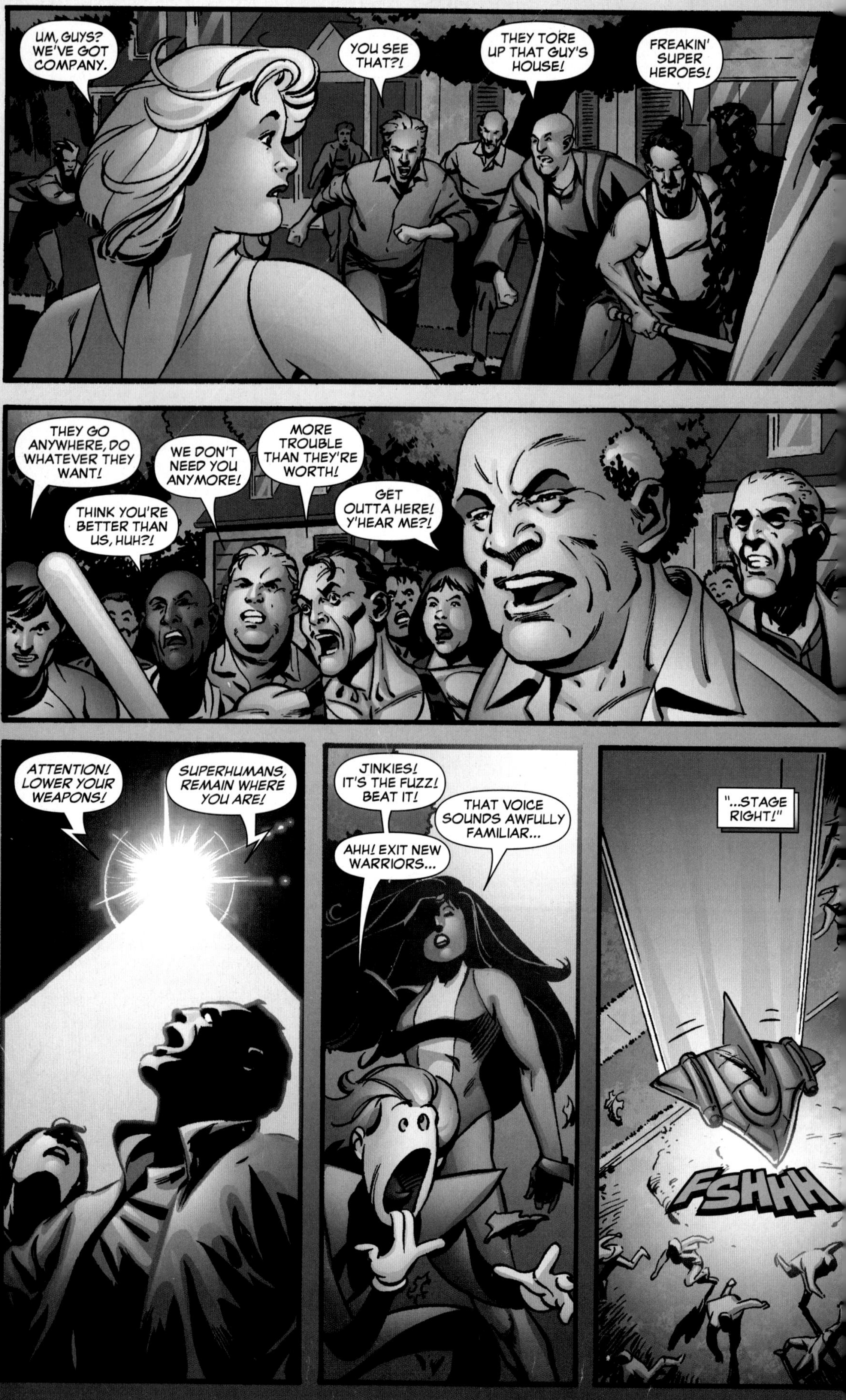

UM, GUYS? WE'VE GOT COMPANY.
YOU SEE THAT?!
THEY TORE UP THAT GUY'S HOUSE!
FREAKIN' SUPER HEROES!
THEY GO ANYWHERE, DO WHATEVER THEY WANT!
THINK YOU'RE BETTER THAN US, HUH?!
WE DON'T NEED YOU ANYMORE!
MORE TROUBLE THAN THEY'RE WORTH!
GET OUTTA HERE! Y'HEAR ME?!
ATTENTION! LOWER YOUR WEAPONS!
SUPERHUMANS, REMAIN WHERE YOU ARE!
JINKIES! IT'S THE FUZZ! BEAT IT!
THAT VOICE SOUNDS AWFULLY FAMILIAR...
AHH! EXIT NEW WARRIORS...
"...STAGE RIGHT!"
FSHHH

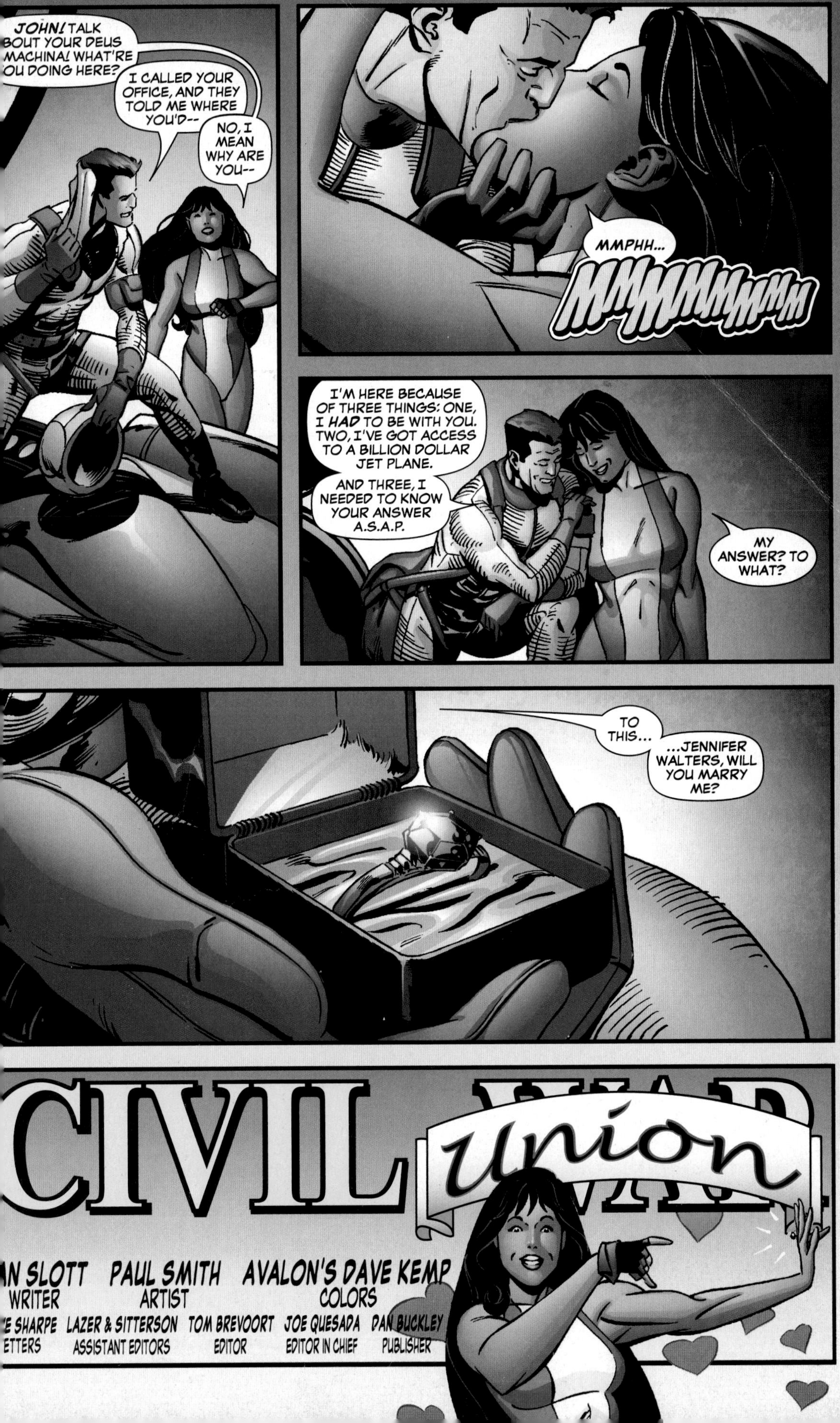
JOHN! TALK BOUT YOUR DEUS MACHINA! WHAT'RE OU DOING HERE?
I CALLED YOUR OFFICE, AND THEY TOLD ME WHERE YOU'D--
NO, I MEAN WHY ARE YOU--
MMPHH...
MMMMMMMMMM
I'M HERE BECAUSE OF THREE THINGS: ONE, I HAD TO BE WITH YOU. TWO, I'VE GOT ACCESS TO A BILLION DOLLAR JET PLANE.
AND THREE, I NEEDED TO KNOW YOUR ANSWER A.S.A.P.
MY ANSWER? TO WHAT?
TO THIS...
...JENNIFER WALTERS, WILL YOU MARRY ME?
CIVIL WAR union
AN SLOTT WRITER
PAUL SMITH ARTIST
AVALON'S DAVE KEMP COLORS
E SHARPE ETTERS
LAZER & SITTERSON ASSISTANT EDITORS
TOM BREVOORT EDITOR
JOE QUESADA EDITOR IN CHIEF
DAN BUCKLEY PUBLISHER

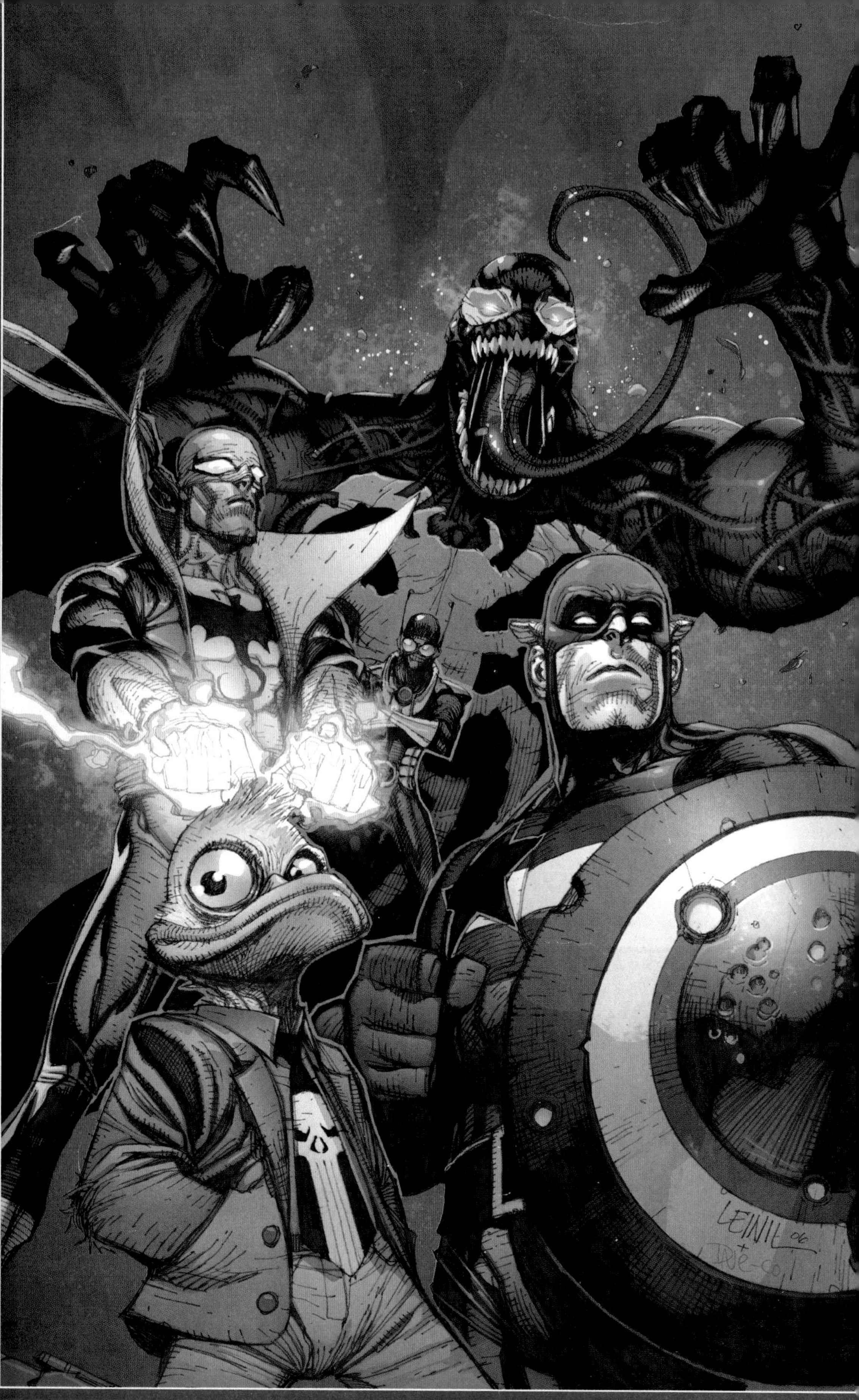

CIVIL WAR: CHOOSING SIDES

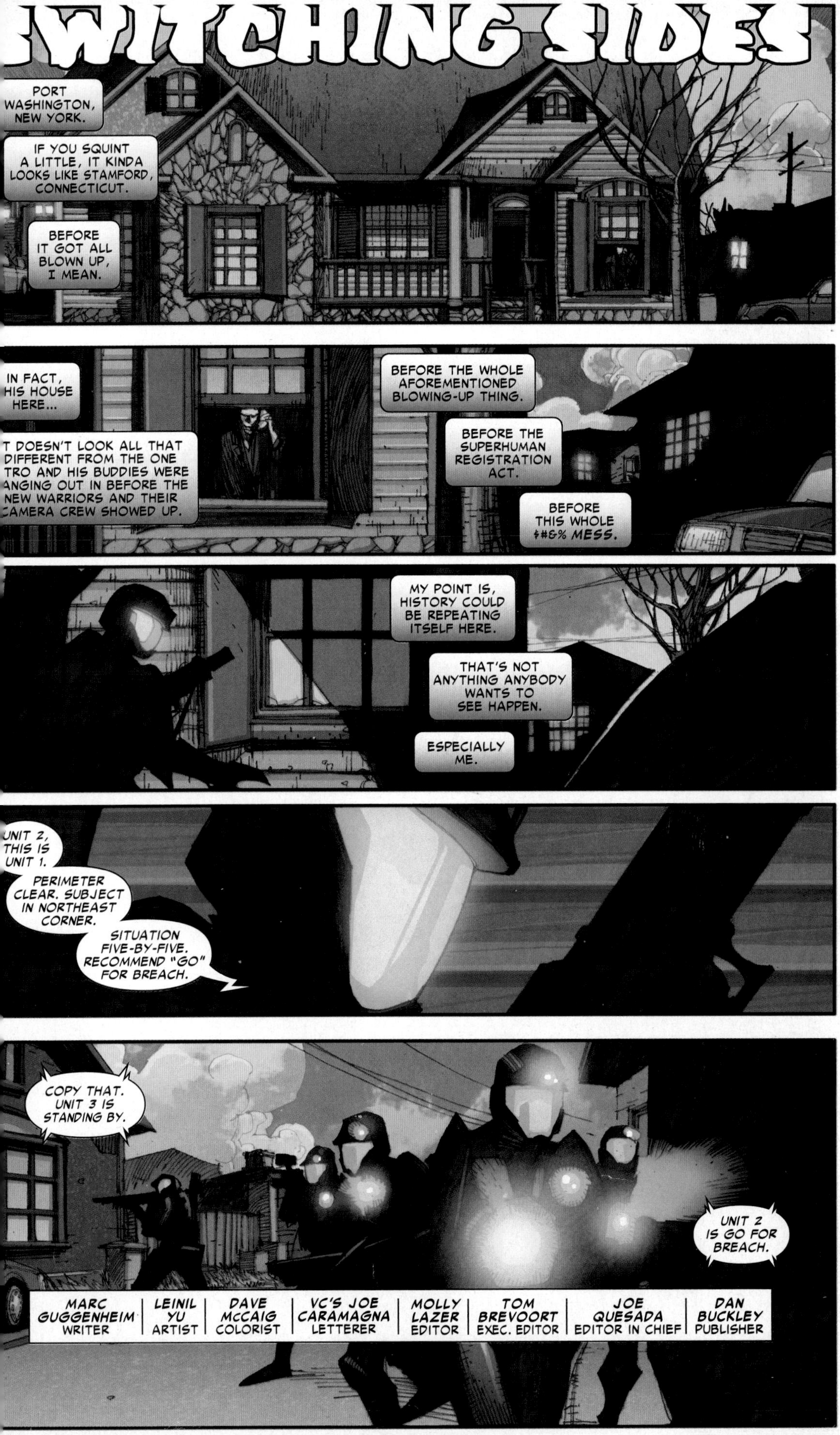
SWITCHING SIDES
PORT WASHINGTON, NEW YORK.
IF YOU SQUINT A LITTLE, IT KINDA LOOKS LIKE STAMFORD, CONNECTICUT.
BEFORE IT GOT ALL BLOWN UP, I MEAN.
IN FACT, HIS HOUSE HERE...
T DOESN'T LOOK ALL THAT DIFFERENT FROM THE ONE TRO AND HIS BUDDIES WERE ANGING OUT IN BEFORE THE NEW WARRIORS AND THEIR CAMERA CREW SHOWED UP.
BEFORE THE WHOLE AFOREMENTIONED BLOWING-UP THING.
BEFORE THE SUPERHUMAN REGISTRATION ACT.
BEFORE THIS WHOLE $#&% MESS.
MY POINT IS, HISTORY COULD BE REPEATING ITSELF HERE.
THAT'S NOT ANYTHING ANYBODY WANTS TO SEE HAPPEN.
ESPECIALLY ME.
UNIT 2, THIS IS UNIT 1.
PERIMETER CLEAR. SUBJECT IN NORTHEAST CORNER.
SITUATION FIVE-BY-FIVE. RECOMMEND "GO" FOR BREACH.
COPY THAT. UNIT 3 IS STANDING BY.
UNIT 2 IS GO FOR BREACH.
MARC GUGGENHEIM WRITER | LEINIL YU ARTIST | DAVE McCAIG COLORIST | VC'S JOE CARAMAGNA LETTERER | MOLLY LAZER EDITOR | TOM BREVOORT EXEC. EDITOR | JOE QUESADA EDITOR IN CHIEF | DAN BUCKLEY PUBLISHER

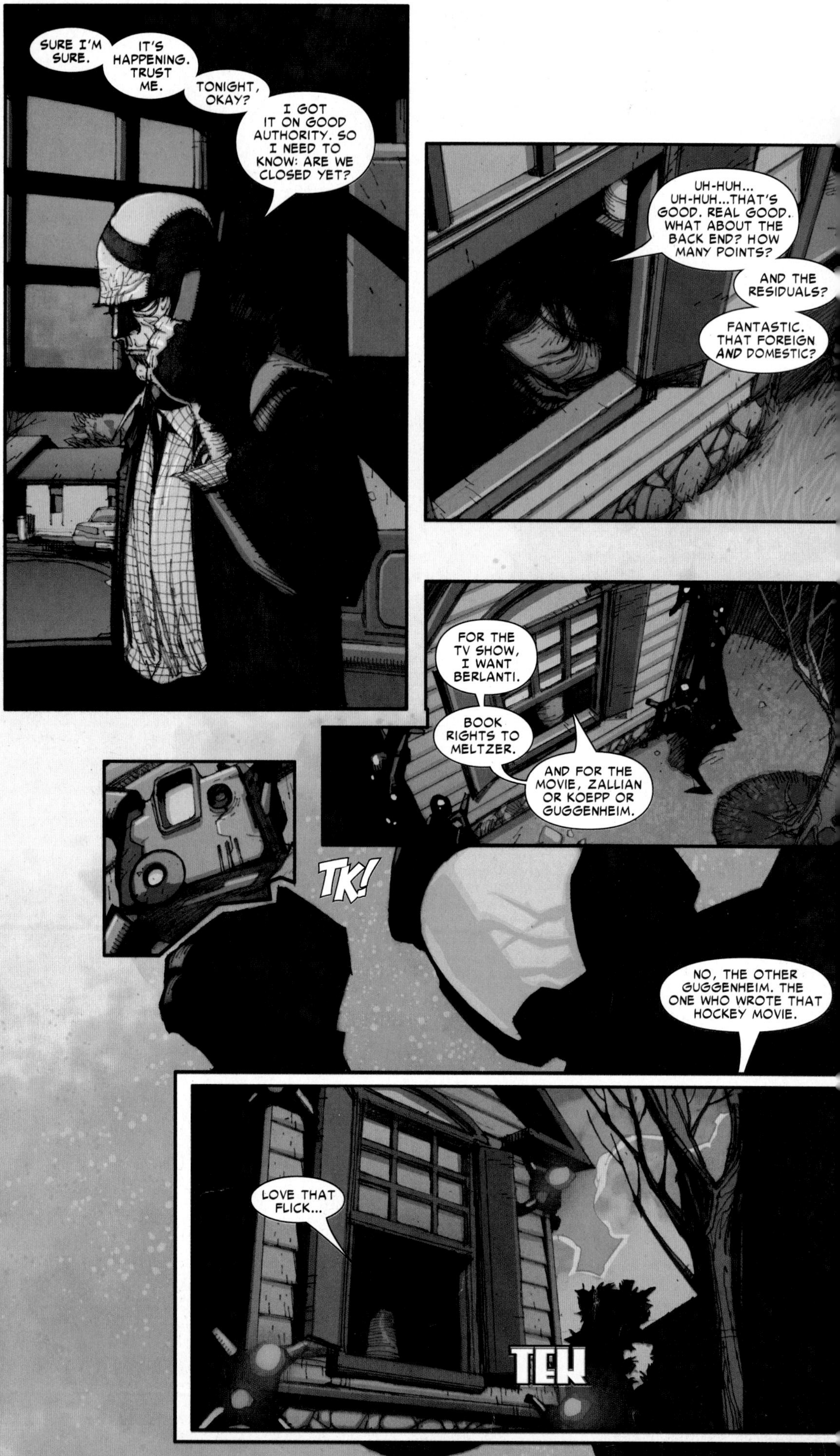
SURE I'M SURE.
IT'S HAPPENING. TRUST ME.
TONIGHT, OKAY?
I GOT IT ON GOOD AUTHORITY. SO I NEED TO KNOW: ARE WE CLOSED YET?
UH-HUH... UH-HUH...THAT'S GOOD. REAL GOOD. WHAT ABOUT THE BACK END? HOW MANY POINTS?
AND THE RESIDUALS?
FANTASTIC. THAT FOREIGN AND DOMESTIC?
FOR THE TV SHOW, I WANT BERLANTI.
BOOK RIGHTS TO MELTZER.
AND FOR THE MOVIE, ZALLIAN OR KOEPP OR GUGGENHEIM.
TK!
NO, THE OTHER GUGGENHEIM. THE ONE WHO WROTE THAT HOCKEY MOVIE.
LOVE THAT FLICK...
TEN

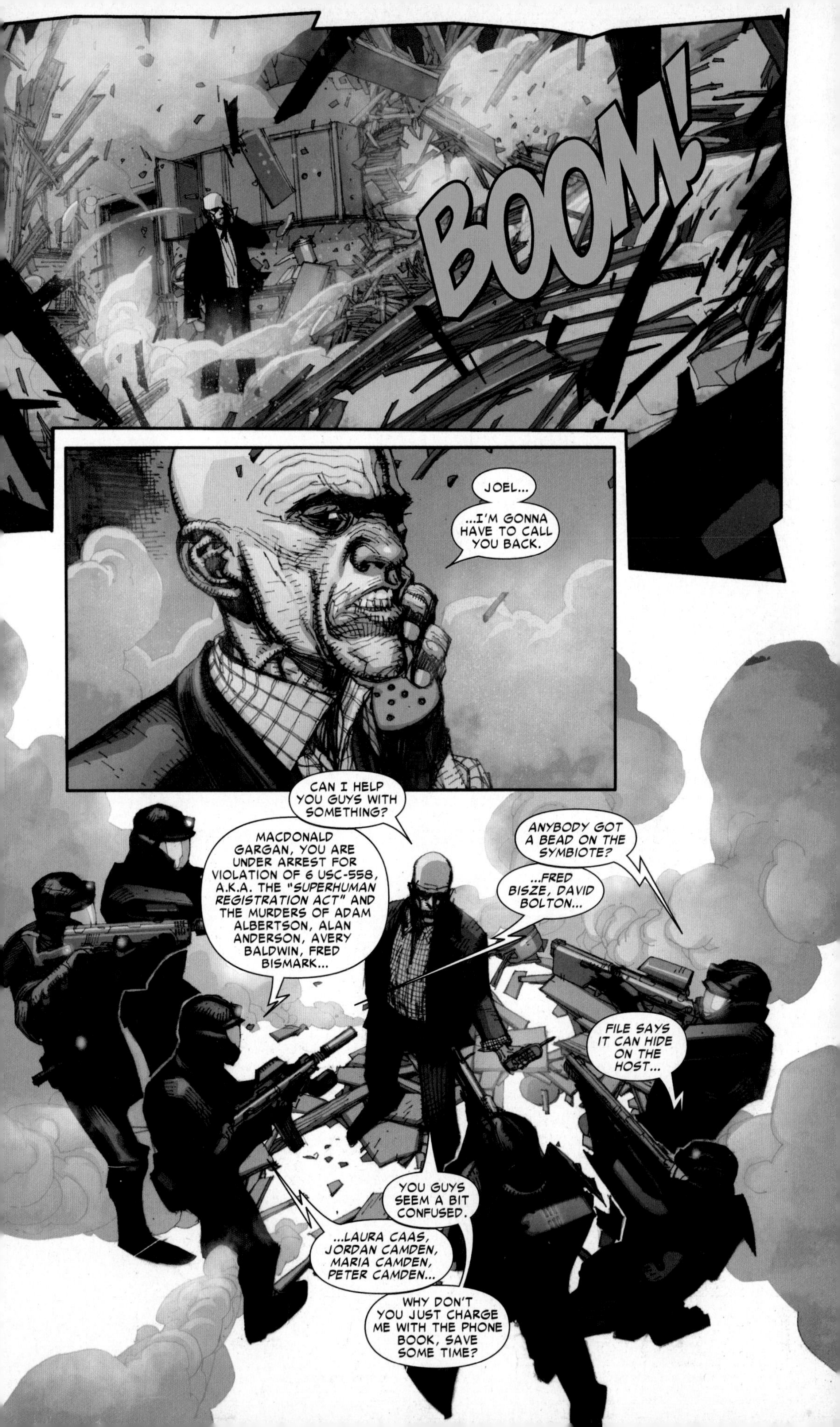
BOOM!
JOEL...
...I'M GONNA HAVE TO CALL YOU BACK.
CAN I HELP YOU GUYS WITH SOMETHING?
MACDONALD GARGAN, YOU ARE UNDER ARREST FOR VIOLATION OF 6 USC-558, A.K.A. THE "SUPERHUMAN REGISTRATION ACT" AND THE MURDERS OF ADAM ALBERTSON, ALAN ANDERSON, AVERY BALDWIN, FRED BISMARK...
...FRED BISZE, DAVID BOLTON...
ANYBODY GOT A BEAD ON THE SYMBIOTE?
FILE SAYS IT CAN HIDE ON THE HOST...
YOU GUYS SEEM A BIT CONFUSED.
...LAURA CAAS, JORDAN CAMDEN, MARIA CAMDEN, PETER CAMDEN...
WHY DON'T YOU JUST CHARGE ME WITH THE PHONE BOOK, SAVE SOME TIME?

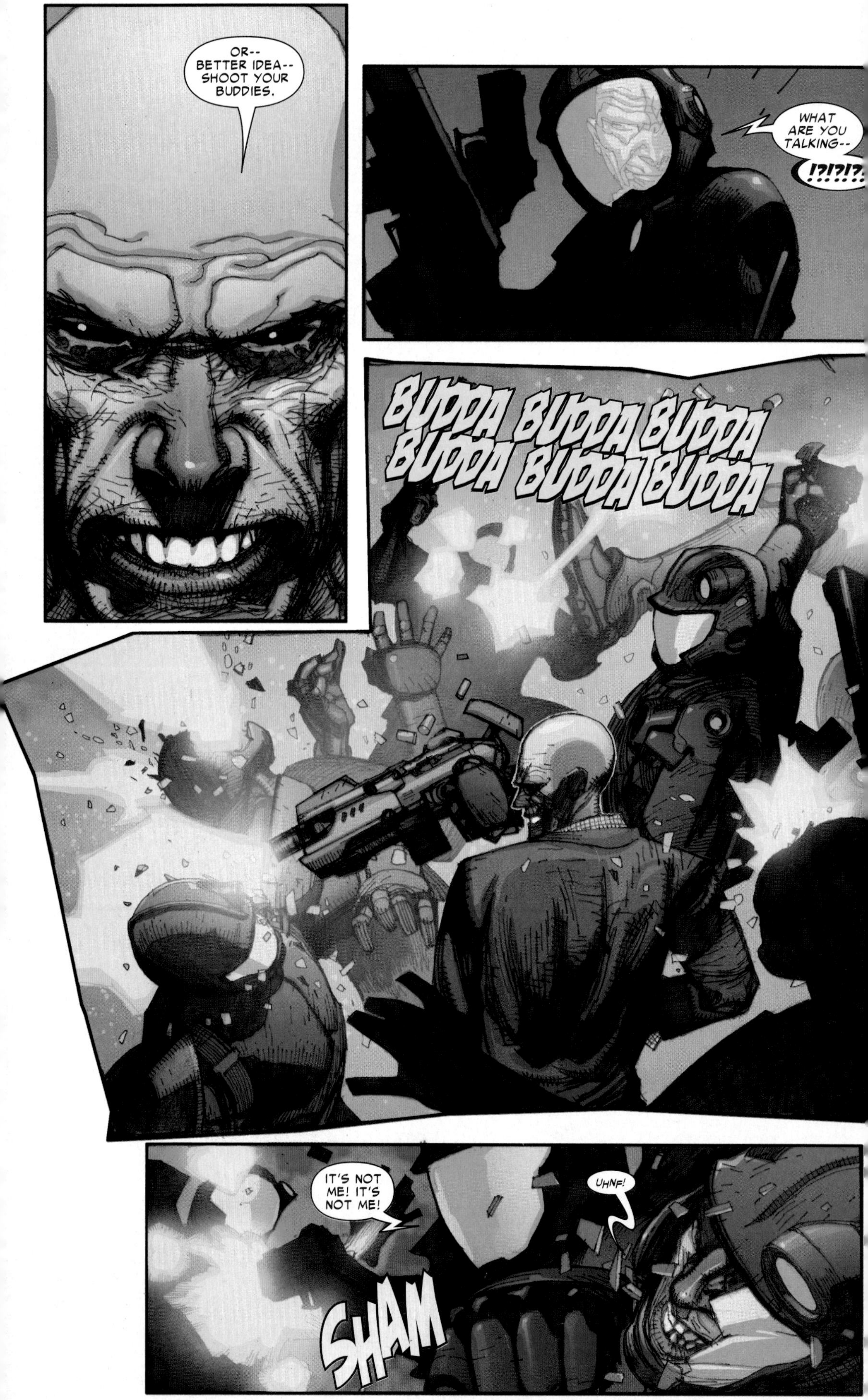
OR-- BETTER IDEA-- SHOOT YOUR BUDDIES.
WHAT ARE YOU TALKING--
!?!?!?
BUDDA BUDDA BUDDA BUDDA BUDDA BUDDA
IT'S NOT ME! IT'S NOT ME!
UHNF!
SHAM

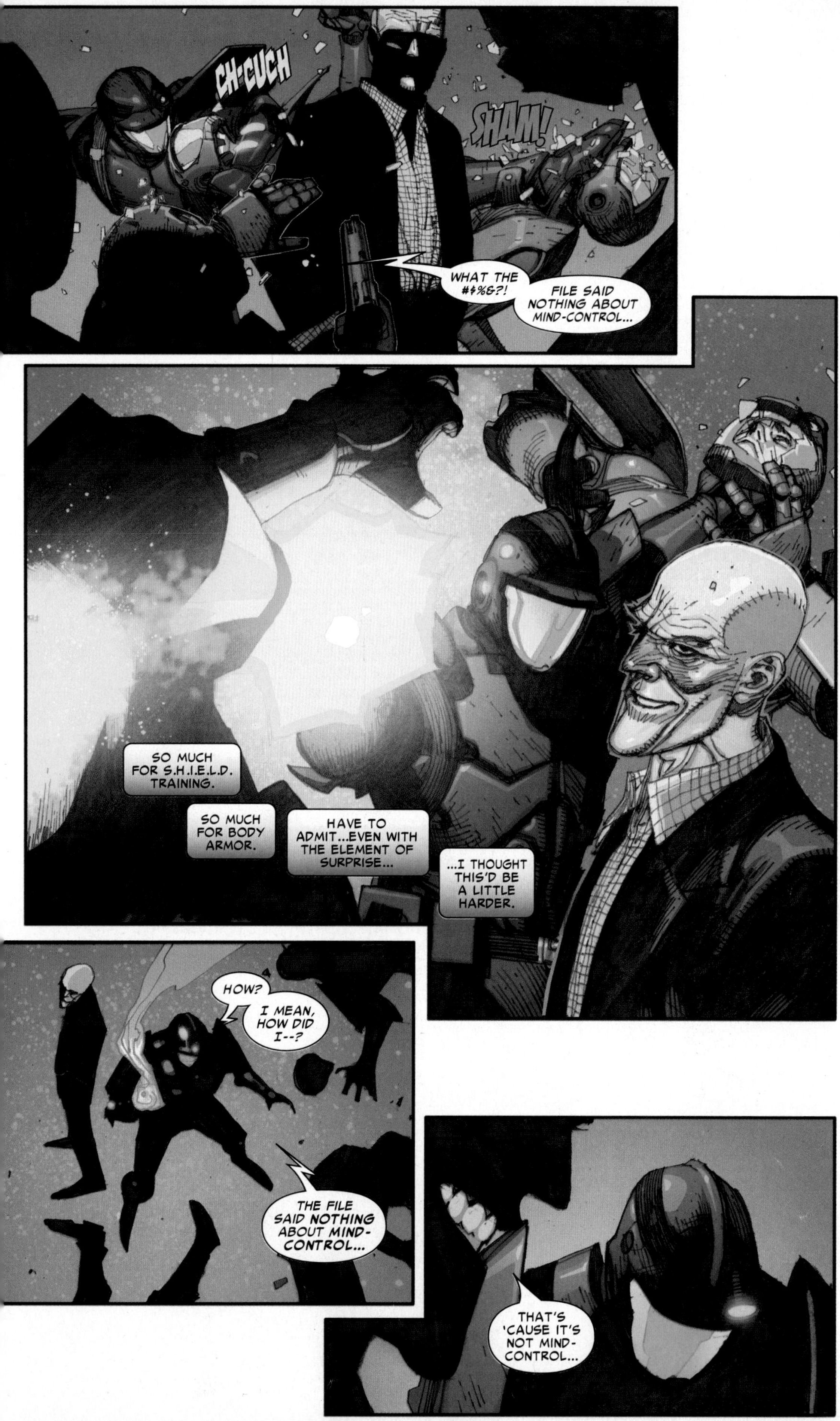
CH-CUCH
SHAM!
WHAT THE #$%&?!
FILE SAID NOTHING ABOUT MIND-CONTROL...
SO MUCH FOR S.H.I.E.L.D. TRAINING.
SO MUCH FOR BODY ARMOR.
HAVE TO ADMIT...EVEN WITH THE ELEMENT OF SURPRISE...
...I THOUGHT THIS'D BE A LITTLE HARDER.
HOW?
I MEAN, HOW DID I--?
THE FILE SAID NOTHING ABOUT MIND-CONTROL...
THAT'S 'CAUSE IT'S NOT MIND-CONTROL...

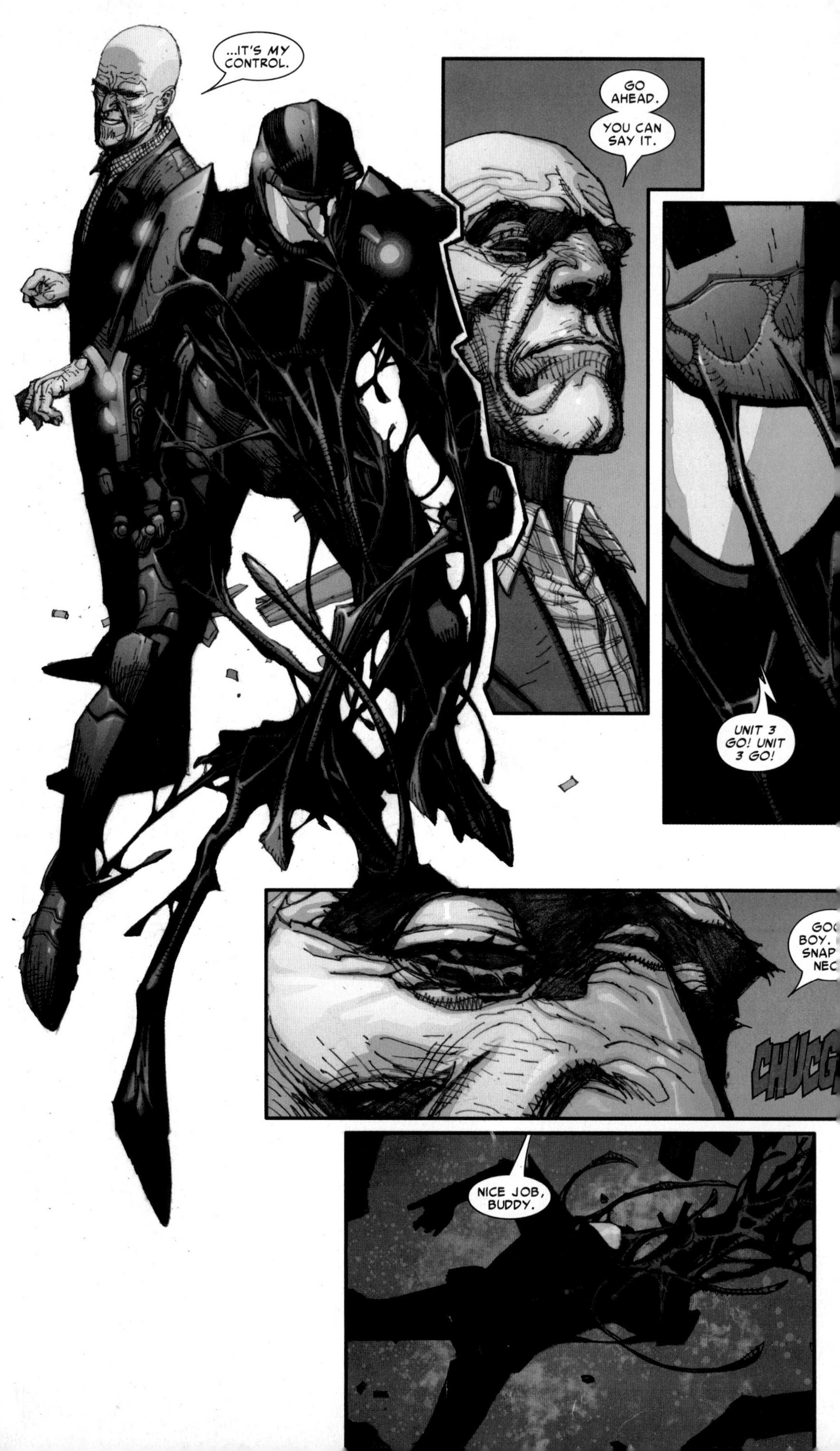

...IT'S MY CONTROL.
GO AHEAD.
YOU CAN SAY IT.
UNIT 3 GO! UNIT 3 GO!
NICE JOB, BUDDY.

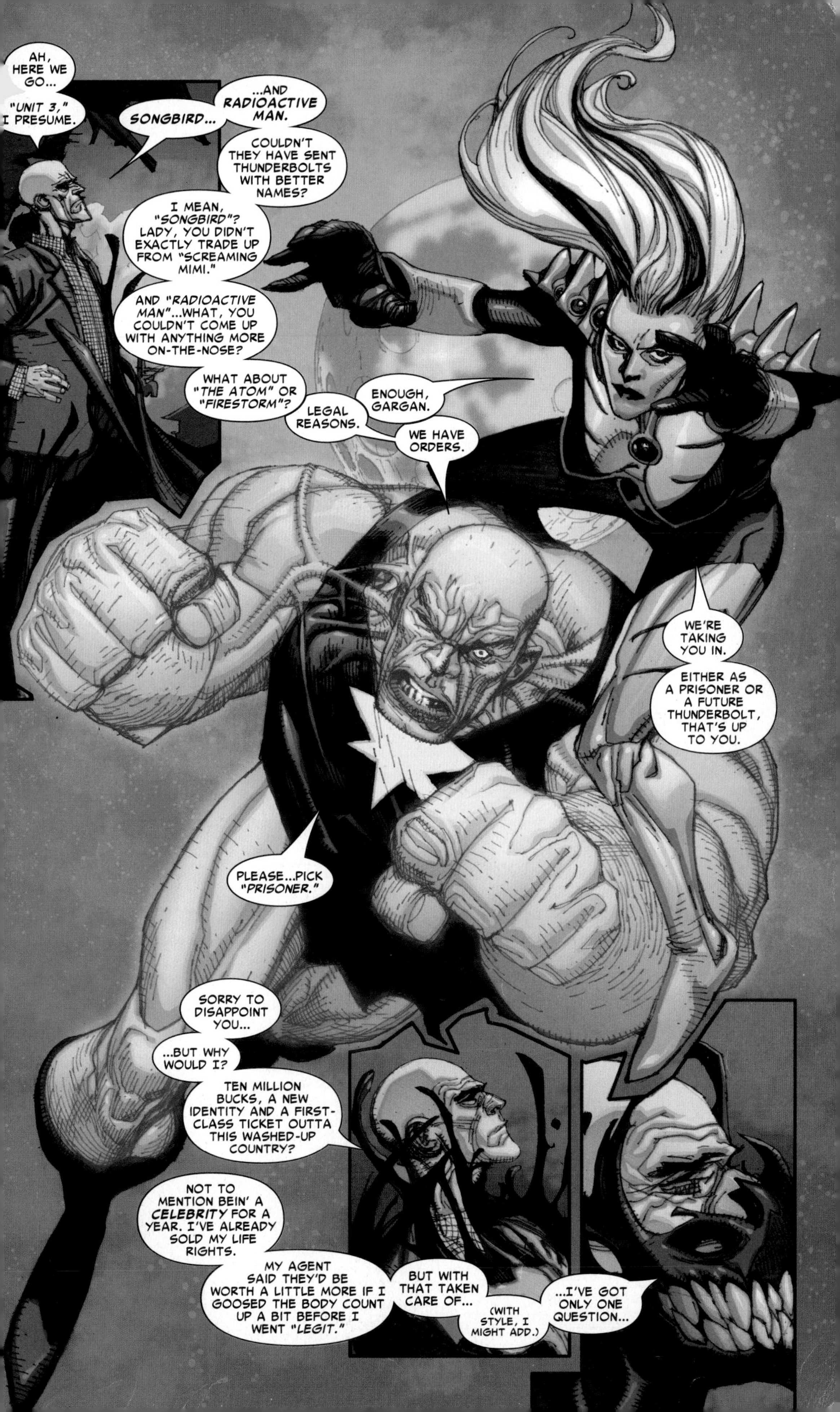
AH, HERE WE GO...
"UNIT 3," I PRESUME.
SONGBIRD...
...AND RADIOACTIVE MAN.
COULDN'T THEY HAVE SENT THUNDERBOLTS WITH BETTER NAMES?
I MEAN, "SONGBIRD"? LADY, YOU DIDN'T EXACTLY TRADE UP FROM "SCREAMING MIMI."
AND "RADIOACTIVE MAN"...WHAT, YOU COULDN'T COME UP WITH ANYTHING MORE ON-THE-NOSE?
WHAT ABOUT "THE ATOM" OR "FIRESTORM"?
LEGAL REASONS.
ENOUGH, GARGAN.
WE HAVE ORDERS.
WE'RE TAKING YOU IN.
EITHER AS A PRISONER OR A FUTURE THUNDERBOLT, THAT'S UP TO YOU.
PLEASE...PICK "PRISONER."
SORRY TO DISAPPOINT YOU...
...BUT WHY WOULD I?
TEN MILLION BUCKS, A NEW IDENTITY AND A FIRST-CLASS TICKET OUTTA THIS WASHED-UP COUNTRY?
NOT TO MENTION BEIN' A CELEBRITY FOR A YEAR. I'VE ALREADY SOLD MY LIFE RIGHTS.
MY AGENT SAID THEY'D BE WORTH A LITTLE MORE IF I GOOSED THE BODY COUNT UP A BIT BEFORE I WENT "LEGIT."
BUT WITH THAT TAKEN CARE OF...
(WITH STYLE, I MIGHT ADD.)
...I'VE GOT ONLY ONE QUESTION...

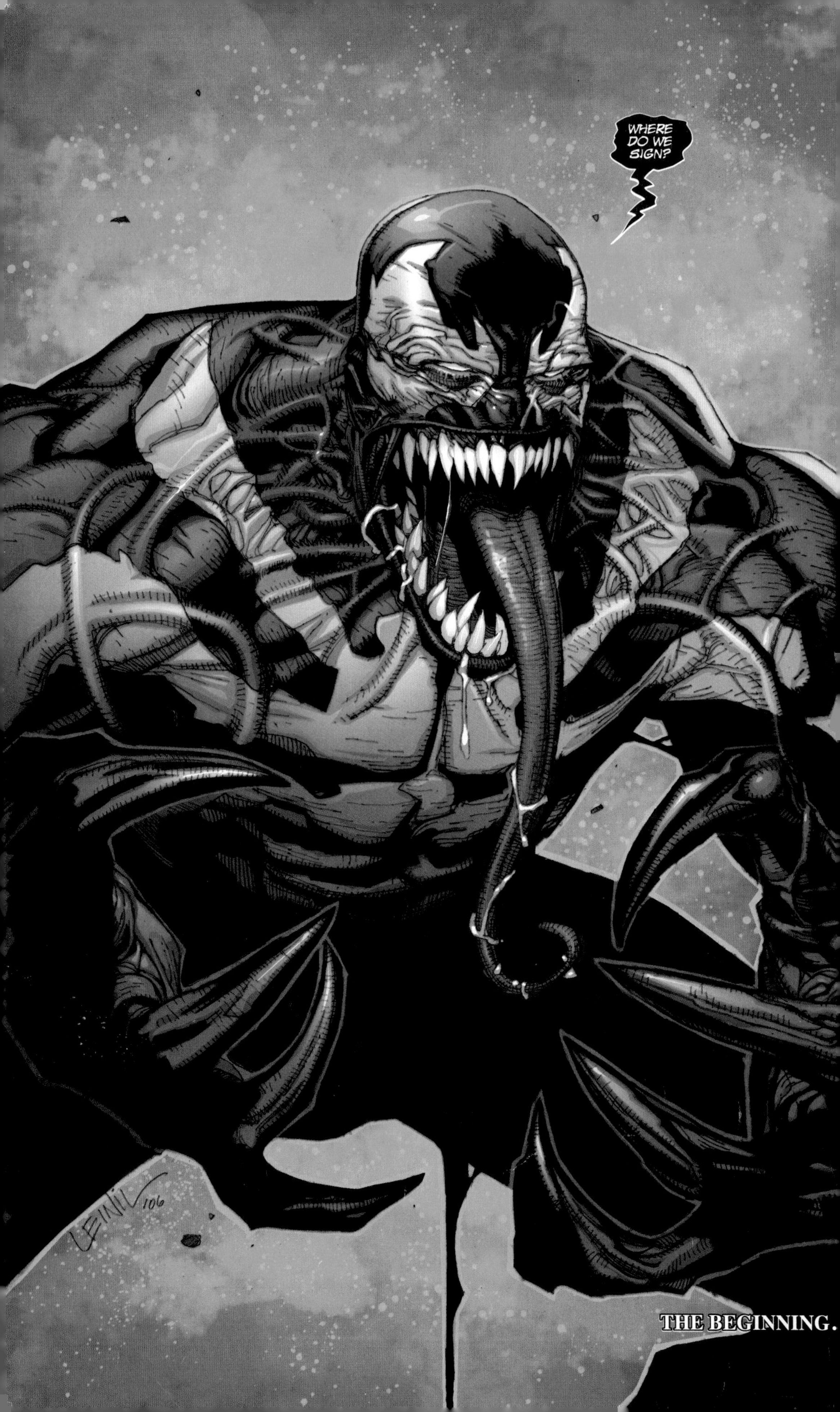
WHERE DO WE SIGN?
LEINIL '06
THE BEGINNING.

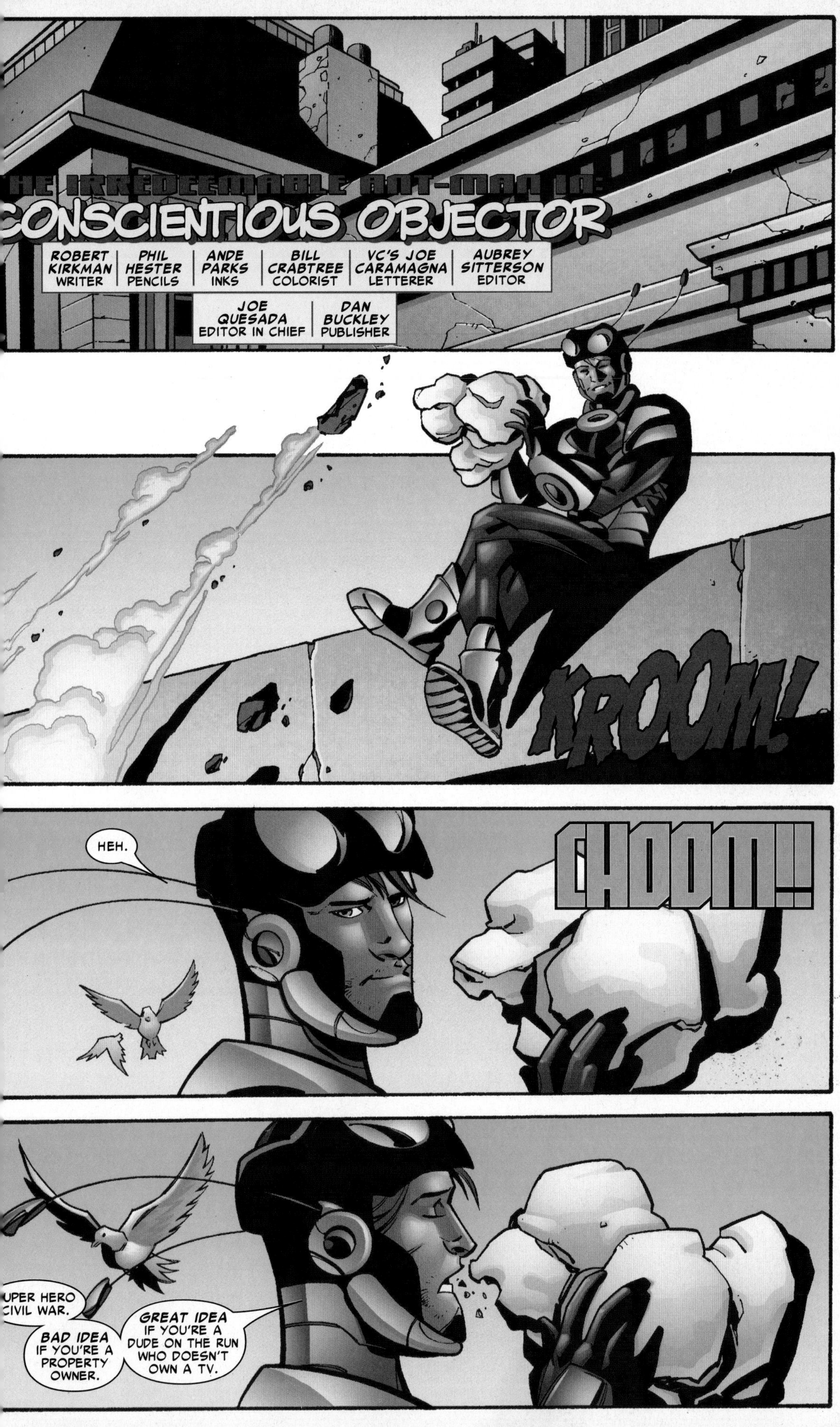
THE IRREDEEMABLE ANT-MAN IN:
CONSCIENTIOUS OBJECTOR
ROBERT KIRKMAN WRITER
PHIL HESTER PENCILS
ANDE PARKS INKS
BILL CRABTREE COLORIST
VC'S JOE CARAMAGNA LETTERER
AUBREY SITTERSON EDITOR
JOE QUESADA EDITOR IN CHIEF
DAN BUCKLEY PUBLISHER
KROOM!
HEH.
CHOOM!!
UPER HERO CIVIL WAR.
BAD IDEA IF YOU'RE A PROPERTY OWNER.
GREAT IDEA IF YOU'RE A DUDE ON THE RUN WHO DOESN'T OWN A TV.

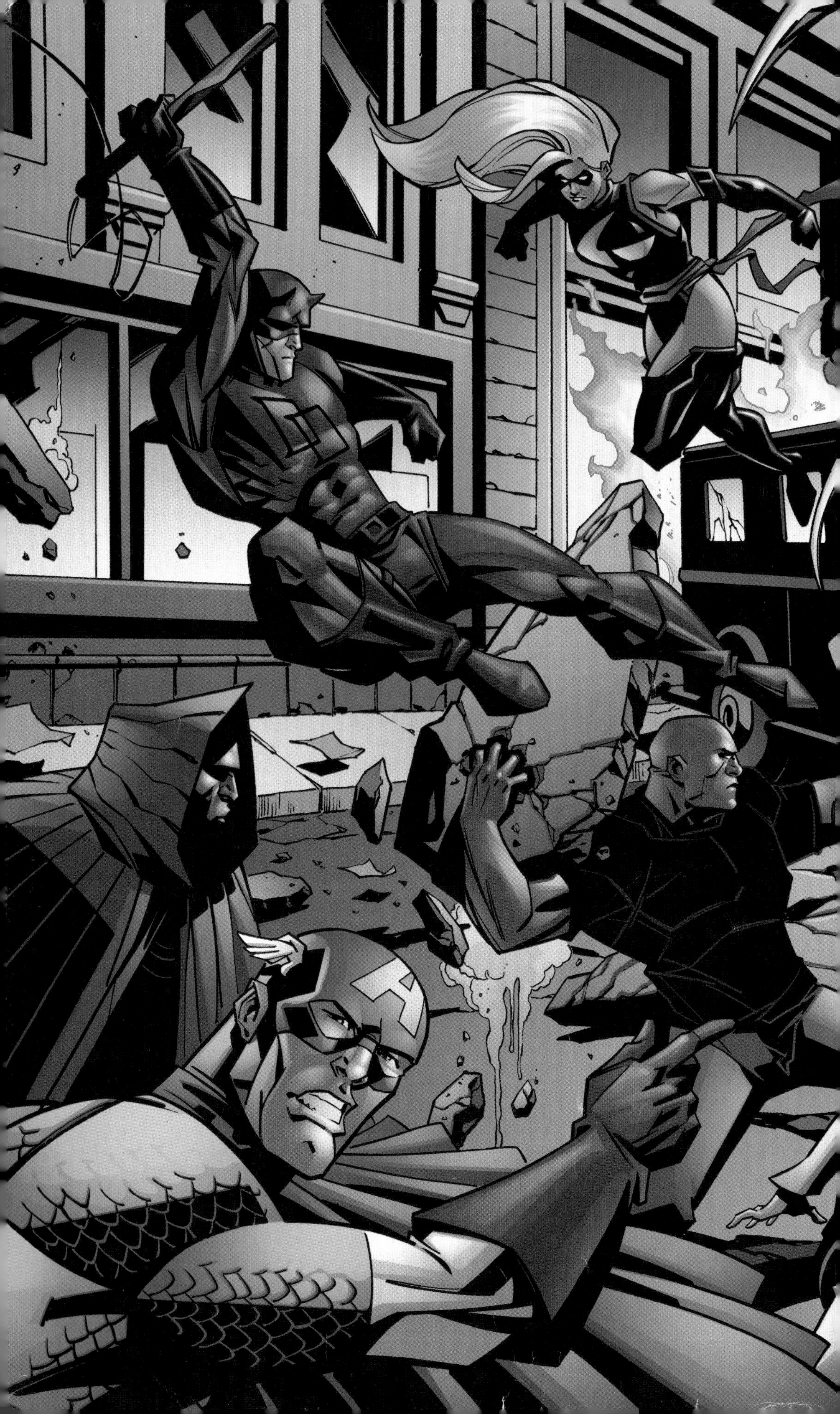

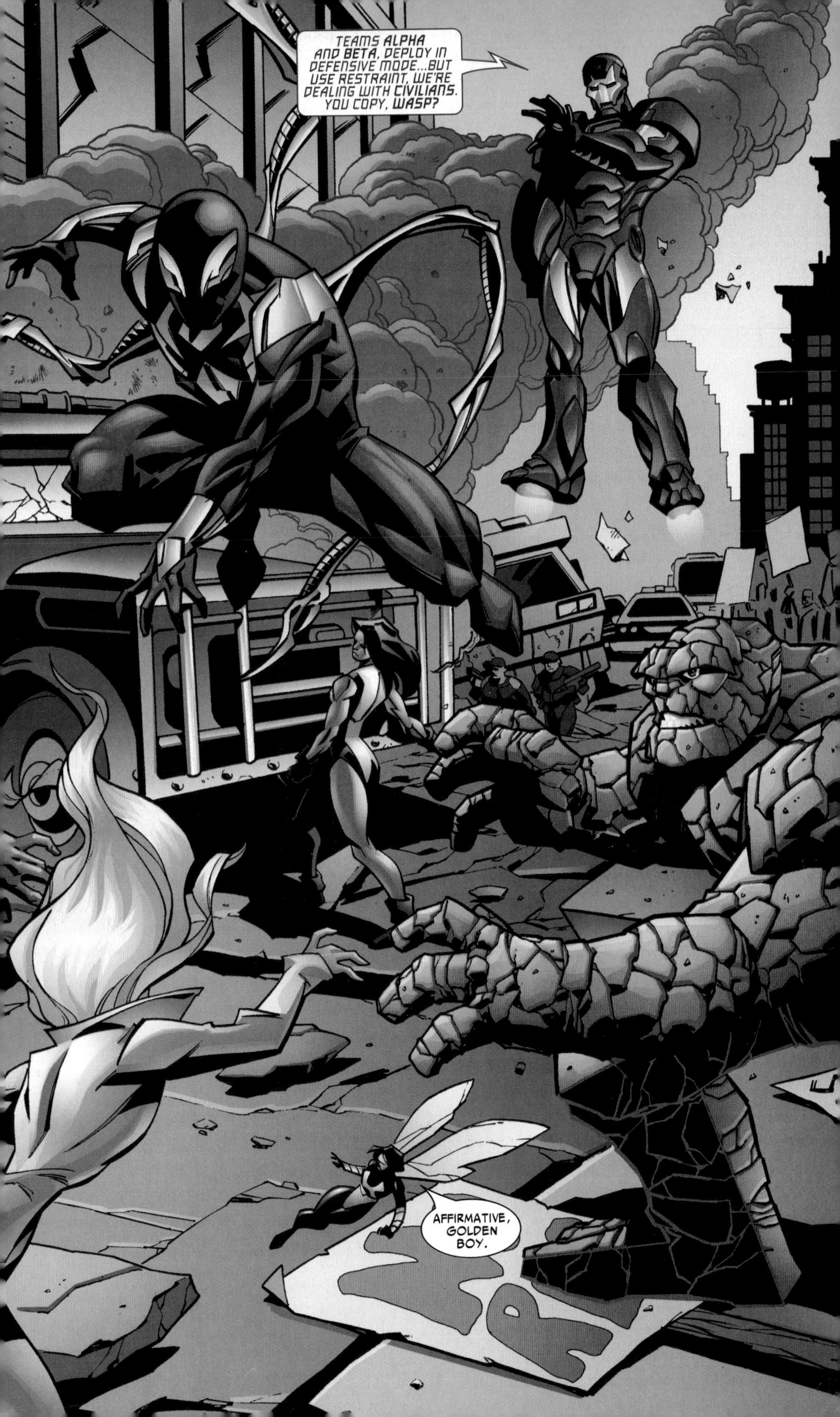
TEAMS ALPHA AND BETA, DEPLOY IN DEFENSIVE MODE...BUT USE RESTRAINT, WE'RE DEALING WITH CIVILIANS. YOU COPY, WASP?
AFFIRMATIVE, GOLDEN BOY.

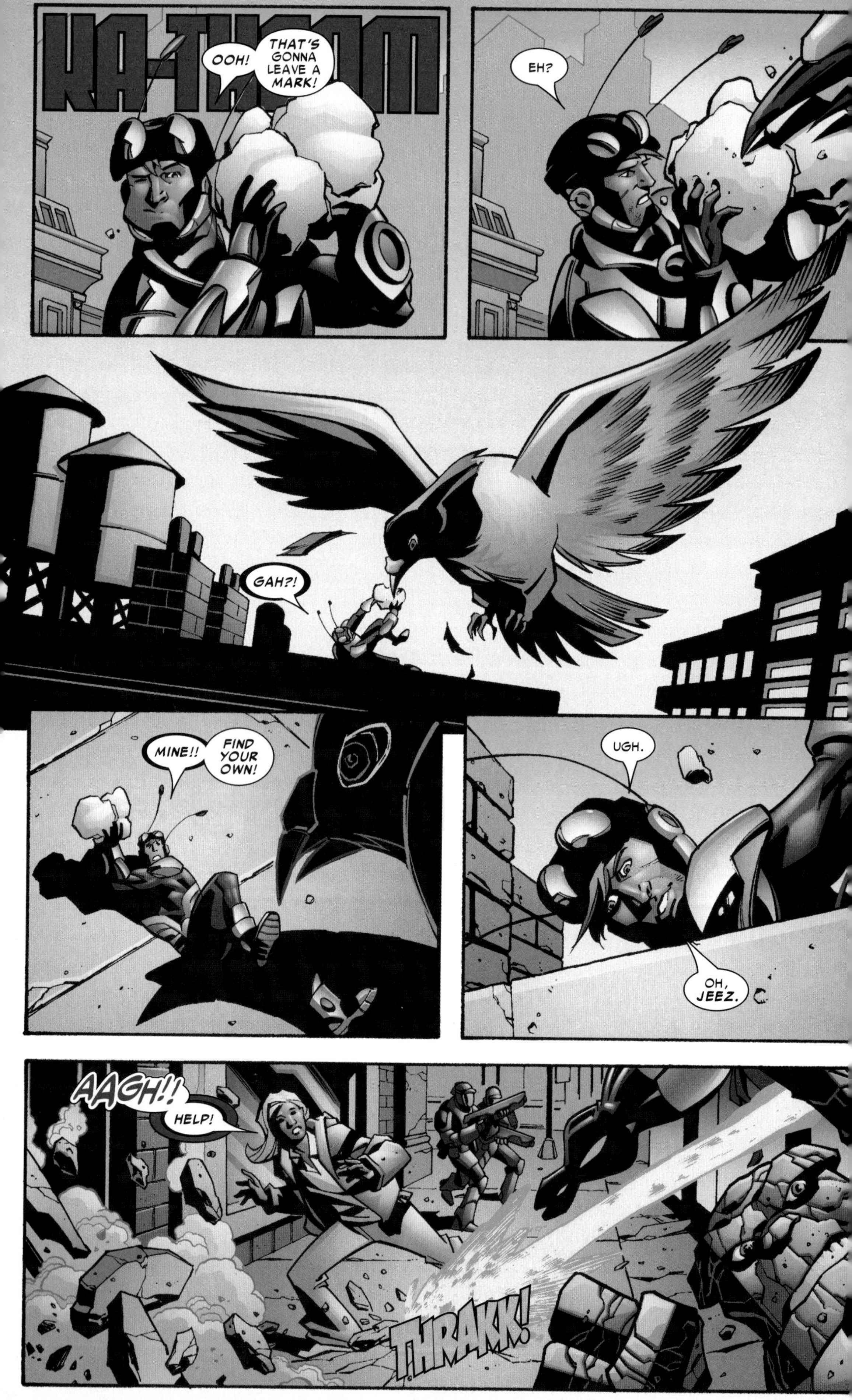
KA-THOOM
OOH!
THAT'S GONNA LEAVE A MARK!
EH?
GAH?!
MINE!!
FIND YOUR OWN!
UGH.
OH, JEEZ.
AAGH!!
HELP!
THRAKK!

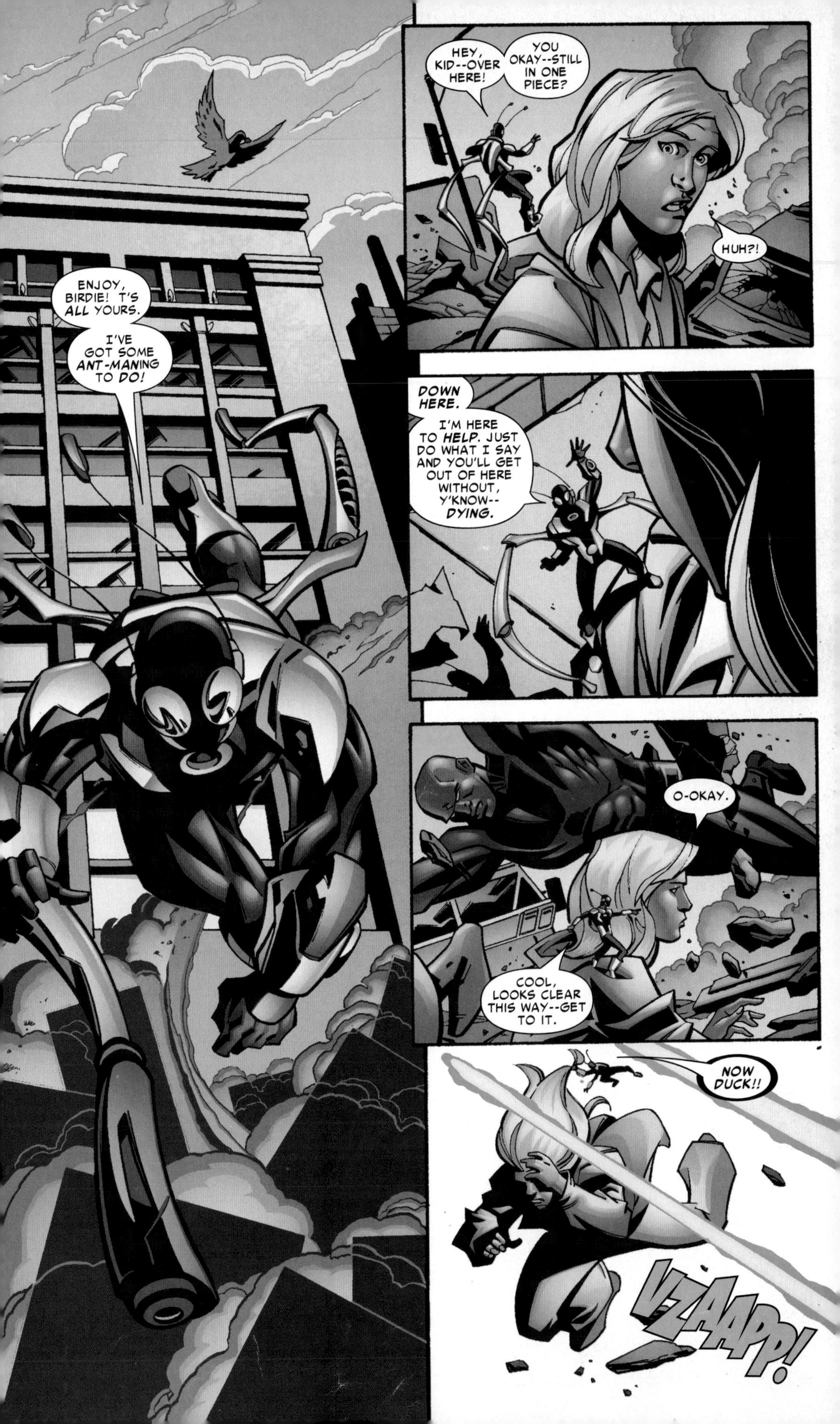
ENJOY, BIRDIE! T'S ALL YOURS.
I'VE GOT SOME ANT-MANING TO DO!
HEY, KID--OVER HERE!
YOU OKAY--STILL IN ONE PIECE?
HUH?!
DOWN HERE.
I'M HERE TO HELP. JUST DO WHAT I SAY AND YOU'LL GET OUT OF HERE WITHOUT, Y'KNOW--DYING.
O-OKAY.
COOL, LOOKS CLEAR THIS WAY--GET TO IT.
NOW DUCK!!
VZAAPP!

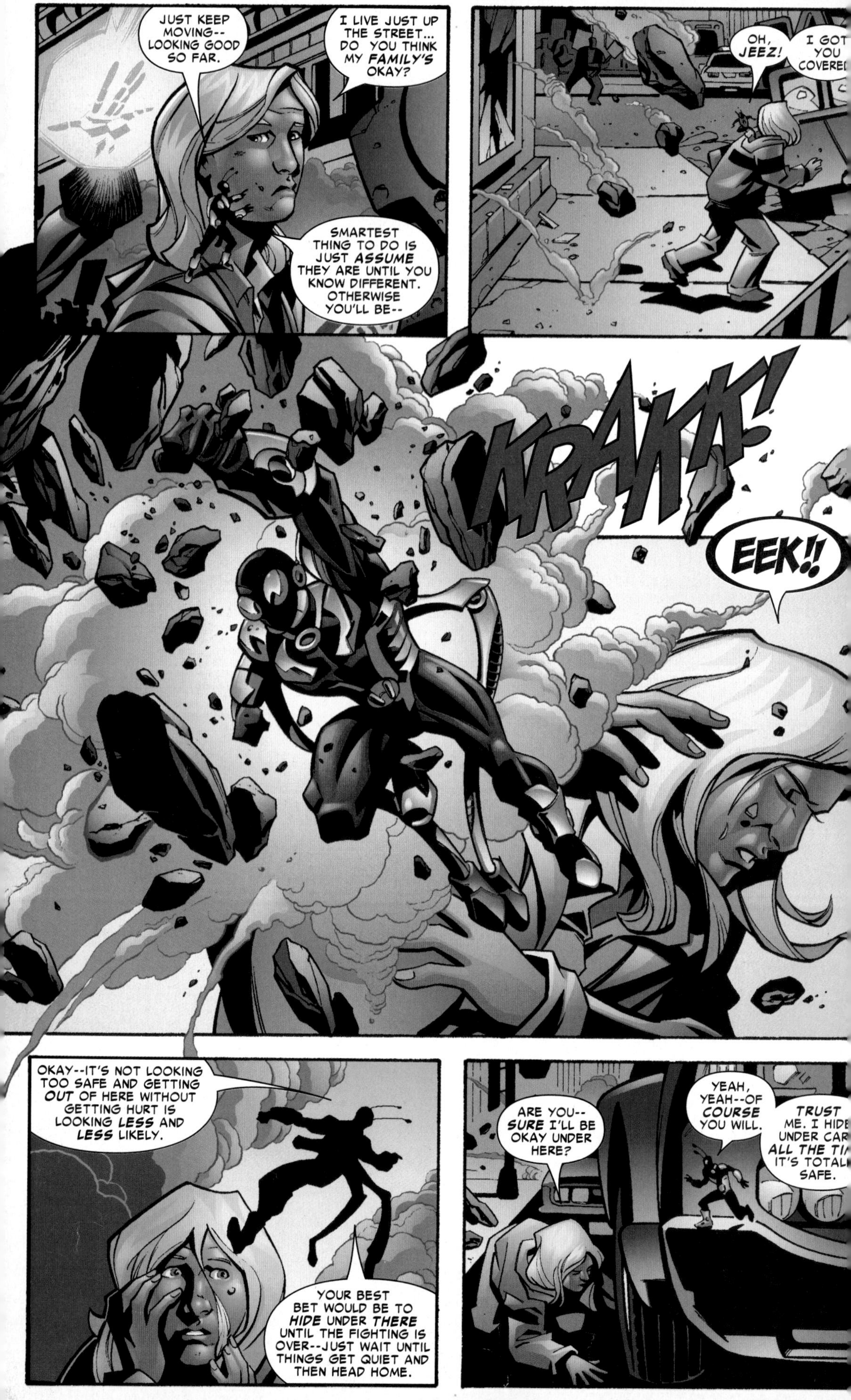

JUST KEEP MOVING-- LOOKING GOOD SO FAR.
I LIVE JUST UP THE STREET... DO YOU THINK MY *FAMILY'S* OKAY?
SMARTEST THING TO DO IS JUST *ASSUME* THEY ARE UNTIL YOU KNOW DIFFERENT. OTHERWISE YOU'LL BE--
OH, *JEEZ!*
I GOT YOU COVERED
KRAKK!
EEK!!
OKAY--IT'S NOT LOOKING TOO SAFE AND GETTING *OUT* OF HERE WITHOUT GETTING HURT IS LOOKING *LESS* AND *LESS* LIKELY.
YOUR BEST BET WOULD BE TO *HIDE* UNDER *THERE* UNTIL THE FIGHTING IS OVER--JUST WAIT UNTIL THINGS GET QUIET AND THEN HEAD HOME.
ARE YOU-- *SURE* I'LL BE OKAY UNDER HERE?
YEAH, YEAH--OF *COURSE* YOU WILL.
TRUST ME. I HIDE UNDER CAR *ALL THE TI* IT'S TOTAL SAFE.

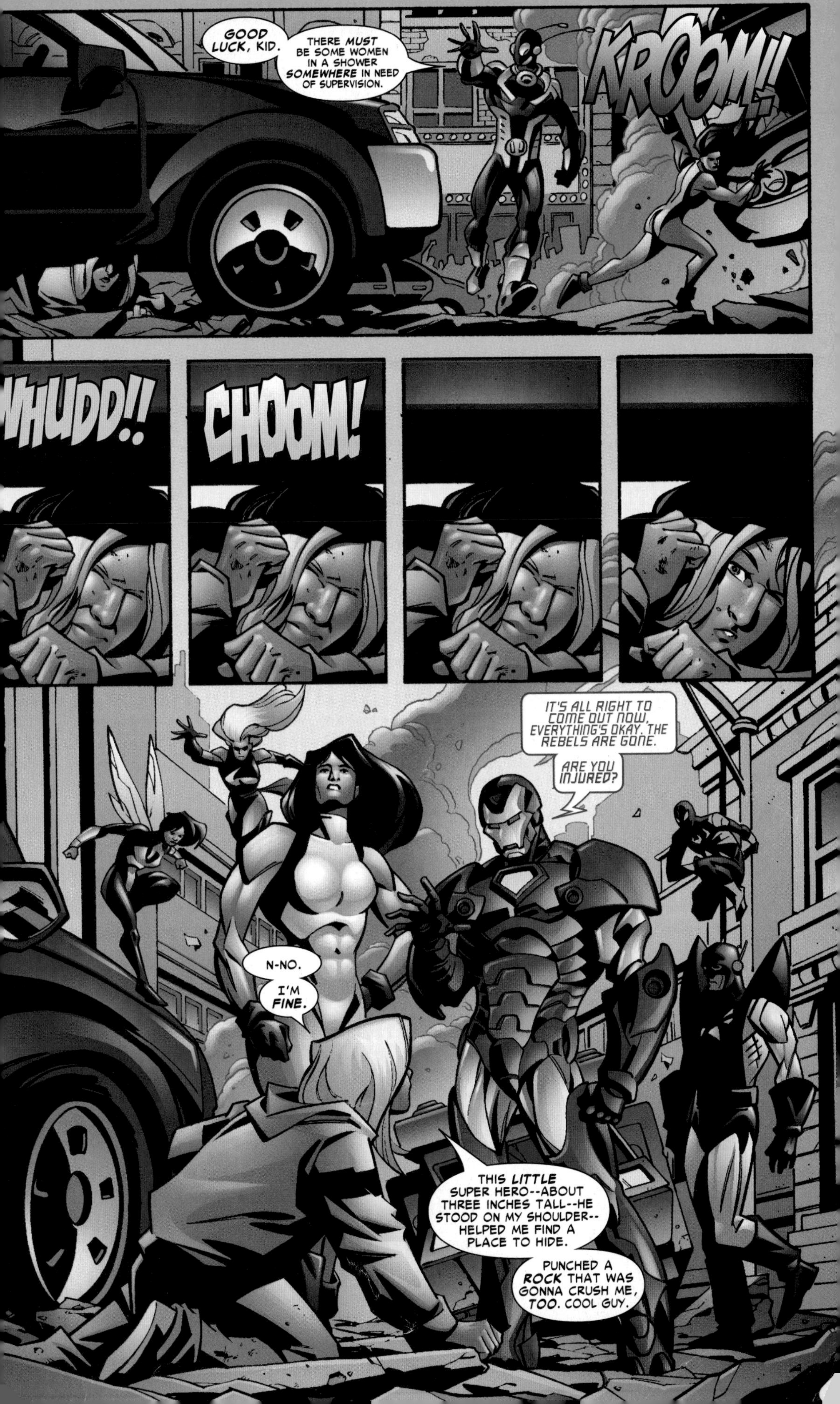
GOOD LUCK, KID.
THERE MUST BE SOME WOMEN IN A SHOWER SOMEWHERE IN NEED OF SUPERVISION.
KROOM!!
WHUDD!!
CHOOM!
IT'S ALL RIGHT TO COME OUT NOW, EVERYTHING'S OKAY. THE REBELS ARE GONE.
ARE YOU INJURED?
N-NO.
I'M FINE.
THIS LITTLE SUPER HERO--ABOUT THREE INCHES TALL--HE STOOD ON MY SHOULDER--HELPED ME FIND A PLACE TO HIDE.
PUNCHED A ROCK THAT WAS GONNA CRUSH ME, TOO. COOL GUY.

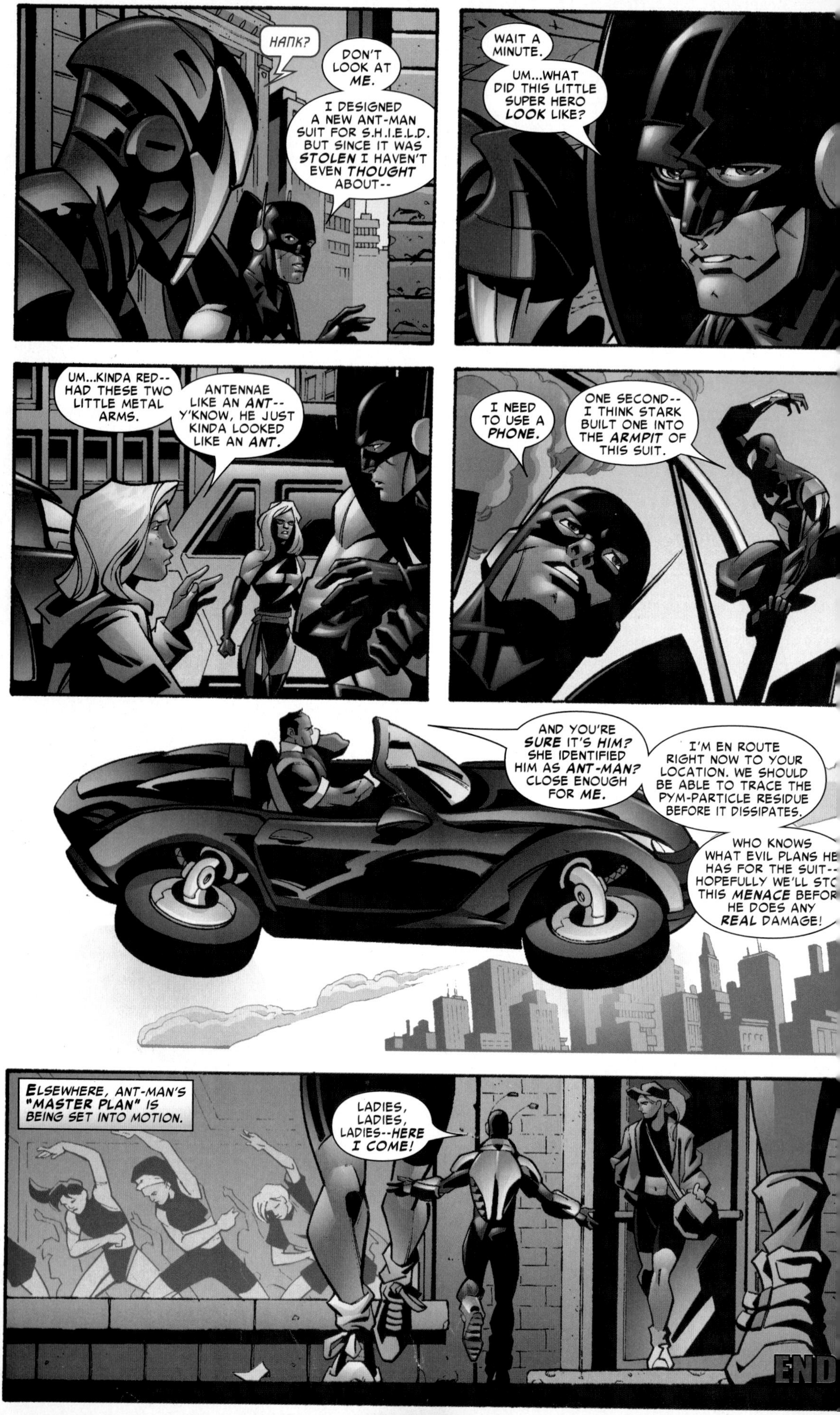
HANK?
DON'T LOOK AT ME.
I DESIGNED A NEW ANT-MAN SUIT FOR S.H.I.E.L.D. BUT SINCE IT WAS STOLEN I HAVEN'T EVEN THOUGHT ABOUT--
WAIT A MINUTE.
UM...WHAT DID THIS LITTLE SUPER HERO LOOK LIKE?
UM...KINDA RED--HAD THESE TWO LITTLE METAL ARMS.
ANTENNAE LIKE AN ANT--Y'KNOW, HE JUST KINDA LOOKED LIKE AN ANT.
I NEED TO USE A PHONE.
ONE SECOND--I THINK STARK BUILT ONE INTO THE ARMPIT OF THIS SUIT.
AND YOU'RE SURE IT'S HIM? SHE IDENTIFIED HIM AS ANT-MAN? CLOSE ENOUGH FOR ME.
I'M EN ROUTE RIGHT NOW TO YOUR LOCATION. WE SHOULD BE ABLE TO TRACE THE PYM-PARTICLE RESIDUE BEFORE IT DISSIPATES.
WHO KNOWS WHAT EVIL PLANS HE HAS FOR THE SUIT--HOPEFULLY WE'LL STO THIS MENACE BEFOR HE DOES ANY REAL DAMAGE!
ELSEWHERE, ANT-MAN'S "MASTER PLAN" IS BEING SET INTO MOTION.
LADIES, LADIES, LADIES--HERE I COME!
END

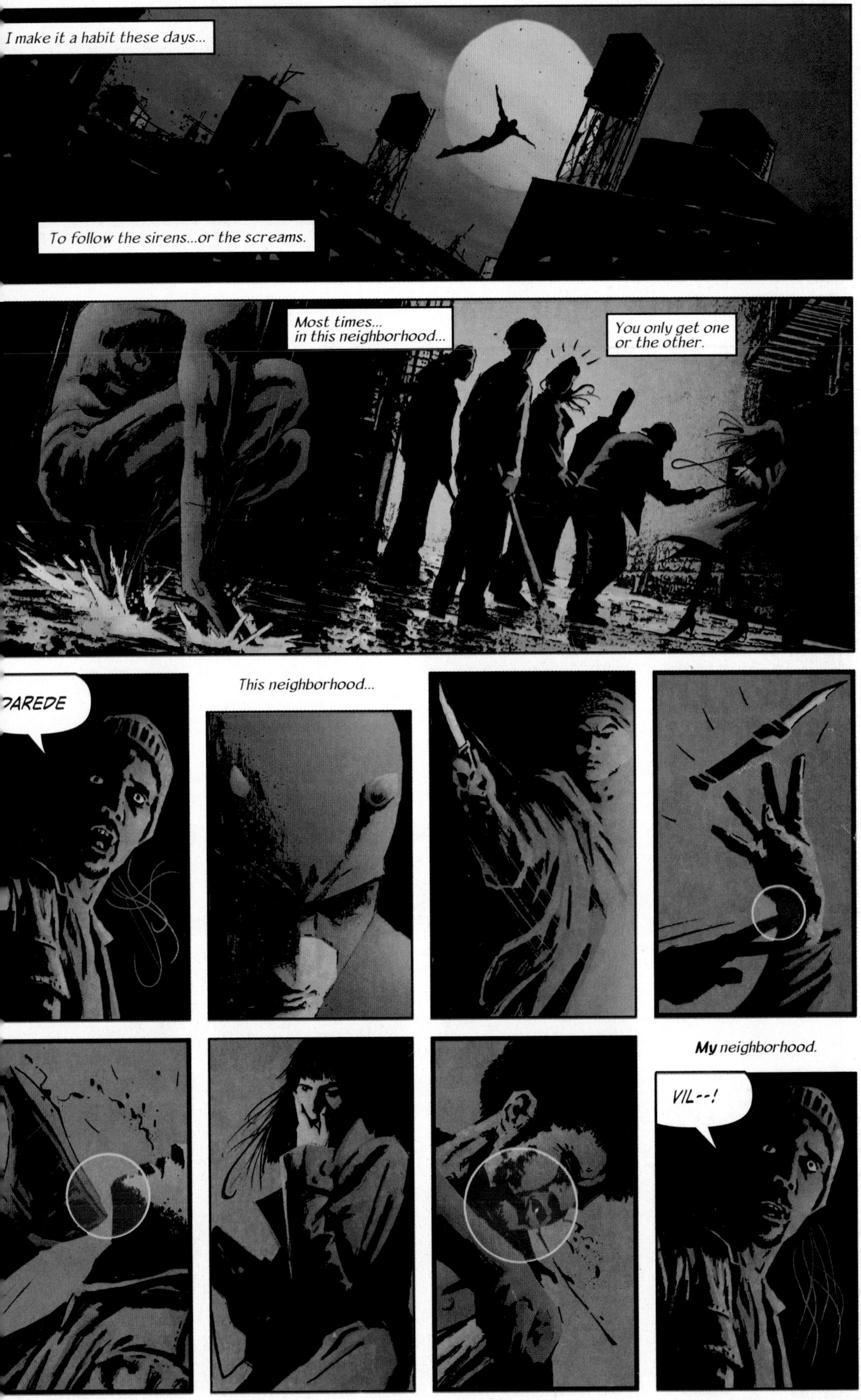
I make it a habit these days...
To follow the sirens...or the screams.
Most times... in this neighborhood...
You only get one or the other.
PAREDE
This neighborhood...
My neighborhood.
VIL--!

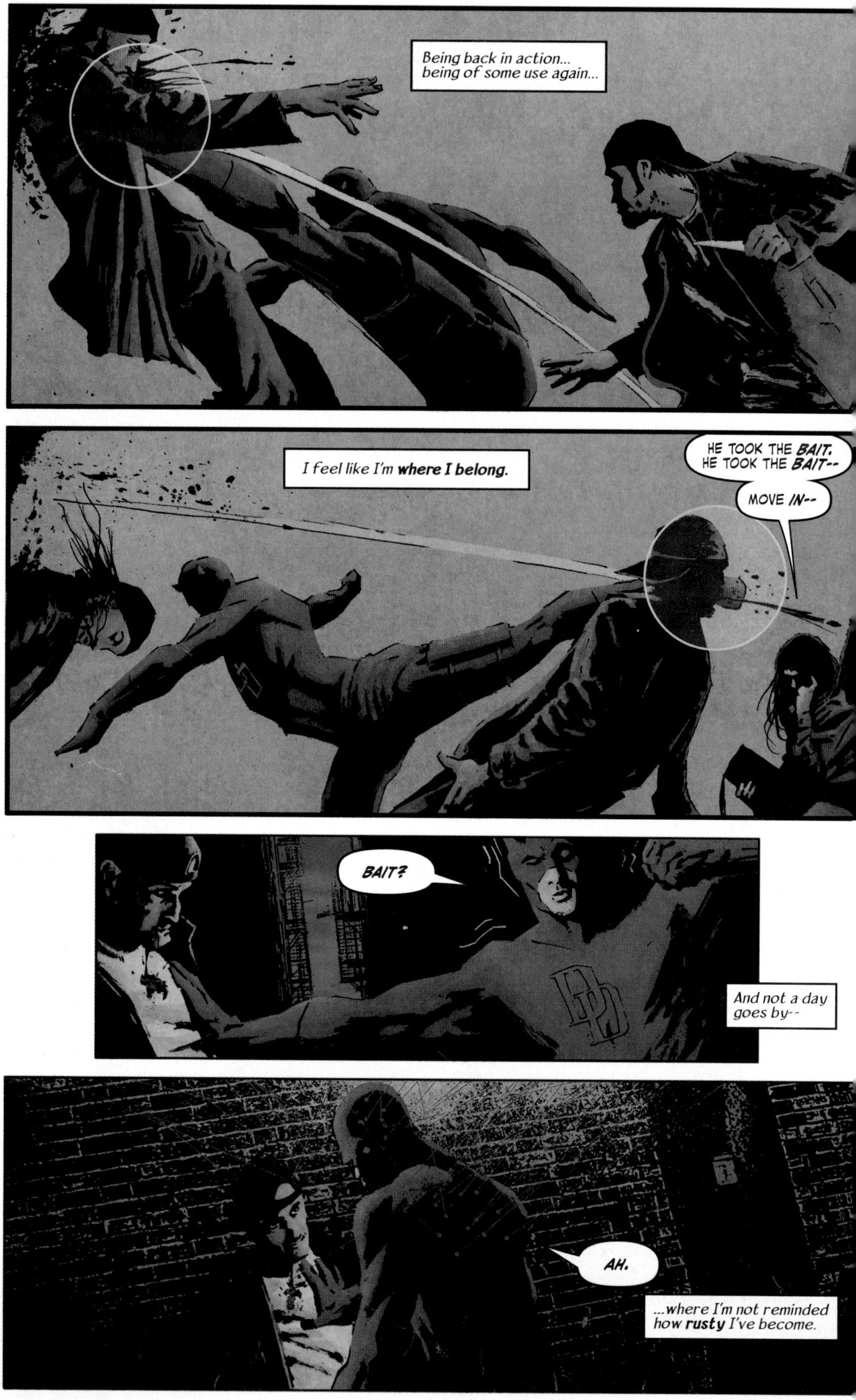
Being back in action...
being of some use again...
I feel like I'm **where I belong.**
HE TOOK THE *BAIT.* HE TOOK THE *BAIT--*
MOVE *IN--*
BAIT?
And not a day goes by--
AH.
...where I'm not reminded how **rusty** I've become.

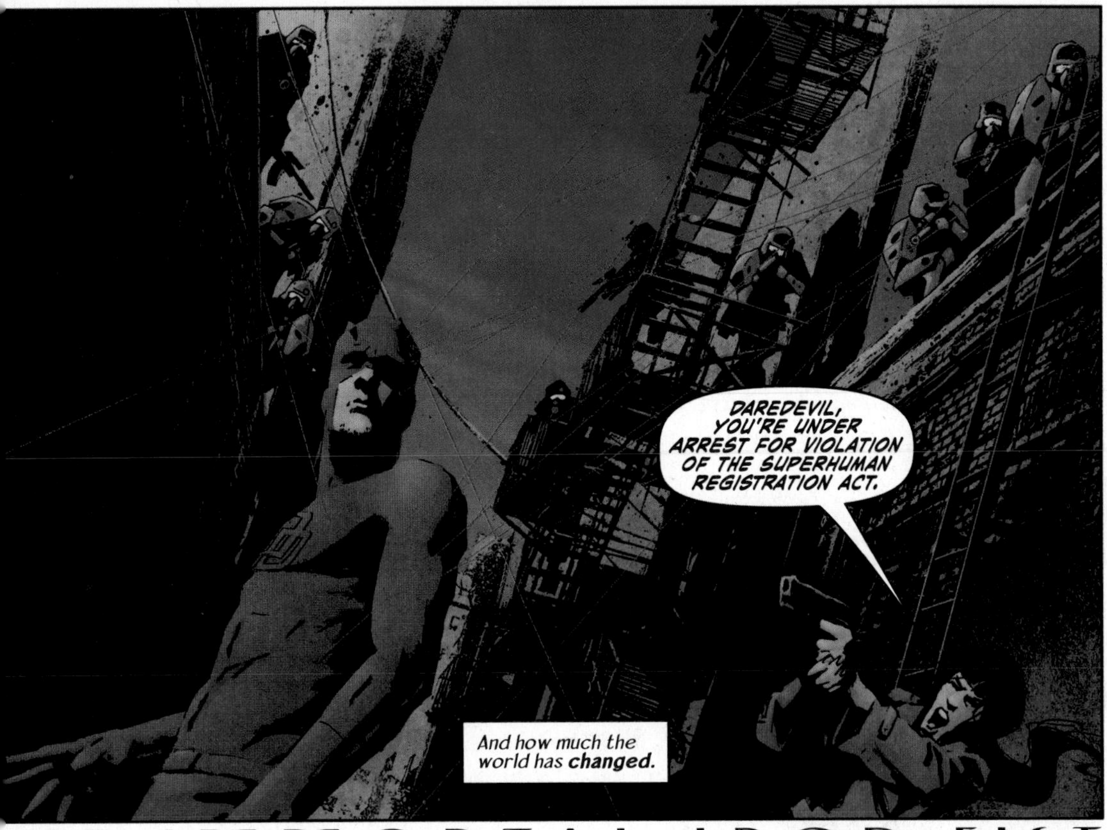
DAREDEVIL, YOU'RE UNDER ARREST FOR VIOLATION OF THE SUPERHUMAN REGISTRATION ACT.
And how much the world has **changed.**

HE IMMORTAL IRON FIST
CHOOSING SIDES"

ED BRUBAKER & MATT FRACTION – WRITERS
DAVID AJA – ARTIST / **MATT HOLLINGSWORTH** – COLORIST
DAVE LANPHEAR – LETTERER / **WARREN SIMONS** – EDITOR

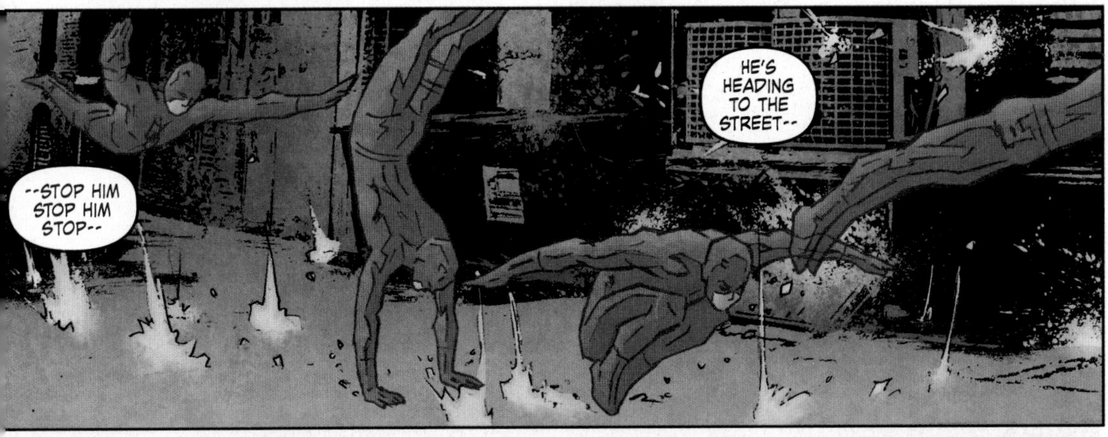
HE'S HEADING TO THE STREET--
--STOP HIM STOP HIM STOP--

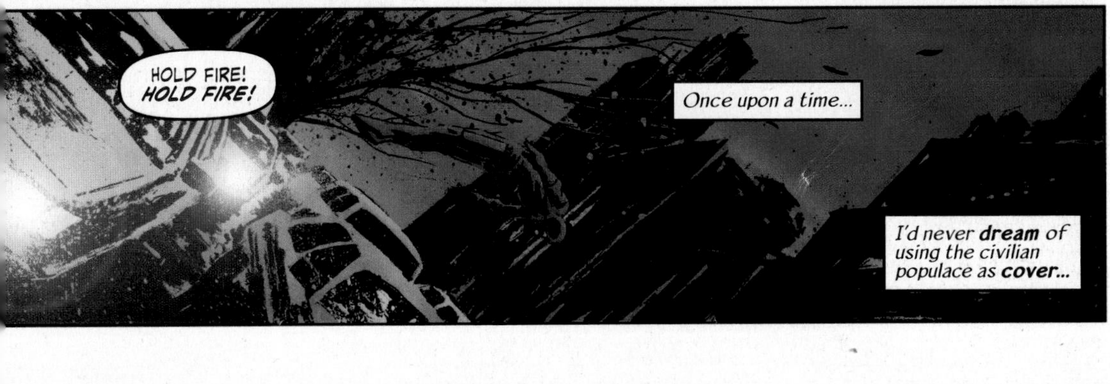
HOLD FIRE! *HOLD FIRE!*
Once upon a time...
I'd never **dream** of using the civilian populace as **cover...**

...but **war** changes everything.

It changes what we do...

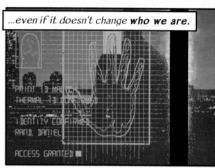

...even if it doesn't change **who we are.**

PRINT ID MATCH
THERMAL ID CONFIRMED

IDENTITY CONFIRMED
RAND, DANIEL

ACCESS GRANTED

YOU HAVE **ONE** MESSAGE.

DANNY, IT'S **JERYN.** LOOK, THIS **THING** COMING UP NEXT WEEK, IT'S PRETTY **BIG** FOR US. LIKE, **BIG** WITH CAPITAL **BILLIONS...**

IT'S **BIG** FOR ME, IT'S **BIG** FOR YOU. IT'S **BIG** FOR RAND...HELL, DANNY, IT'S **BIG** FOR **ALL OF CHINA...**

...AND EVERY-BODY HERE CA... APPRECIATE THA... YOU WANT TO G... **INVOLVED** AND MAKE AN APPEARANCE A... THE **FINISH LIN...** BUT...

...WELL, DANNY, IT'S NOT LIKE YOU'VE MADE ANY **SECRET** OF NOT BEING AROUND FOR THE LAST, UH, **FEW YEARS** OR ANYTHING...

AND IF YOU'RE COMING INTO **THE ROOM** ON THIS THING...

...I WANT YOU TO REMEMBER **WHO YOU ARE...**

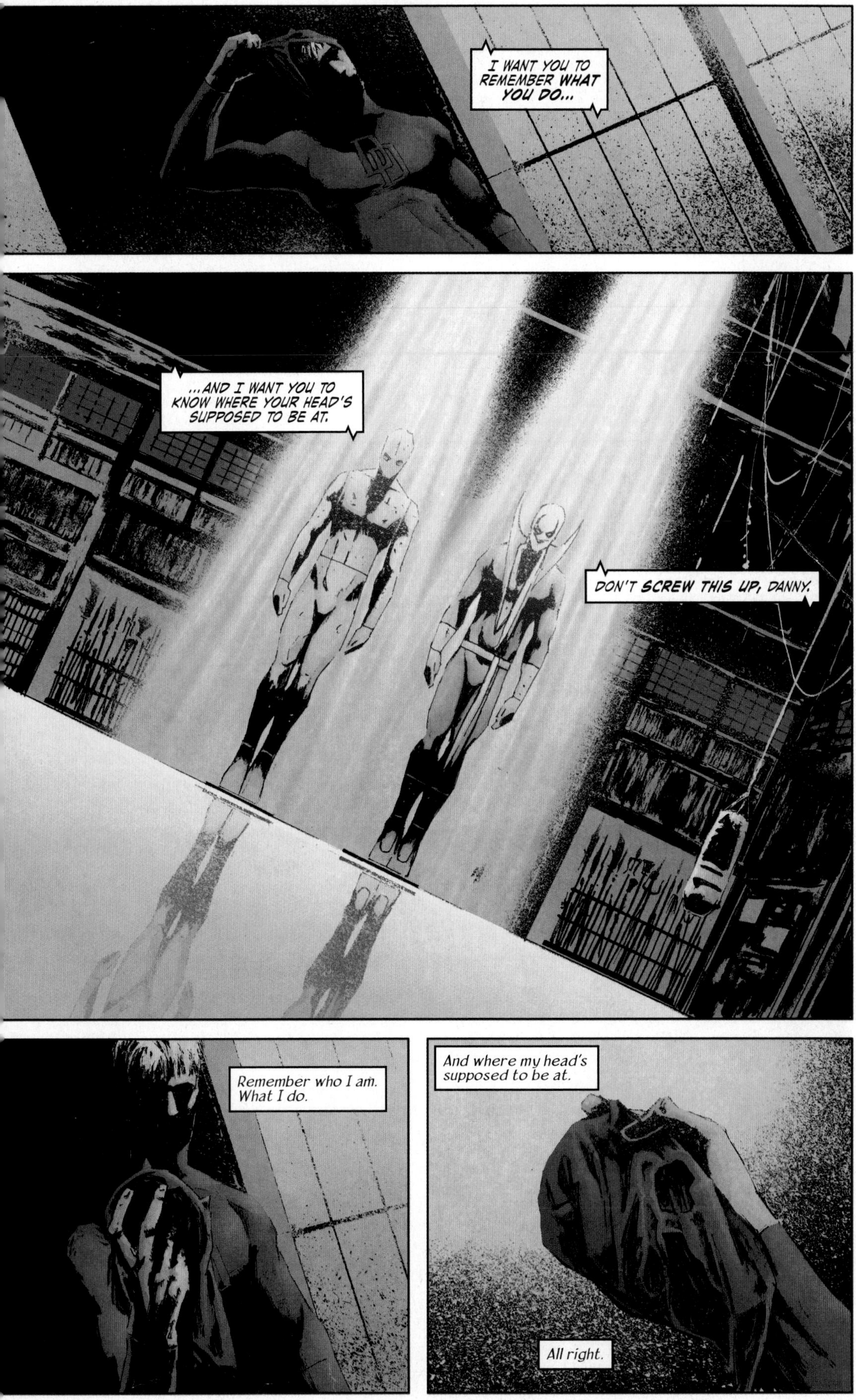
I WANT YOU TO REMEMBER WHAT YOU DO...
...AND I WANT YOU TO KNOW WHERE YOUR HEAD'S SUPPOSED TO BE AT.
DON'T SCREW THIS UP, DANNY.
Remember who I am. What I do.
And where my head's supposed to be at.
All right.

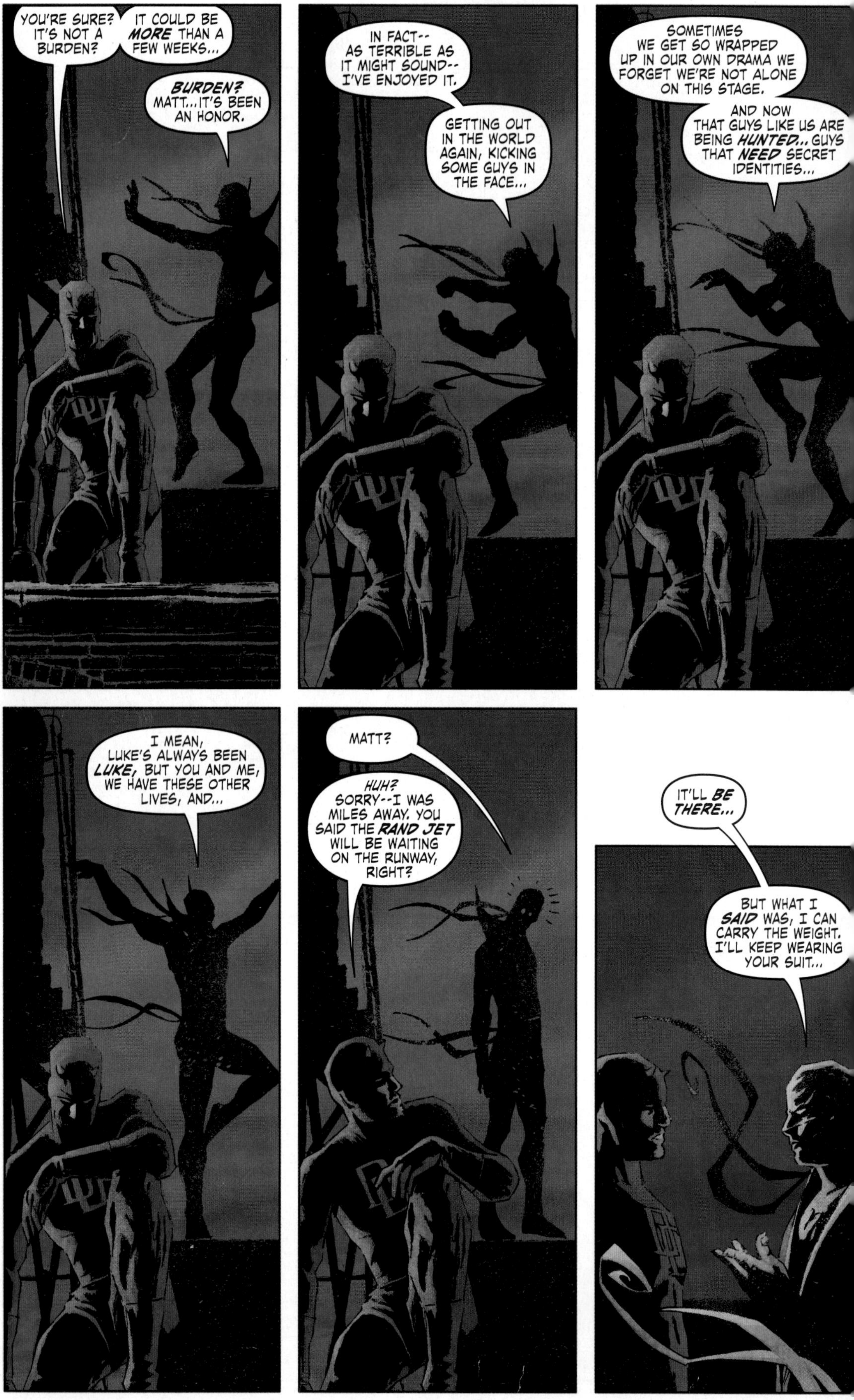
YOU'RE SURE? IT'S NOT A BURDEN?
IT COULD BE MORE THAN A FEW WEEKS...
BURDEN? MATT...IT'S BEEN AN HONOR.
IN FACT-- AS TERRIBLE AS IT MIGHT SOUND-- I'VE ENJOYED IT.
GETTING OUT IN THE WORLD AGAIN, KICKING SOME GUYS IN THE FACE...
SOMETIMES WE GET SO WRAPPED UP IN OUR OWN DRAMA WE FORGET WE'RE NOT ALONE ON THIS STAGE.
AND NOW THAT GUYS LIKE US ARE BEING HUNTED... GUYS THAT NEED SECRET IDENTITIES...
I MEAN, LUKE'S ALWAYS BEEN LUKE, BUT YOU AND ME, WE HAVE THESE OTHER LIVES, AND...
MATT?
HUH? SORRY--I WAS MILES AWAY. YOU SAID THE RAND JET WILL BE WAITING ON THE RUNWAY, RIGHT?
IT'LL BE THERE...
BUT WHAT I SAID WAS, I CAN CARRY THE WEIGHT. I'LL KEEP WEARING YOUR SUIT...

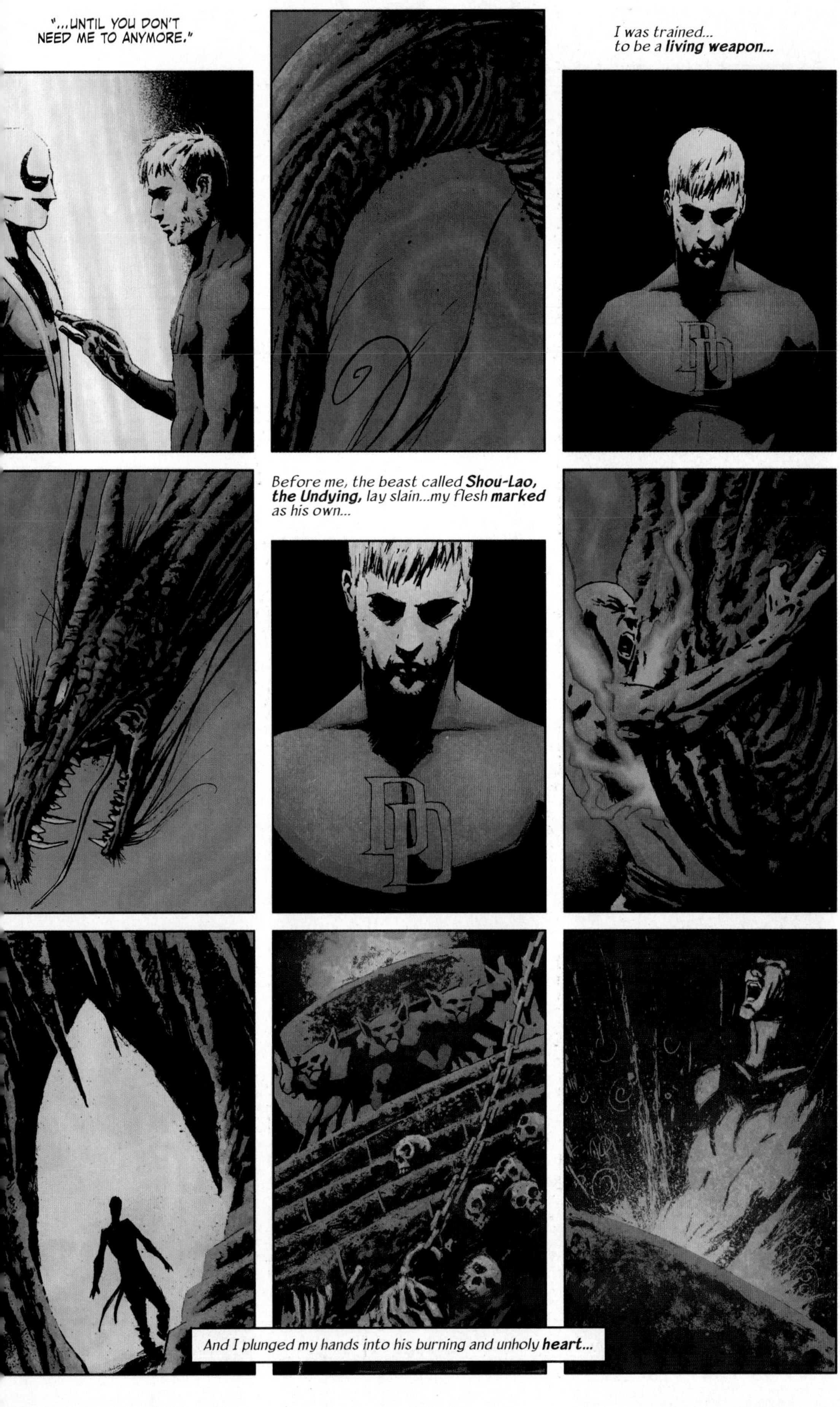
"...UNTIL YOU DON'T NEED ME TO ANYMORE."
I was trained... to be a **living weapon...**
Before me, the beast called **Shou-Lao, the Undying,** lay slain...my flesh **marked** as his own...
And I plunged my hands into his burning and unholy **heart...**

And my fist became like unto...

..a thing of **iron**.

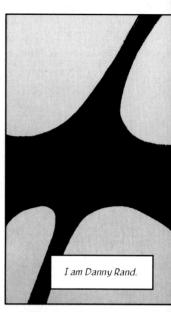

I am Danny Rand.

The Immortal Iron Fist.

I made a promise to Matt Murdock to wear his mask...I've fought this war in his place... And I'll continue to.

But I haven't **forgotten** who I am...

...and soon it will be time to carry my **own** burdens again.

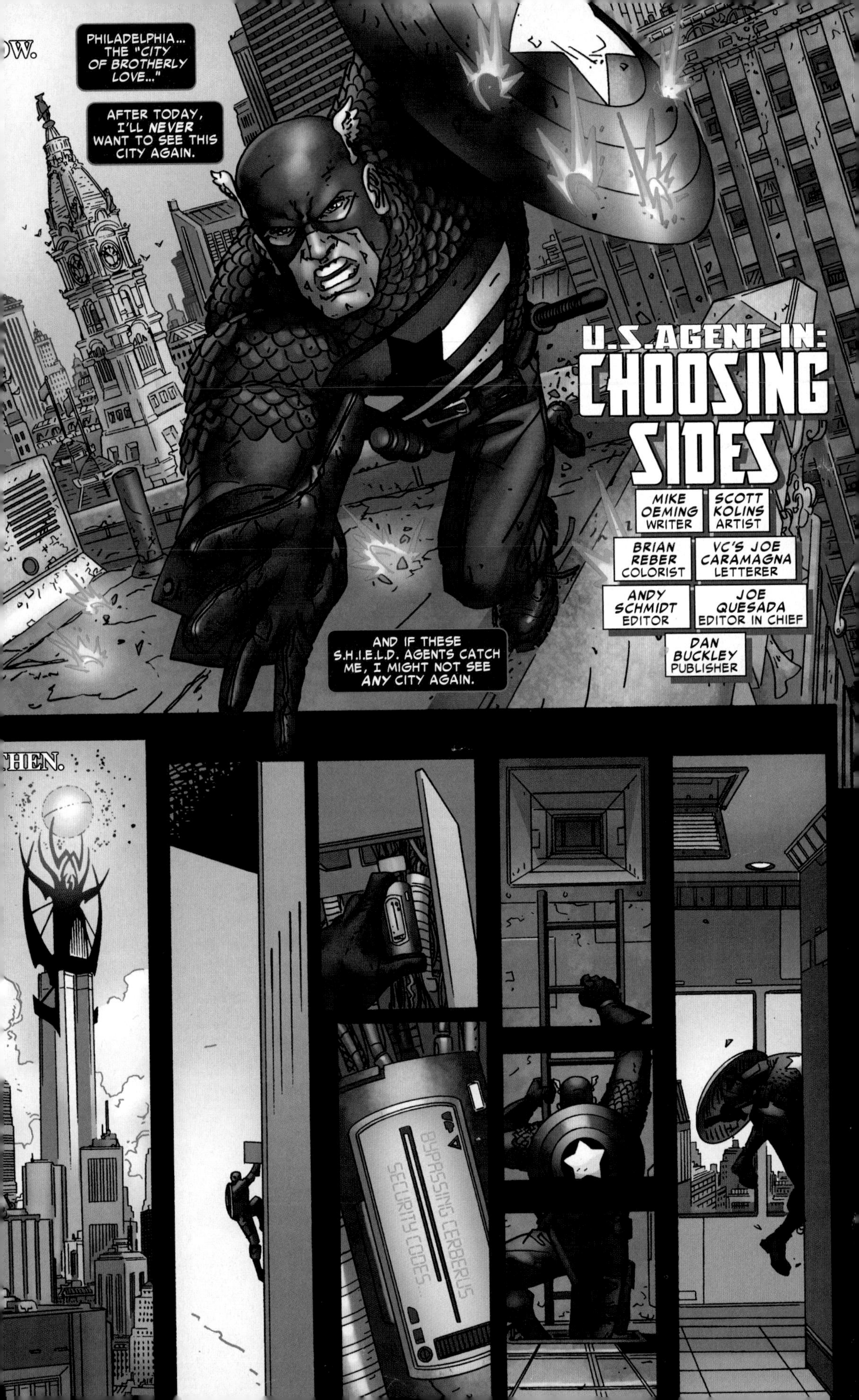
PHILADELPHIA... THE "CITY OF BROTHERLY LOVE..."
AFTER TODAY, I'LL NEVER WANT TO SEE THIS CITY AGAIN.
U.S. AGENT IN:
CHOOSING SIDES
MIKE OEMING WRITER
SCOTT KOLINS ARTIST
BRIAN REBER COLORIST
VC'S JOE CARAMAGNA LETTERER
ANDY SCHMIDT EDITOR
JOE QUESADA EDITOR IN CHIEF
DAN BUCKLEY PUBLISHER
AND IF THESE S.H.I.E.L.D. AGENTS CATCH ME, I MIGHT NOT SEE ANY CITY AGAIN.
BYPASSING CERBERUS SECURITY CODES...

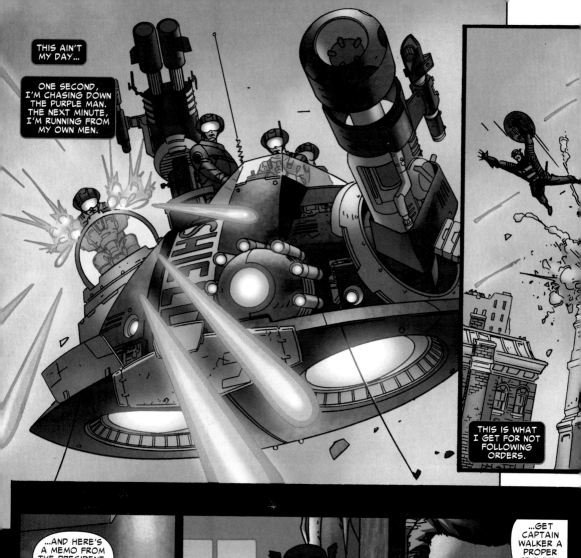

THIS AIN'T MY DAY...

ONE SECOND, I'M CHASING DOWN THE PURPLE MAN. THE NEXT MINUTE, I'M RUNNING FROM MY OWN MEN.

THIS IS WHAT I GET FOR NOT FOLLOWING ORDERS.

...AND HERE'S A MEMO FROM THE PRESIDENT, MR. STARK. JUST CAME IN.

...GET CAPTAIN WALKER A PROPER SECURITY PASS.

THANKS... OH, AND ONE MORE THING...

I'D HATE FOR HIM TO BE A VICTIM OF A MISUNDERSTANDING WITH OUR SECURITY SYSTEM.

CRUD.

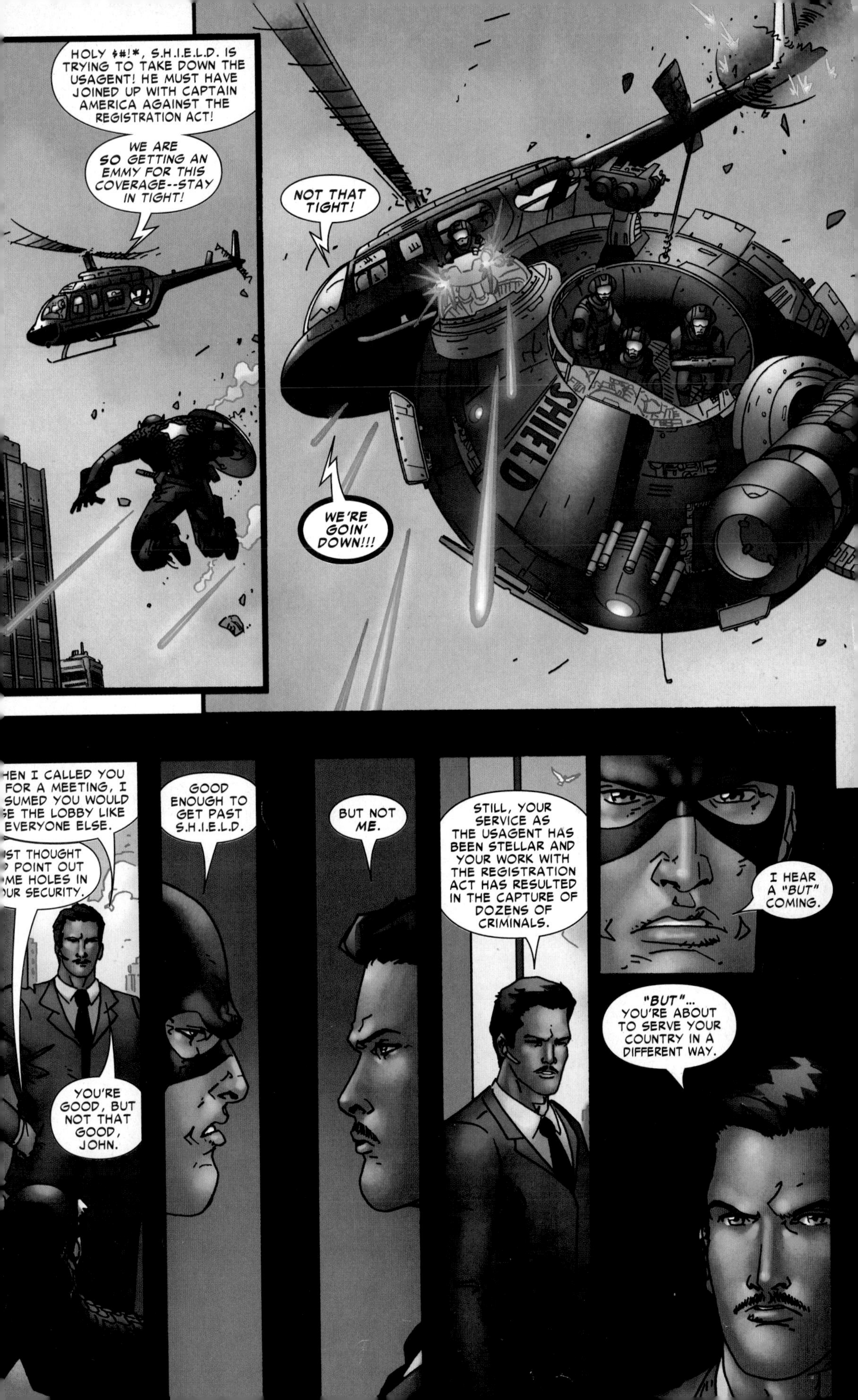
HOLY $#!*, S.H.I.E.L.D. IS TRYING TO TAKE DOWN THE USAGENT! HE MUST HAVE JOINED UP WITH CAPTAIN AMERICA AGAINST THE REGISTRATION ACT!
WE ARE SO GETTING AN EMMY FOR THIS COVERAGE--STAY IN TIGHT!
NOT THAT TIGHT!
WE'RE GOIN' DOWN!!!
SHIELD
HEN I CALLED YOU FOR A MEETING, I SUMED YOU WOULD SE THE LOBBY LIKE EVERYONE ELSE.
ST THOUGHT POINT OUT ME HOLES IN UR SECURITY.
GOOD ENOUGH TO GET PAST S.H.I.E.L.D.
YOU'RE GOOD, BUT NOT THAT GOOD, JOHN.
BUT NOT ME.
STILL, YOUR SERVICE AS THE USAGENT HAS BEEN STELLAR AND YOUR WORK WITH THE REGISTRATION ACT HAS RESULTED IN THE CAPTURE OF DOZENS OF CRIMINALS.
I HEAR A "BUT" COMING.
"BUT"... YOU'RE ABOUT TO SERVE YOUR COUNTRY IN A DIFFERENT WAY.

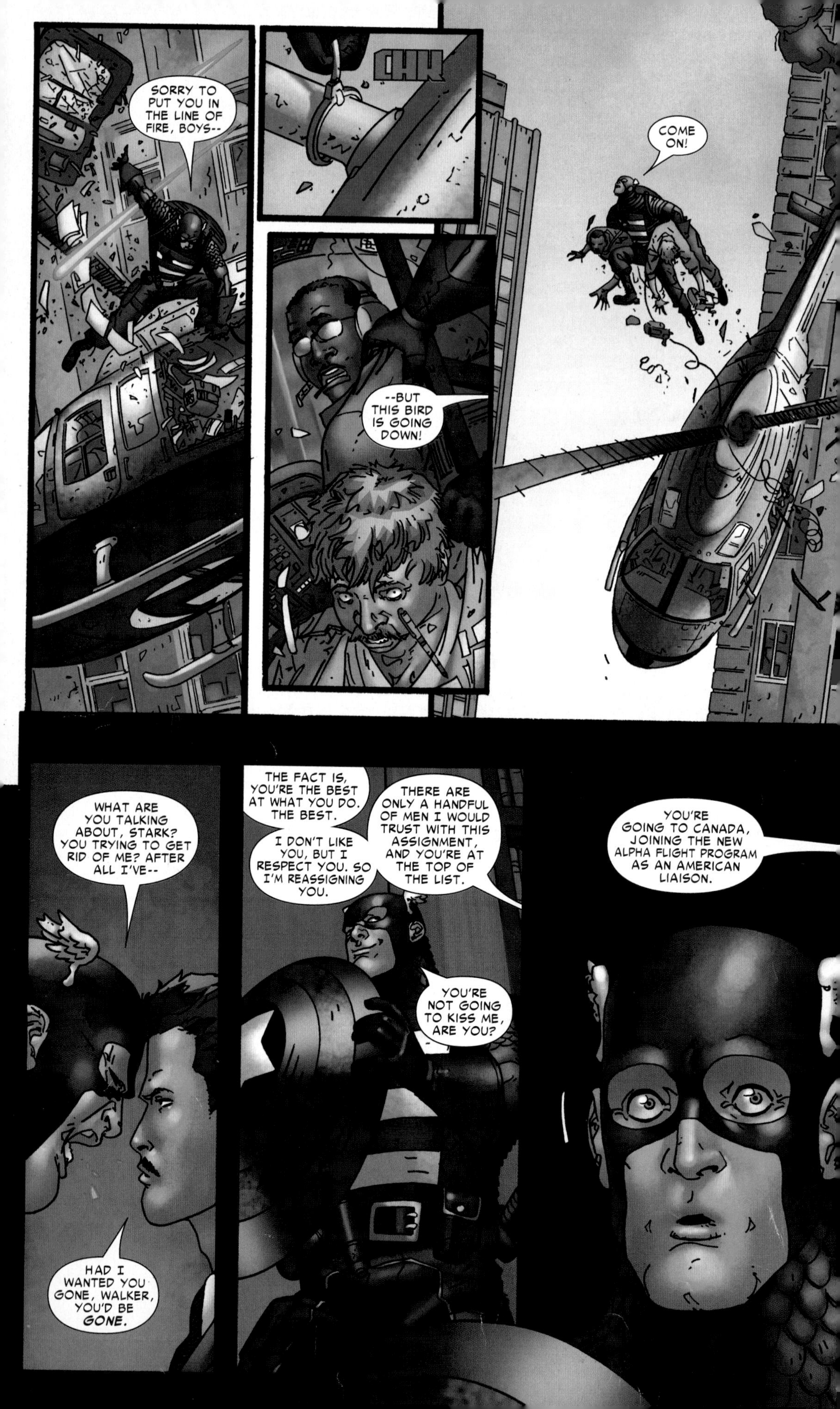
SORRY TO PUT YOU IN THE LINE OF FIRE, BOYS--
CHK
--BUT THIS BIRD IS GOING DOWN!
COME ON!
WHAT ARE YOU TALKING ABOUT, STARK? YOU TRYING TO GET RID OF ME? AFTER ALL I'VE--
HAD I WANTED YOU GONE, WALKER, YOU'D BE GONE.
THE FACT IS, YOU'RE THE BEST AT WHAT YOU DO. THE BEST.
I DON'T LIKE YOU, BUT I RESPECT YOU. SO I'M REASSIGNING YOU.
THERE ARE ONLY A HANDFUL OF MEN I WOULD TRUST WITH THIS ASSIGNMENT, AND YOU'RE AT THE TOP OF THE LIST.
YOU'RE NOT GOING TO KISS ME, ARE YOU?
YOU'RE GOING TO CANADA, JOINING THE NEW ALPHA FLIGHT PROGRAM AS AN AMERICAN LIAISON.

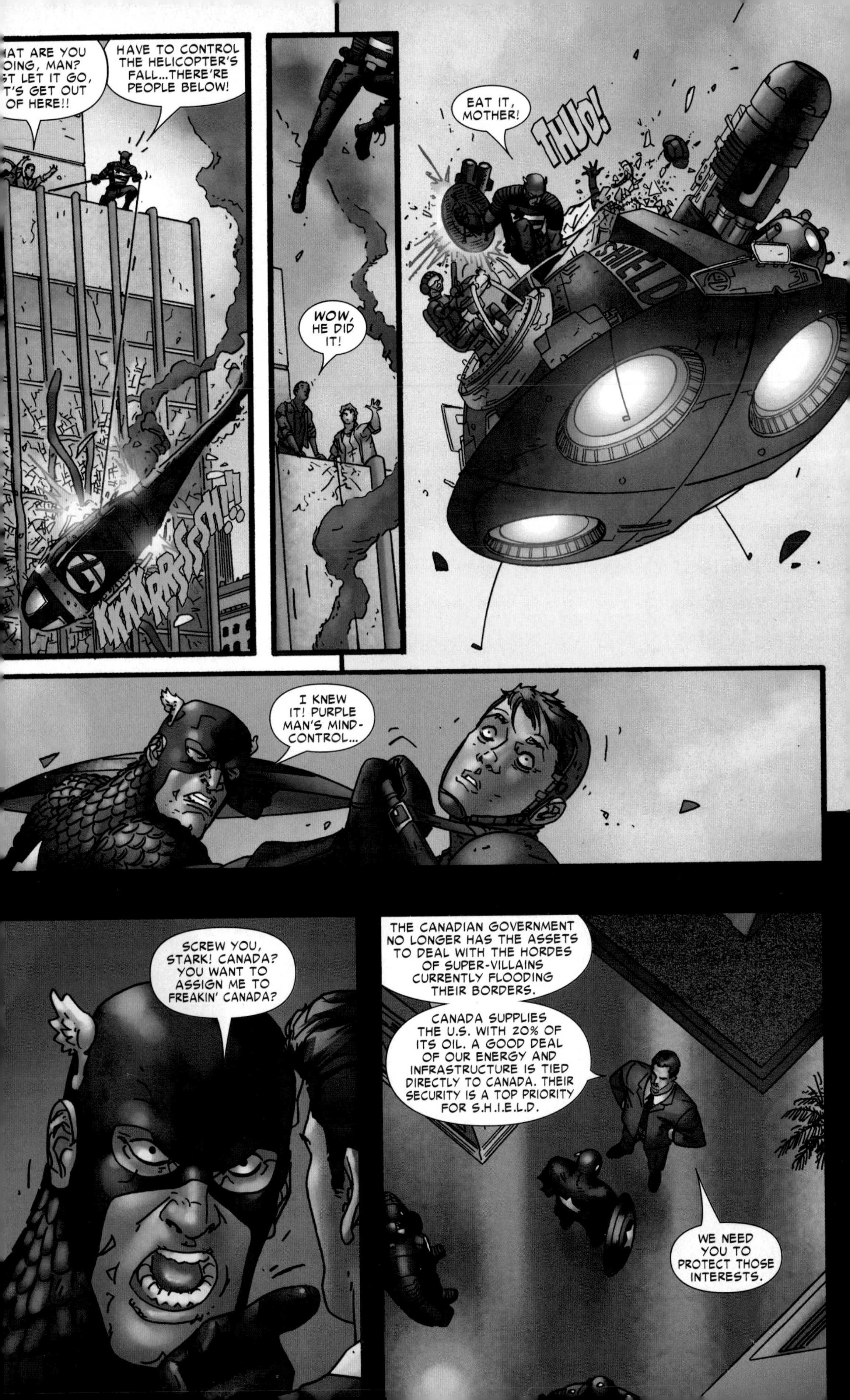

HAT ARE YOU OING, MAN? ST LET IT GO, T'S GET OUT OF HERE!!
HAVE TO CONTROL THE HELICOPTER'S FALL...THERE'RE PEOPLE BELOW!
KKKRRSSSH!!
WOW, HE DID IT!
EAT IT, MOTHER!
THUD!
I KNEW IT! PURPLE MAN'S MIND-CONTROL...
SCREW YOU, STARK! CANADA? YOU WANT TO ASSIGN ME TO FREAKIN' CANADA?
THE CANADIAN GOVERNMENT NO LONGER HAS THE ASSETS TO DEAL WITH THE HORDES OF SUPER-VILLAINS CURRENTLY FLOODING THEIR BORDERS.
CANADA SUPPLIES THE U.S. WITH 20% OF ITS OIL. A GOOD DEAL OF OUR ENERGY AND INFRASTRUCTURE IS TIED DIRECTLY TO CANADA. THEIR SECURITY IS A TOP PRIORITY FOR S.H.I.E.L.D.
WE NEED YOU TO PROTECT THOSE INTERESTS.

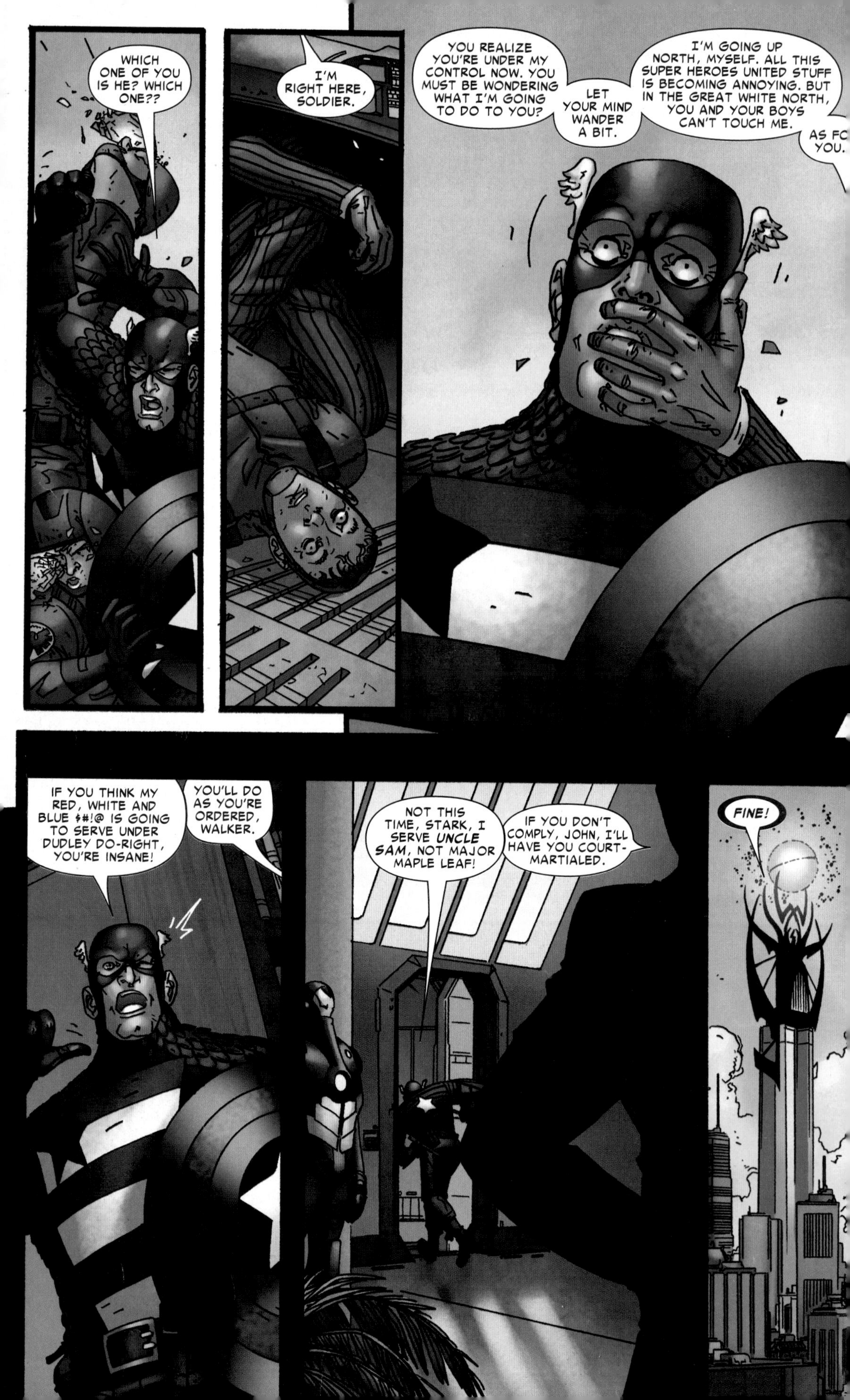
WHICH ONE OF YOU IS HE? WHICH ONE??
I'M RIGHT HERE, SOLDIER.
YOU REALIZE YOU'RE UNDER MY CONTROL NOW. YOU MUST BE WONDERING WHAT I'M GOING TO DO TO YOU?
LET YOUR MIND WANDER A BIT.
I'M GOING UP NORTH, MYSELF. ALL THIS SUPER HEROES UNITED STUFF IS BECOMING ANNOYING. BUT IN THE GREAT WHITE NORTH, YOU AND YOUR BOYS CAN'T TOUCH ME.
AS FO YOU.
IF YOU THINK MY RED, WHITE AND BLUE $#!@ IS GOING TO SERVE UNDER DUDLEY DO-RIGHT, YOU'RE INSANE!
YOU'LL DO AS YOU'RE ORDERED, WALKER.
NOT THIS TIME, STARK, I SERVE UNCLE SAM, NOT MAJOR MAPLE LEAF!
IF YOU DON'T COMPLY, JOHN, I'LL HAVE YOU COURT-MARTIALED.
FINE!

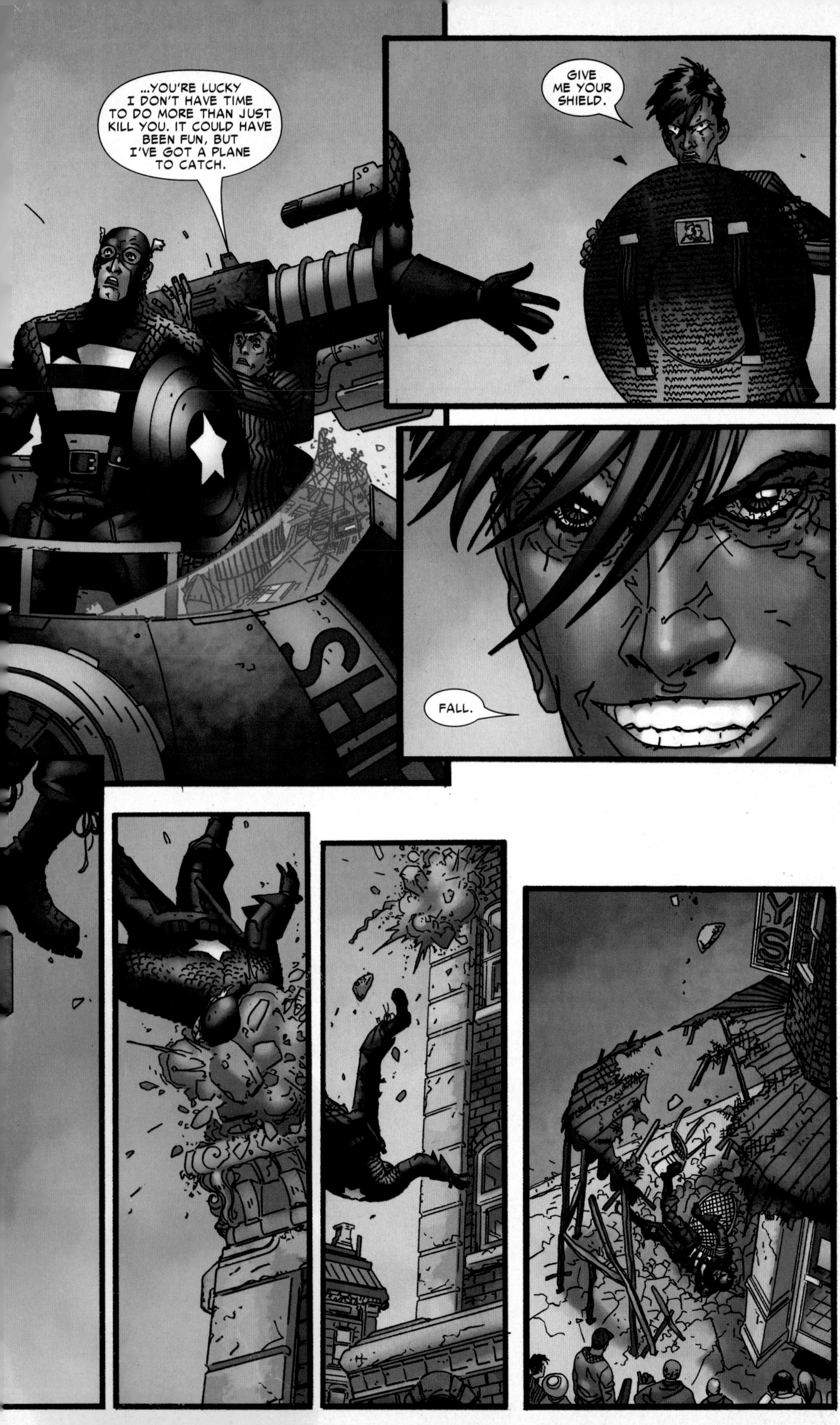
...YOU'RE LUCKY I DON'T HAVE TIME TO DO MORE THAN JUST KILL YOU. IT COULD HAVE BEEN FUN, BUT I'VE GOT A PLANE TO CATCH.
GIVE ME YOUR SHIELD.
FALL.
SH
S

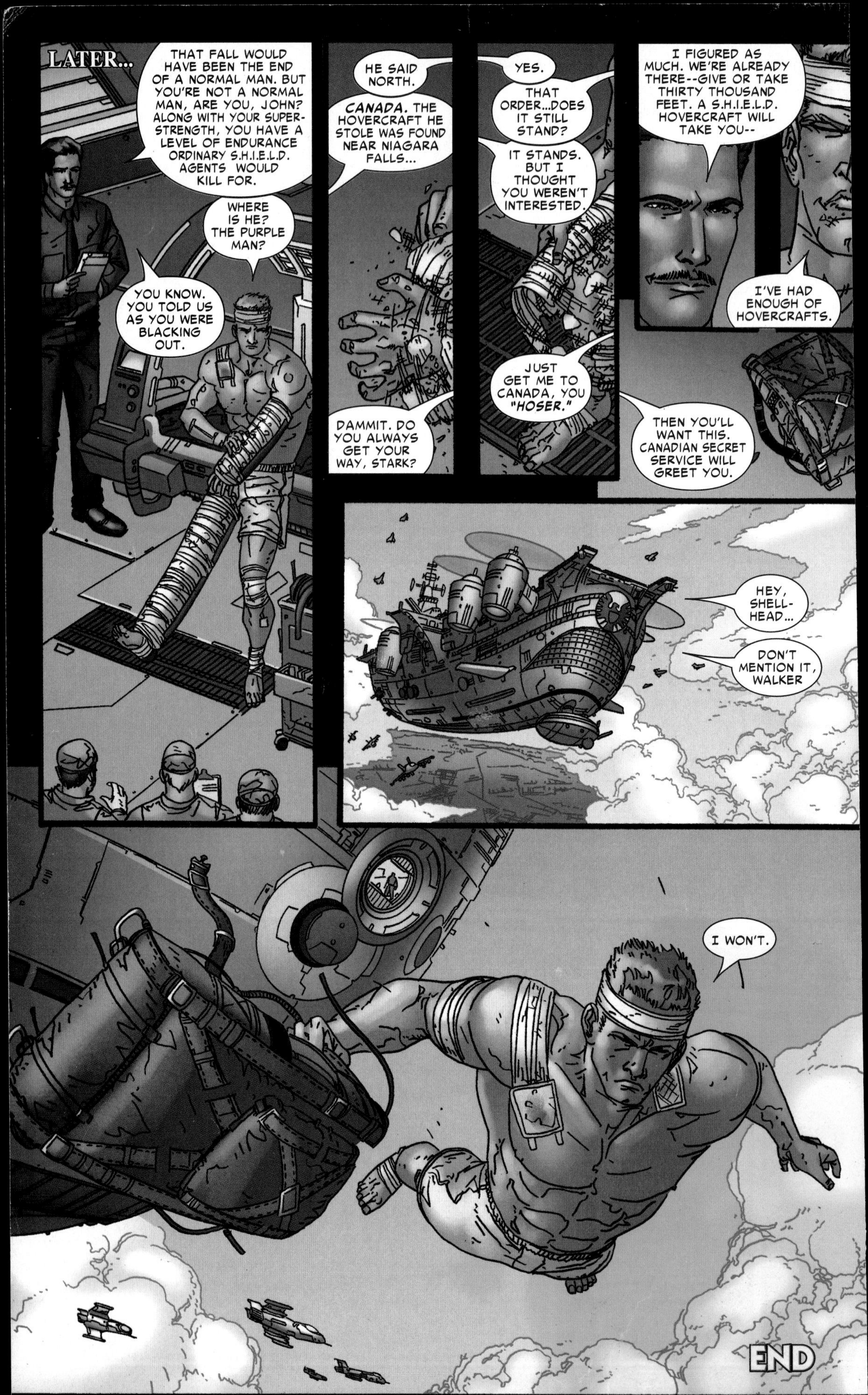
LATER...
THAT FALL WOULD HAVE BEEN THE END OF A NORMAL MAN. BUT YOU'RE NOT A NORMAL MAN, ARE YOU, JOHN? ALONG WITH YOUR SUPER-STRENGTH, YOU HAVE A LEVEL OF ENDURANCE ORDINARY S.H.I.E.L.D. AGENTS WOULD KILL FOR.
WHERE IS HE? THE PURPLE MAN?
YOU KNOW. YOU TOLD US AS YOU WERE BLACKING OUT.
HE SAID NORTH.
CANADA. THE HOVERCRAFT HE STOLE WAS FOUND NEAR NIAGARA FALLS...
DAMMIT. DO YOU ALWAYS GET YOUR WAY, STARK?
YES.
THAT ORDER...DOES IT STILL STAND?
IT STANDS. BUT I THOUGHT YOU WEREN'T INTERESTED.
JUST GET ME TO CANADA, YOU "HOSER."
I FIGURED AS MUCH. WE'RE ALREADY THERE--GIVE OR TAKE THIRTY THOUSAND FEET. A S.H.I.E.L.D. HOVERCRAFT WILL TAKE YOU--
I'VE HAD ENOUGH OF HOVERCRAFTS.
THEN YOU'LL WANT THIS. CANADIAN SECRET SERVICE WILL GREET YOU.
HEY, SHELL-HEAD...
DON'T MENTION IT, WALKER
I WON'T.
END

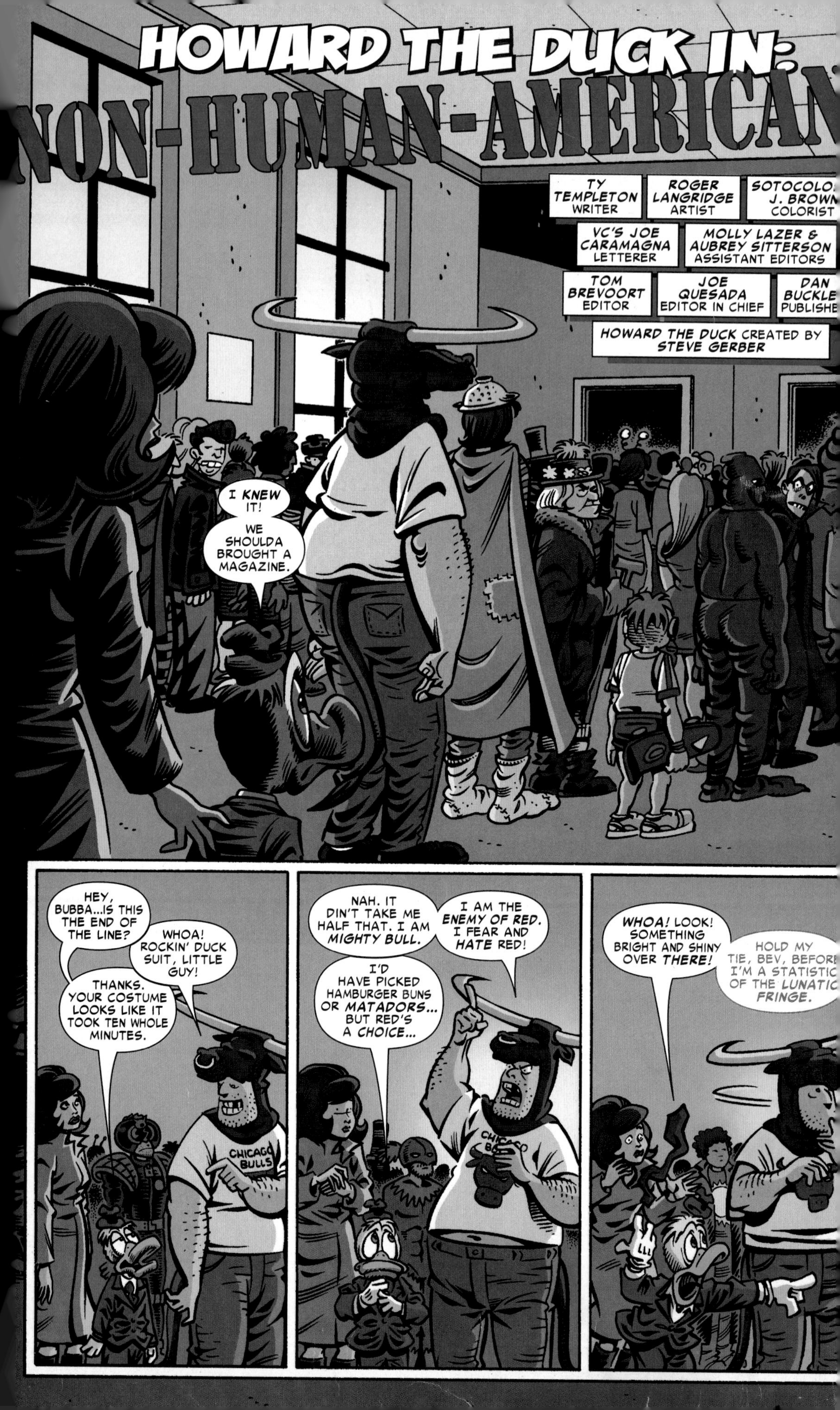

HOWARD THE DUCK IN:
NON-HUMAN-AMERICAN
TY TEMPLETON WRITER
ROGER LANGRIDGE ARTIST
SOTOCOLO J. BROWN COLORIST
VC'S JOE CARAMAGNA LETTERER
MOLLY LAZER & AUBREY SITTERSON ASSISTANT EDITORS
TOM BREVOORT EDITOR
JOE QUESADA EDITOR IN CHIEF
DAN BUCKLE PUBLISHE
HOWARD THE DUCK CREATED BY STEVE GERBER
I KNEW IT!
WE SHOULDA BROUGHT A MAGAZINE.
HEY, BUBBA...IS THIS THE END OF THE LINE?
WHOA! ROCKIN' DUCK SUIT, LITTLE GUY!
THANKS. YOUR COSTUME LOOKS LIKE IT TOOK TEN WHOLE MINUTES.
CHICAGO BULLS
NAH. IT DIN'T TAKE ME HALF THAT. I AM MIGHTY BULL.
I AM THE ENEMY OF RED. I FEAR AND HATE RED!
I'D HAVE PICKED HAMBURGER BUNS OR MATADORS... BUT RED'S A CHOICE...
WHOA! LOOK! SOMETHING BRIGHT AND SHINY OVER THERE!
HOLD MY TIE, BEV, BEFOR I'M A STATISTIC OF THE LUNATIC FRINGE.

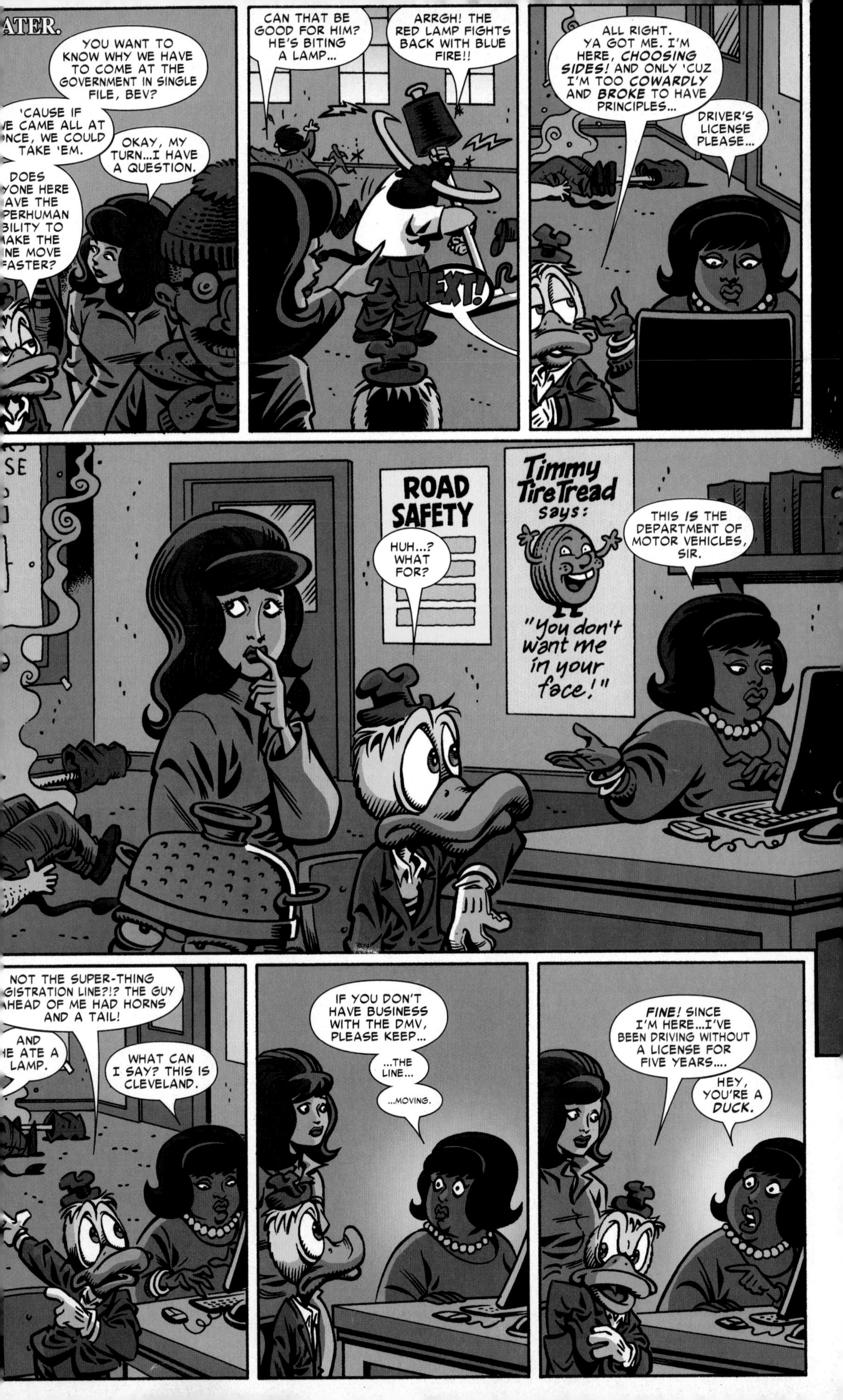

ATER.
YOU WANT TO KNOW WHY WE HAVE TO COME AT THE GOVERNMENT IN SINGLE FILE, BEV?
'CAUSE IF E CAME ALL AT NCE, WE COULD TAKE 'EM.
OKAY, MY TURN...I HAVE A QUESTION.
DOES YONE HERE AVE THE PERHUMAN BILITY TO AKE THE NE MOVE FASTER?
CAN THAT BE GOOD FOR HIM? HE'S BITING A LAMP...
ARRGH! THE RED LAMP FIGHTS BACK WITH BLUE FIRE!!
NEXT!
ALL RIGHT. YA GOT ME. I'M HERE, CHOOSING SIDES! AND ONLY 'CUZ I'M TOO COWARDLY AND BROKE TO HAVE PRINCIPLES...
DRIVER'S LICENSE PLEASE...
ROAD SAFETY
Timmy TireTread says:
"You don't want me in your face!"
HUH...? WHAT FOR?
THIS IS THE DEPARTMENT OF MOTOR VEHICLES, SIR.
NOT THE SUPER-THING GISTRATION LINE?!? THE GUY HEAD OF ME HAD HORNS AND A TAIL!
AND HE ATE A LAMP.
WHAT CAN I SAY? THIS IS CLEVELAND.
IF YOU DON'T HAVE BUSINESS WITH THE DMV, PLEASE KEEP...
...THE LINE...
...MOVING.
FINE! SINCE I'M HERE...I'VE BEEN DRIVING WITHOUT A LICENSE FOR FIVE YEARS....
HEY, YOU'RE A DUCK.

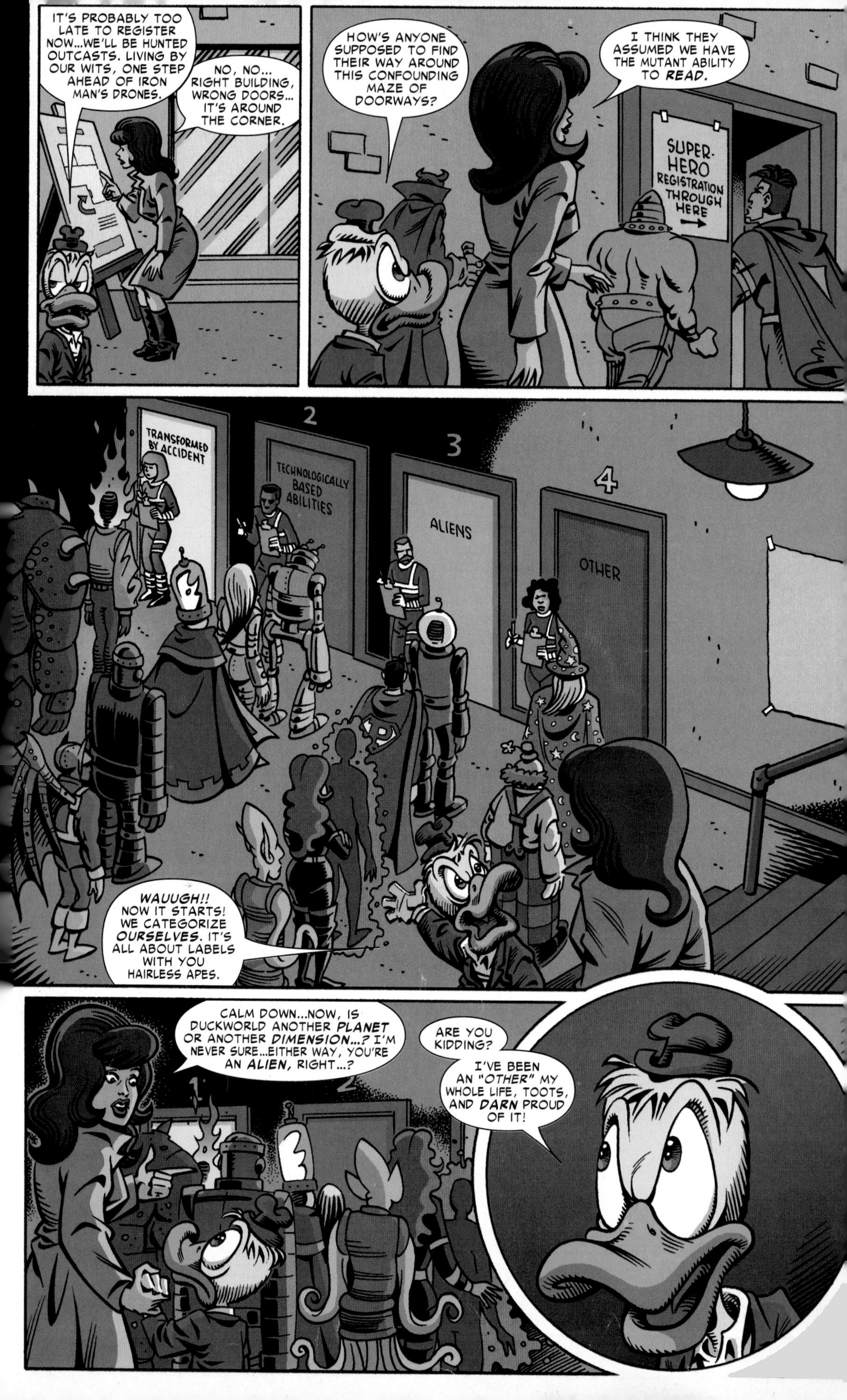
IT'S PROBABLY TOO LATE TO REGISTER NOW...WE'LL BE HUNTED OUTCASTS. LIVING BY OUR WITS, ONE STEP AHEAD OF IRON MAN'S DRONES.
NO, NO... RIGHT BUILDING, WRONG DOORS... IT'S AROUND THE CORNER.
HOW'S ANYONE SUPPOSED TO FIND THEIR WAY AROUND THIS CONFOUNDING MAZE OF DOORWAYS?
I THINK THEY ASSUMED WE HAVE THE MUTANT ABILITY TO *READ.*
SUPER-HERO REGISTRATION THROUGH HERE
TRANSFORMED BY ACCIDENT
2
TECHNOLOGICALLY BASED ABILITIES
3
ALIENS
4
OTHER
WAUUGH!! NOW IT STARTS! WE CATEGORIZE *OURSELVES.* IT'S ALL ABOUT LABELS WITH YOU HAIRLESS APES.
CALM DOWN...NOW, IS DUCKWORLD ANOTHER *PLANET* OR ANOTHER *DIMENSION...?* I'M NEVER SURE...EITHER WAY, YOU'RE AN *ALIEN,* RIGHT...?
ARE YOU KIDDING?
I'VE BEEN AN *"OTHER"* MY WHOLE LIFE, TOOTS, AND *DARN* PROUD OF IT!

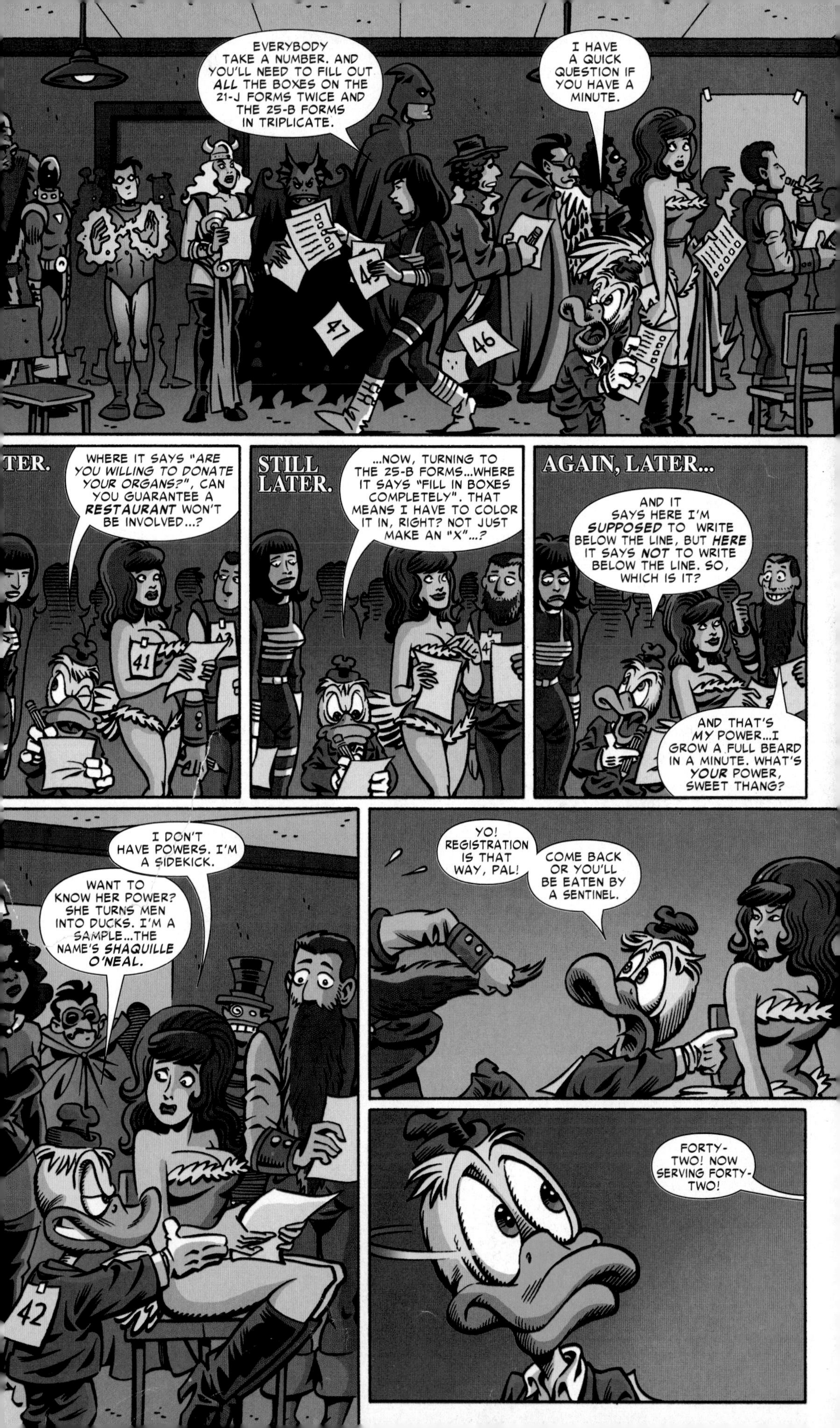
EVERYBODY TAKE A NUMBER. AND YOU'LL NEED TO FILL OUT ALL THE BOXES ON THE 21-J FORMS TWICE AND THE 25-B FORMS IN TRIPLICATE.
I HAVE A QUICK QUESTION IF YOU HAVE A MINUTE.
47
46
TER.
WHERE IT SAYS "ARE YOU WILLING TO DONATE YOUR ORGANS?", CAN YOU GUARANTEE A RESTAURANT WON'T BE INVOLVED...?
41
STILL LATER.
...NOW, TURNING TO THE 25-B FORMS...WHERE IT SAYS "FILL IN BOXES COMPLETELY". THAT MEANS I HAVE TO COLOR IT IN, RIGHT? NOT JUST MAKE AN "X"...?
AGAIN, LATER...
AND IT SAYS HERE I'M SUPPOSED TO WRITE BELOW THE LINE, BUT HERE IT SAYS NOT TO WRITE BELOW THE LINE. SO, WHICH IS IT?
AND THAT'S MY POWER...I GROW A FULL BEARD IN A MINUTE. WHAT'S YOUR POWER, SWEET THANG?
I DON'T HAVE POWERS. I'M A SIDEKICK.
WANT TO KNOW HER POWER? SHE TURNS MEN INTO DUCKS. I'M A SAMPLE...THE NAME'S SHAQUILLE O'NEAL.
42
YO! REGISTRATION IS THAT WAY, PAL!
COME BACK OR YOU'LL BE EATEN BY A SENTINEL.
FORTY-TWO! NOW SERVING FORTY-TWO!

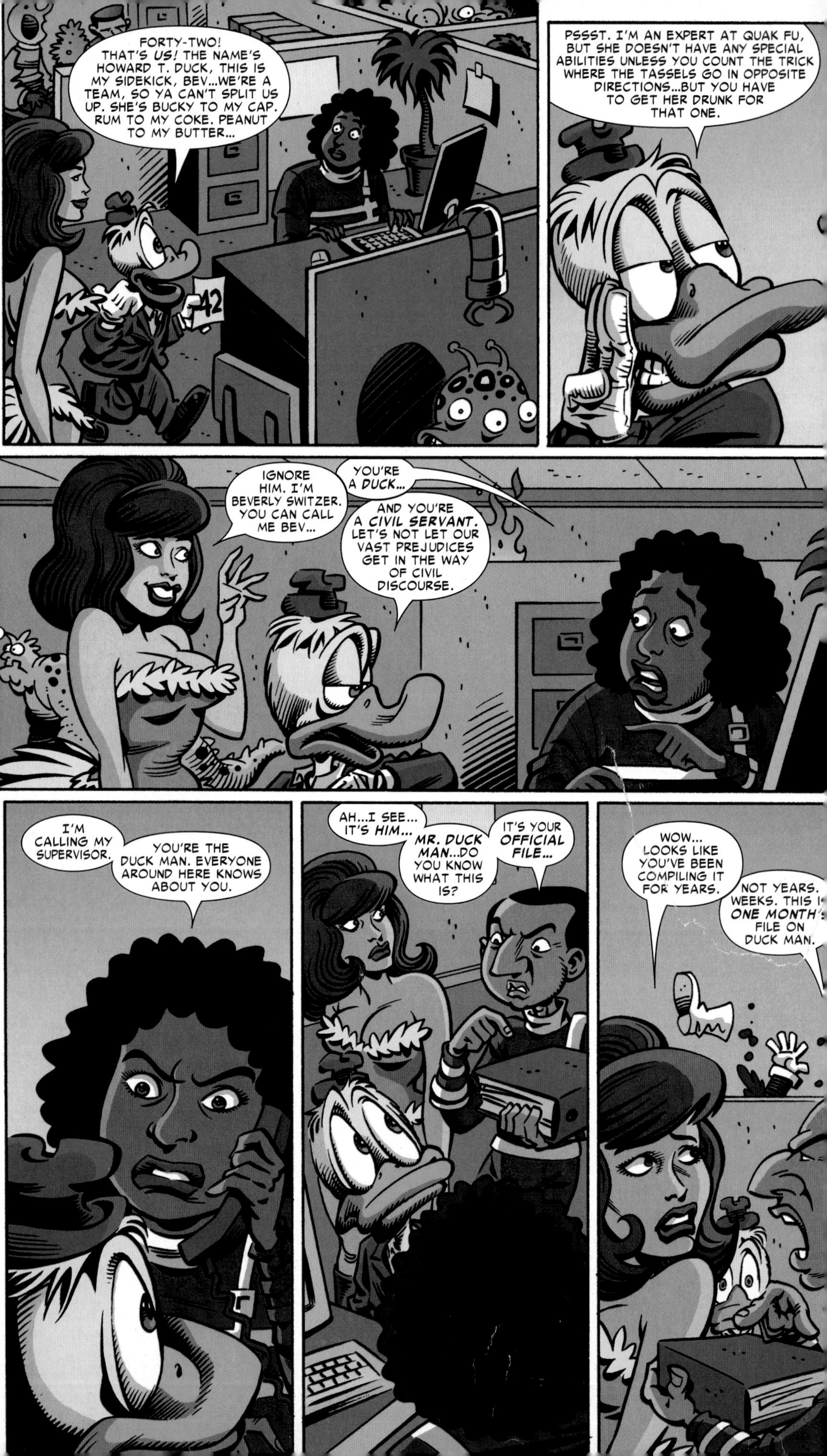
FORTY-TWO! THAT'S US! THE NAME'S HOWARD T. DUCK, THIS IS MY SIDEKICK, BEV...WE'RE A TEAM, SO YA CAN'T SPLIT US UP. SHE'S BUCKY TO MY CAP. RUM TO MY COKE. PEANUT TO MY BUTTER...
42
PSSST. I'M AN EXPERT AT QUAK FU, BUT SHE DOESN'T HAVE ANY SPECIAL ABILITIES UNLESS YOU COUNT THE TRICK WHERE THE TASSELS GO IN OPPOSITE DIRECTIONS...BUT YOU HAVE TO GET HER DRUNK FOR THAT ONE.
IGNORE HIM. I'M BEVERLY SWITZER. YOU CAN CALL ME BEV...
YOU'RE A DUCK...
AND YOU'RE A CIVIL SERVANT. LET'S NOT LET OUR VAST PREJUDICES GET IN THE WAY OF CIVIL DISCOURSE.
I'M CALLING MY SUPERVISOR.
YOU'RE THE DUCK MAN. EVERYONE AROUND HERE KNOWS ABOUT YOU.
AH...I SEE... IT'S HIM...
MR. DUCK MAN...DO YOU KNOW WHAT THIS IS?
IT'S YOUR OFFICIAL FILE...
WOW... LOOKS LIKE YOU'VE BEEN COMPILING IT FOR YEARS.
NOT YEARS. WEEKS. THIS IS ONE MONTH'S FILE ON DUCK MAN.

SINCE I BECAME S.H.I.E.L.D. REGIONAL DIRECTOR OF SUPERNORMAL AFFAIRS FOR OHIO, FOUR YEARS AGO, EACH AND *EVERY* MONTH, WE GET OVER THREE HUNDRED EYEWITNESS REPORTS ABOUT THE FAMOUS *"DUCK MAN OF CLEVELAND"*.

DUCK MAN DRIVING A CAB...DUCK MAN CURSING AT HOT DOG VENDORS...DUCK MAN CHASING EXOTIC DANCERS AND SCRAWLING GRAFFITI ON BUS STOPS...DOZENS OF REPORTS ON MY DESK *EVERY DAY!*

AND EACH TIME IT HAPPENS, WE TELL THE WITNESSES THAT THEY ARE DRUNK, OR UNBALANCED, AND WE TOSS THE FILE INTO THE GARBAGE AT THE END OF THIRTY DAYS...UNTIL IT STARTS UP AGAIN.

ONE YEAR, FOUR MONTHS AND EIGHT DAYS AGO, IT BECAME THE OFFICIAL POLICY OF THIS OFFICE THAT YOU DO NOT EXIST. IT SAVES PAPERWORK AND TIME!

WELL, HERE'S A TASTY MOUTHFUL OF REALITY, PAL.

I'M *HERE*...I'M *FEATHERED*...GET *USED* TO IT.

I DON'T HAVE TO DO ANY SUCH THING.

I'VE *KNOWN* YOU ACTUALLY EXISTED FOR SIX MONTHS NOW.

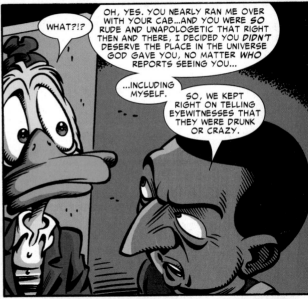

WHAT?!?

OH, YES. YOU NEARLY RAN ME OVER WITH YOUR CAB...AND YOU WERE *SO* RUDE AND UNAPOLOGETIC THAT RIGHT THEN AND THERE, I DECIDED YOU *DIDN'T* DESERVE THE PLACE IN THE UNIVERSE GOD GAVE YOU, NO MATTER *WHO* REPORTS SEEING YOU...

...INCLUDING MYSELF.

SO, WE KEPT RIGHT ON TELLING EYEWITNESSES THAT THEY WERE DRUNK OR CRAZY.

THAT'S *OFFICIAL GOVERNMENT* POLICY.

WAUUGH! YOU CAN'T WISH REALITY AWAY WHEN IT DOESN'T FIT *POLICY!* I *EXIST* AND YOU CAN'T MAKE ME INTO A NON-PERSON WITH THE WAVE OF YOUR FINGER!

OF COURSE YOU'RE A NON-PERSON.

YOU'RE A *DUCK.*

WAAAAGH!!

I'LL KILL HIM!

IN TRIPLICATE!

LET ME AT HIM.

AND STAY OUT!

HAA! HAAA

BOOT!

NO PARKING
NOT EVEN FOR EMERGENCIES

TRUST US, YOUR EXCUSE WILL NOT WORK WITH A JUDGE

YOU OKAY, HOWARD? I THOUGHT YOU WERE GOING TO MOLT, YOU WERE SO ANGRY...

ANGRY?!? ARE YOU KIDDING?!? THIS IS THE GREATEST THING THAT COULD EVER HAPPEN TO ME.

FOR THE REST OF MY LIFE...NO MORE PARKING TICKETS...NO MORE TAXES...OR JURY DUTY. HECK, I COULDN'T EVEN VOTE IF I WANTED TO!

THIS IS BETTER THAN CHRISTMAS IN VEGAS. I NO LONGER OFFICIALLY EXIST!

HEY! BULL BOY! YOU LOOKING FOR THE PLACE FOR THE SUPER HERO REGISTRATION?!?

I AM MIGHTY BULL! I CRUSH RED!

LET ME GIVE YOU SOME ADVICE, AND TRUST ME ON THIS...

...HEAD FOR LINE FOUR...

SUPER HERO REGISTRATION THROUGH HERE

THE END.

THE RETURN

A MARVEL COMICS EVENT

CIVIL WAR

CIVIL WAR

THE RETURN

A Superhuman Registration Act has been passed which requires all people possessir
paranormal abilities to register with the government. Those who do not register a
considered criminals. Some heroes, such as Iron Man, see this as a natural evolution
the role of superhumans in society and a reasonable request. Others view the Act as a
assault on their civil liberties. Captain America currently leads an underground resistance
movement against the new law.

After a brutal battle, Bill Foster--the anti-registration hero known as Goliath--has bee
killed. Other members of Captain America's resistance have been captured and brough
to the pro-registration faction's holding facility in the Negative Zone. Both sides hav
retreated in order to regroup and plan their next move.

Meanwhile, across the country, super heroes continue to weigh the cost of registerin
against the price of freedom...

PAUL JENKINS
WRITER

TOM RANEY
PENCILER

SCOTT HANNA
INKER

GINA GOING (PAGES 1-13)
SOTOCOLOR'S A. CROSSLEY (PAGES 14-23)
COLORISTS

DAVE SHARP
LETTERER

ANTHONY DIAL
PRODUCTION

MOLLY LAZER & AUBREY SITTERSON
ASSISTANT EDITORS

STEPHEN WACKER
EDITOR

JOE QUESADA
EDITOR IN CHIEF

DAN BUCKLE
PUBLISHER

VARIANT COVER **BY ED MCGUINNESS & DAVE MCCAIG**

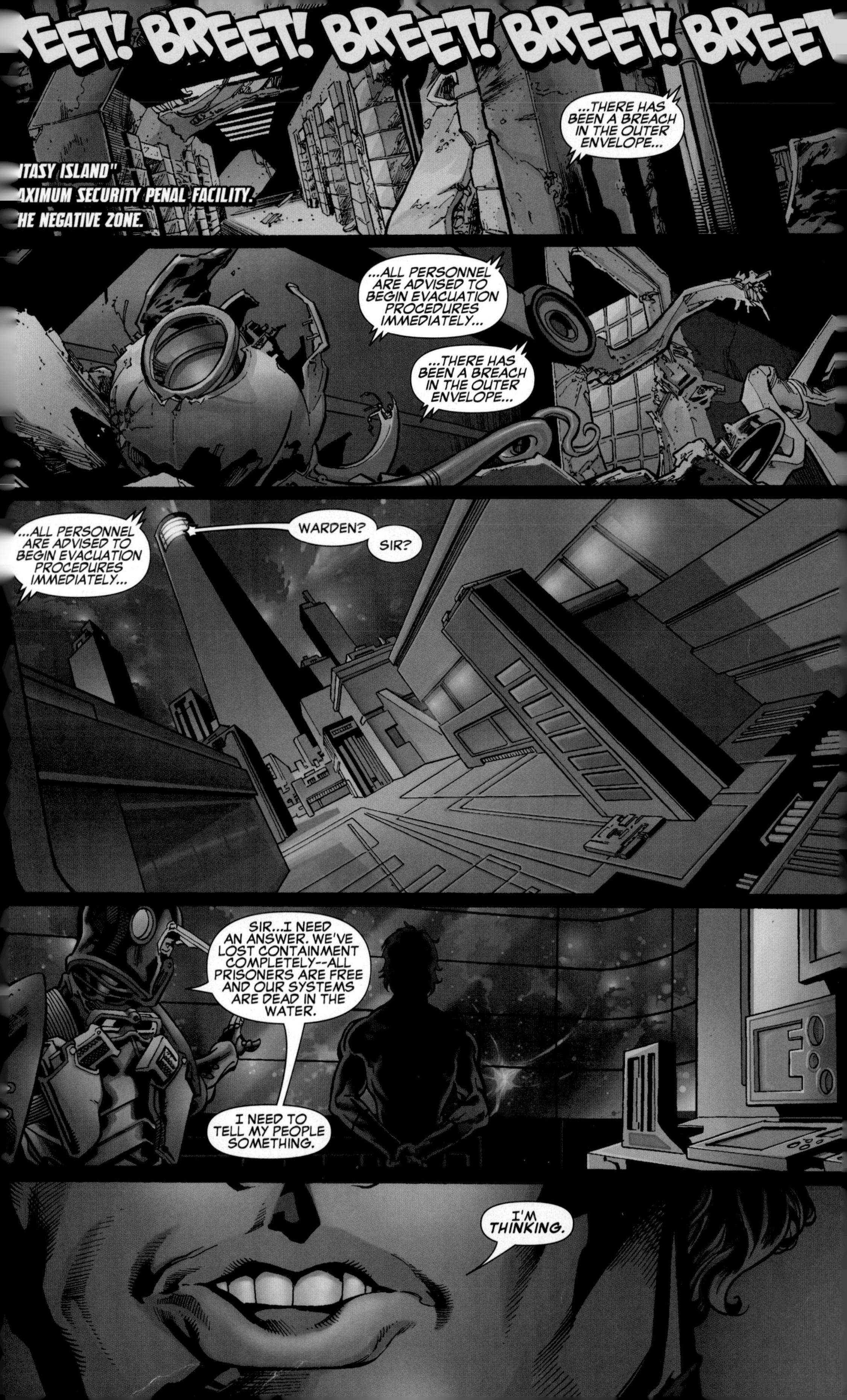
EET! BREET! BREET! BREET! BREE
...THERE HAS BEEN A BREACH IN THE OUTER ENVELOPE...
ITASY ISLAND"
AXIMUM SECURITY PENAL FACILITY.
HE NEGATIVE ZONE.
...ALL PERSONNEL ARE ADVISED TO BEGIN EVACUATION PROCEDURES IMMEDIATELY...
...THERE HAS BEEN A BREACH IN THE OUTER ENVELOPE...
...ALL PERSONNEL ARE ADVISED TO BEGIN EVACUATION PROCEDURES IMMEDIATELY...
WARDEN?
SIR?
SIR...I NEED AN ANSWER. WE'VE LOST CONTAINMENT COMPLETELY--ALL PRISONERS ARE FREE AND OUR SYSTEMS ARE DEAD IN THE WATER.
I NEED TO TELL MY PEOPLE SOMETHING.
I'M THINKING.

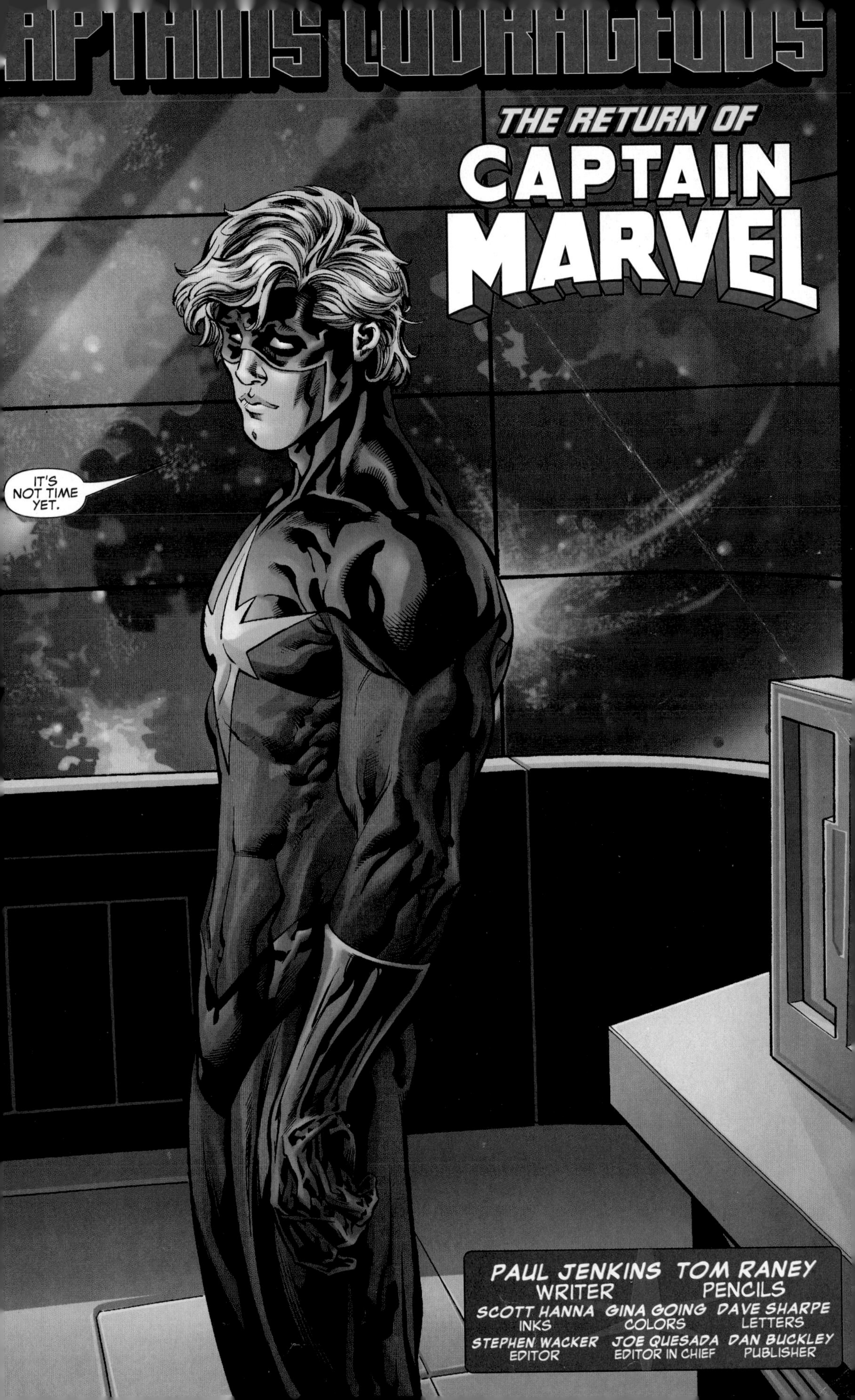
THE RETURN OF
CAPTAIN MARVEL
IT'S NOT TIME YET.
PAUL JENKINS WRITER
TOM RANEY PENCILS
SCOTT HANNA INKS
GINA GOING COLORS
DAVE SHARPE LETTERS
STEPHEN WACKER EDITOR
JOE QUESADA EDITOR IN CHIEF
DAN BUCKLEY PUBLISHER

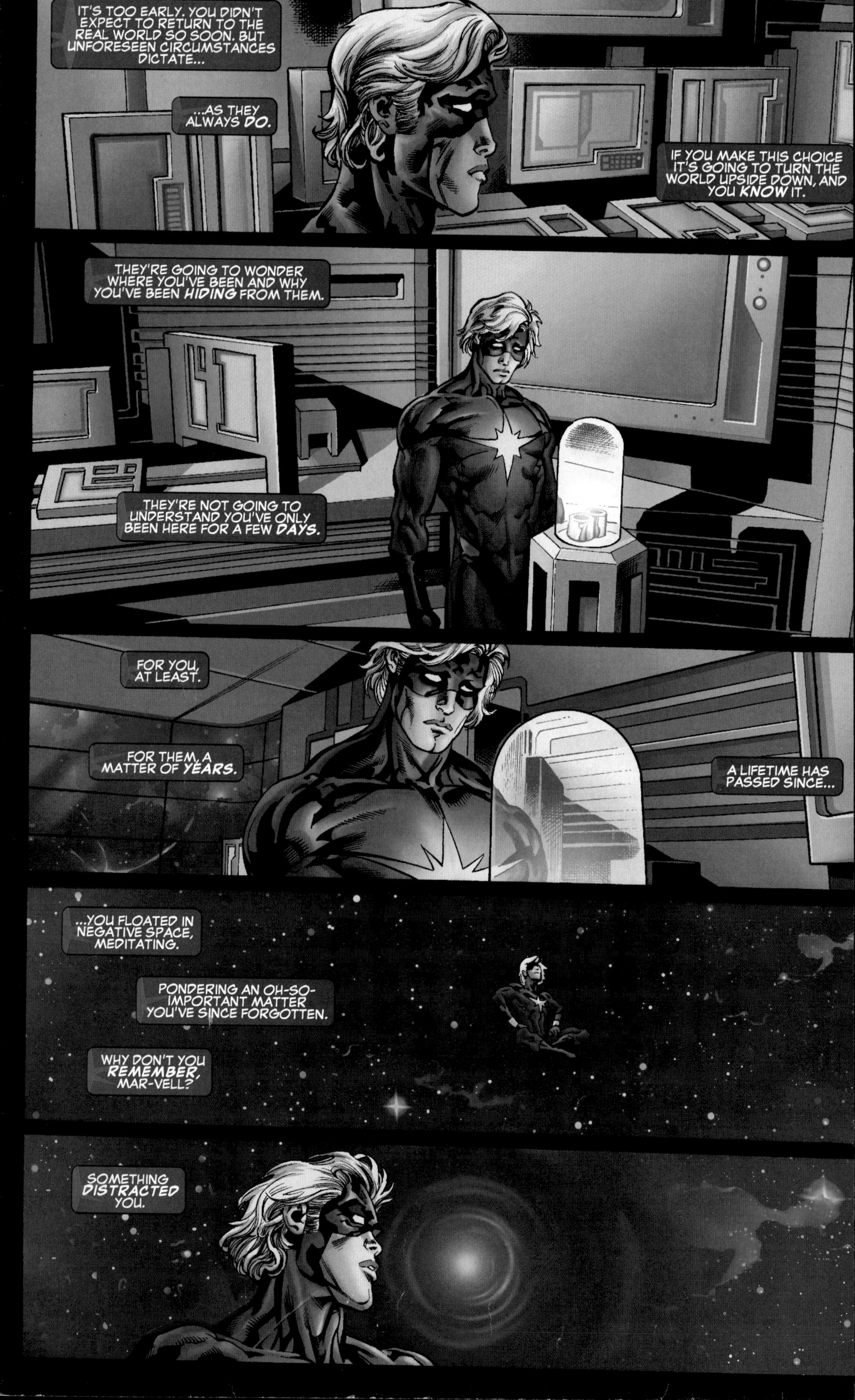
IT'S TOO EARLY. YOU DIDN'T EXPECT TO RETURN TO THE REAL WORLD SO SOON. BUT UNFORESEEN CIRCUMSTANCES DICTATE...
...AS THEY ALWAYS DO.
IF YOU MAKE THIS CHOICE IT'S GOING TO TURN THE WORLD UPSIDE DOWN, AND YOU KNOW IT.
THEY'RE GOING TO WONDER WHERE YOU'VE BEEN AND WHY YOU'VE BEEN HIDING FROM THEM.
THEY'RE NOT GOING TO UNDERSTAND YOU'VE ONLY BEEN HERE FOR A FEW DAYS.
FOR YOU, AT LEAST.
FOR THEM, A MATTER OF YEARS.
A LIFETIME HAS PASSED SINCE...
...YOU FLOATED IN NEGATIVE SPACE, MEDITATING.
PONDERING AN OH-SO-IMPORTANT MATTER YOU'VE SINCE FORGOTTEN.
WHY DON'T YOU REMEMBER, MAR-VELL?
SOMETHING DISTRACTED YOU.

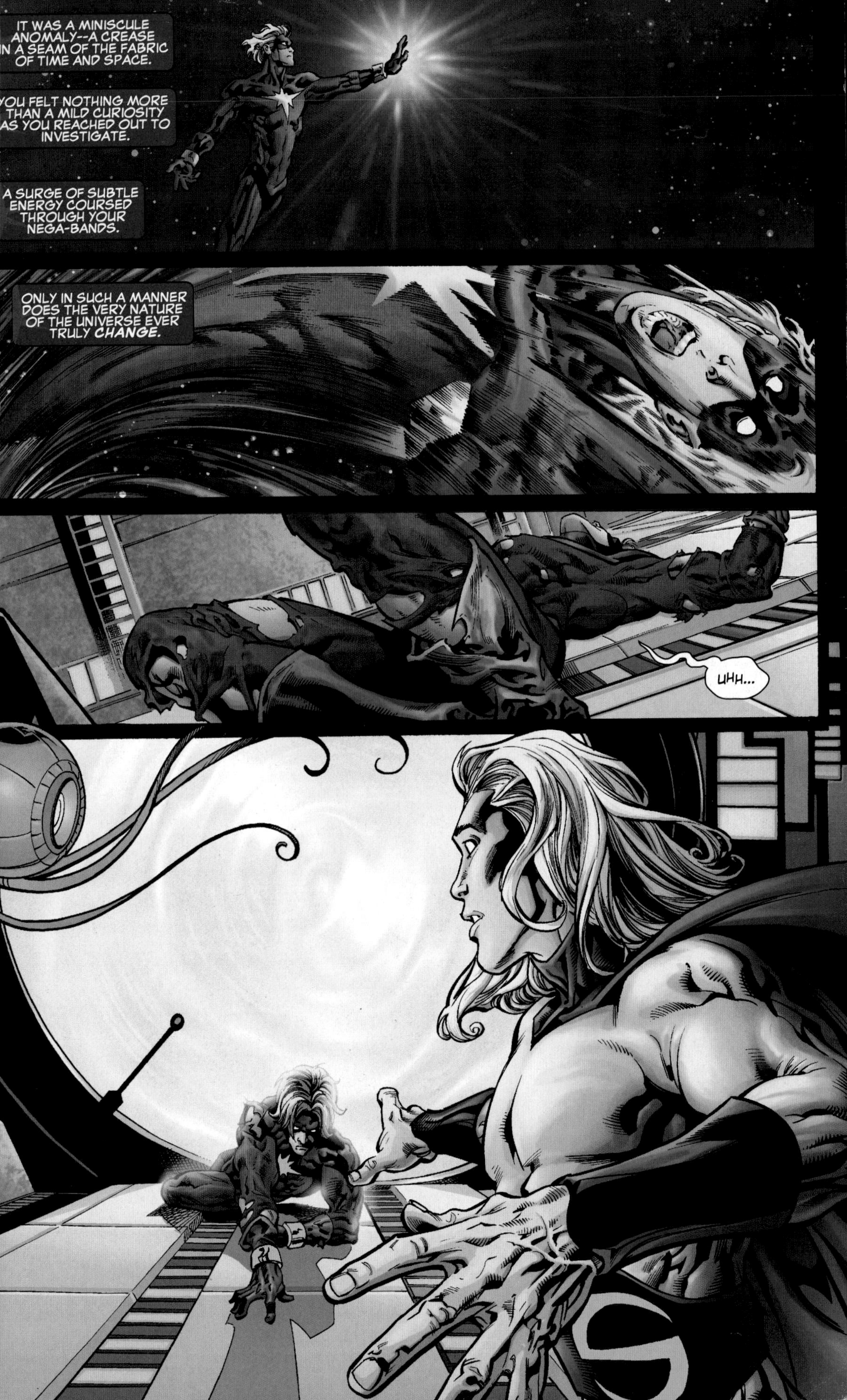
IT WAS A MINISCULE ANOMALY--A CREASE IN A SEAM OF THE FABRIC OF TIME AND SPACE.
YOU FELT NOTHING MORE THAN A MILD CURIOSITY AS YOU REACHED OUT TO INVESTIGATE.
A SURGE OF SUBTLE ENERGY COURSED THROUGH YOUR NEGA-BANDS.
ONLY IN SUCH A MANNER DOES THE VERY NATURE OF THE UNIVERSE EVER TRULY CHANGE.
UHH...

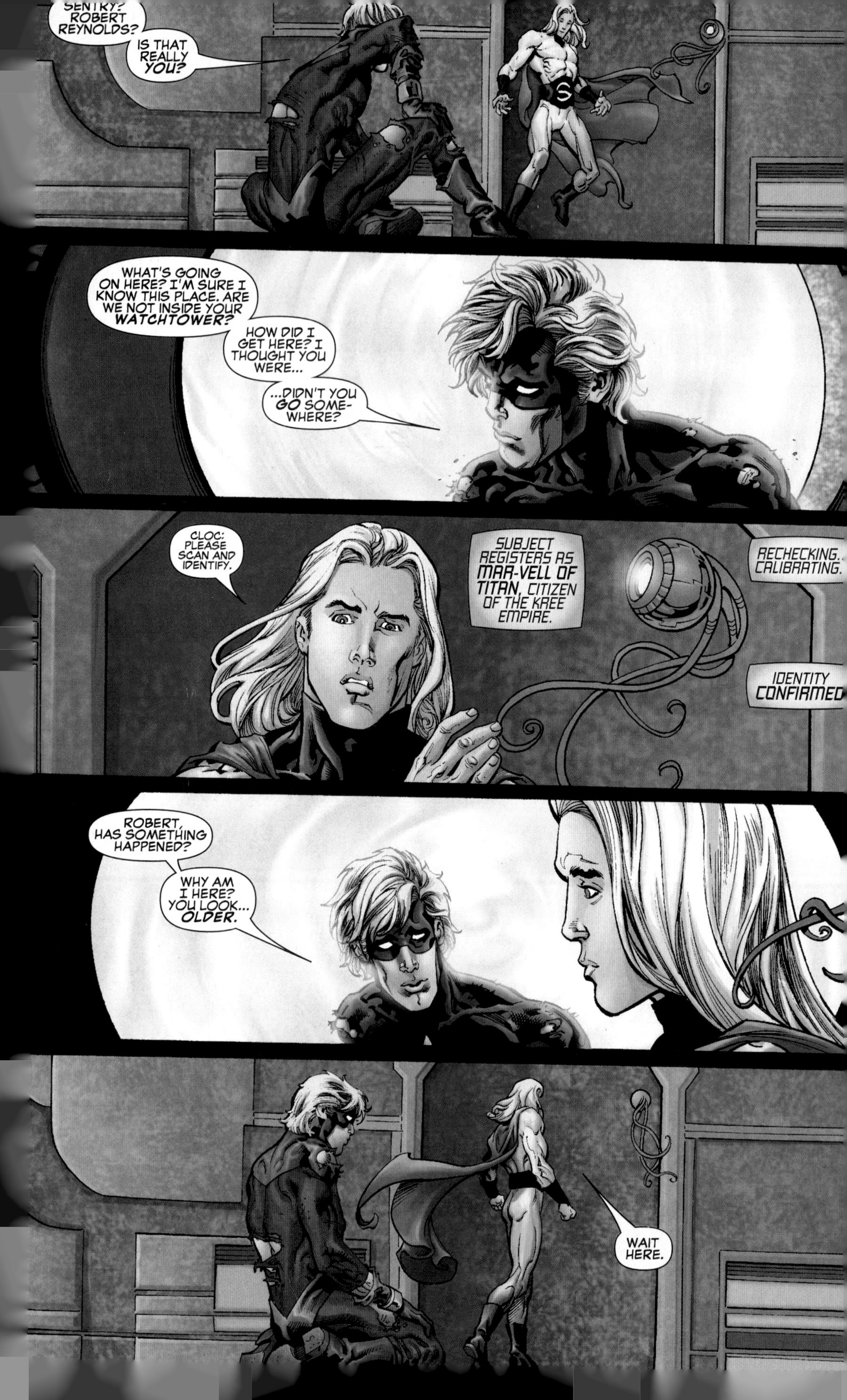
SENTRY? ROBERT REYNOLDS?
IS THAT REALLY YOU?
WHAT'S GOING ON HERE? I'M SURE I KNOW THIS PLACE. ARE WE NOT INSIDE YOUR WATCHTOWER?
HOW DID I GET HERE? I THOUGHT YOU WERE...
...DIDN'T YOU GO SOME-WHERE?
CLOC: PLEASE SCAN AND IDENTIFY.
SUBJECT REGISTERS AS MAR-VELL OF TITAN, CITIZEN OF THE KREE EMPIRE.
RECHECKING. CALIBRATING.
IDENTITY CONFIRMED
ROBERT, HAS SOMETHING HAPPENED?
WHY AM I HERE? YOU LOOK... OLDER.
WAIT HERE.

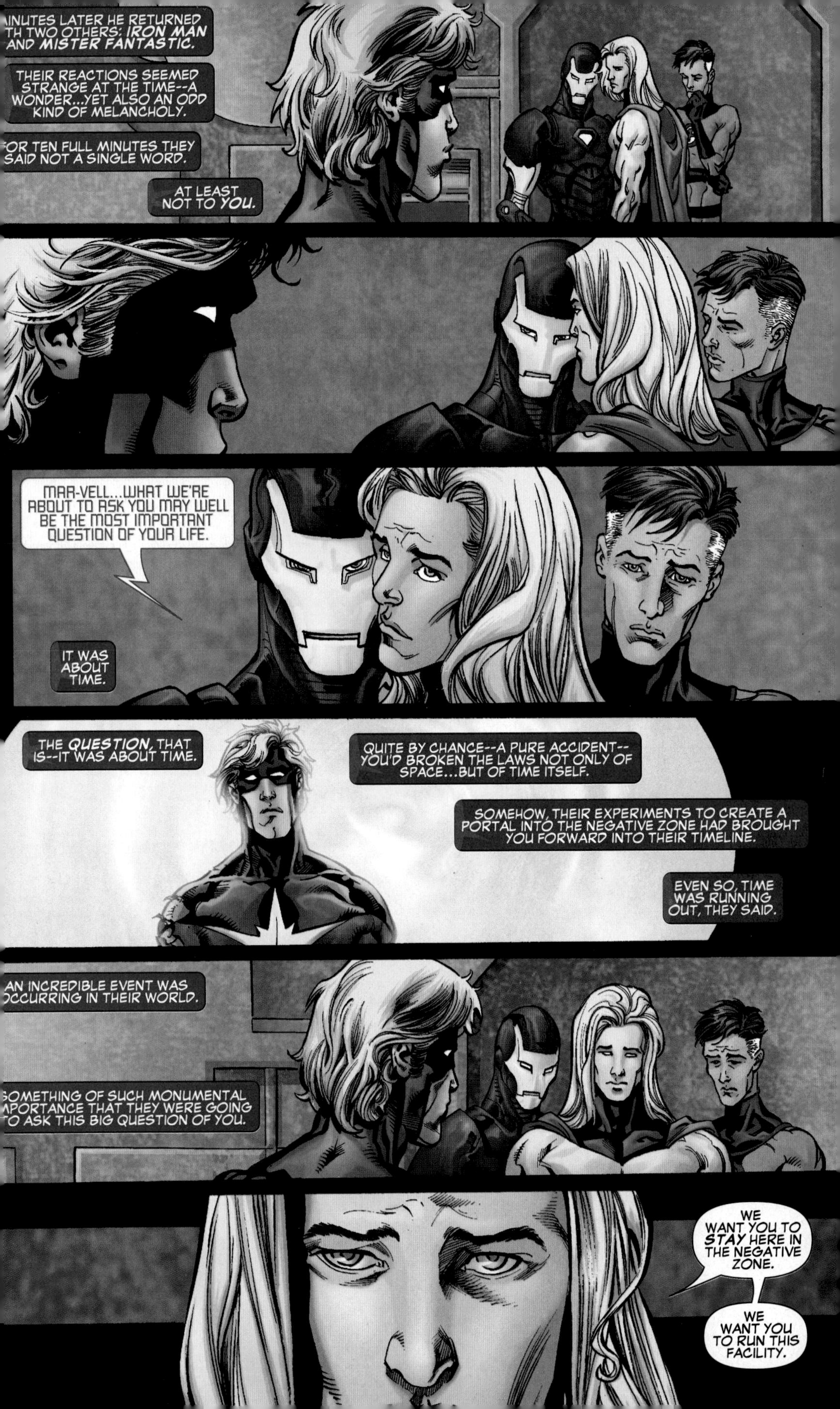

...INUTES LATER HE RETURNED ...TH TWO OTHERS: IRON MAN AND MISTER FANTASTIC.
THEIR REACTIONS SEEMED STRANGE AT THE TIME--A WONDER...YET ALSO AN ODD KIND OF MELANCHOLY.
...OR TEN FULL MINUTES THEY SAID NOT A SINGLE WORD.
AT LEAST NOT TO YOU.
MAR-VELL...WHAT WE'RE ABOUT TO ASK YOU MAY WELL BE THE MOST IMPORTANT QUESTION OF YOUR LIFE.
IT WAS ABOUT TIME.
THE QUESTION, THAT IS--IT WAS ABOUT TIME.
QUITE BY CHANCE--A PURE ACCIDENT--YOU'D BROKEN THE LAWS NOT ONLY OF SPACE...BUT OF TIME ITSELF.
SOMEHOW, THEIR EXPERIMENTS TO CREATE A PORTAL INTO THE NEGATIVE ZONE HAD BROUGHT YOU FORWARD INTO THEIR TIMELINE.
EVEN SO, TIME WAS RUNNING OUT, THEY SAID.
AN INCREDIBLE EVENT WAS ...CCURRING IN THEIR WORLD.
...OMETHING OF SUCH MONUMENTAL ...PORTANCE THAT THEY WERE GOING TO ASK THIS BIG QUESTION OF YOU.
WE WANT YOU TO STAY HERE IN THE NEGATIVE ZONE.
WE WANT YOU TO RUN THIS FACILITY.

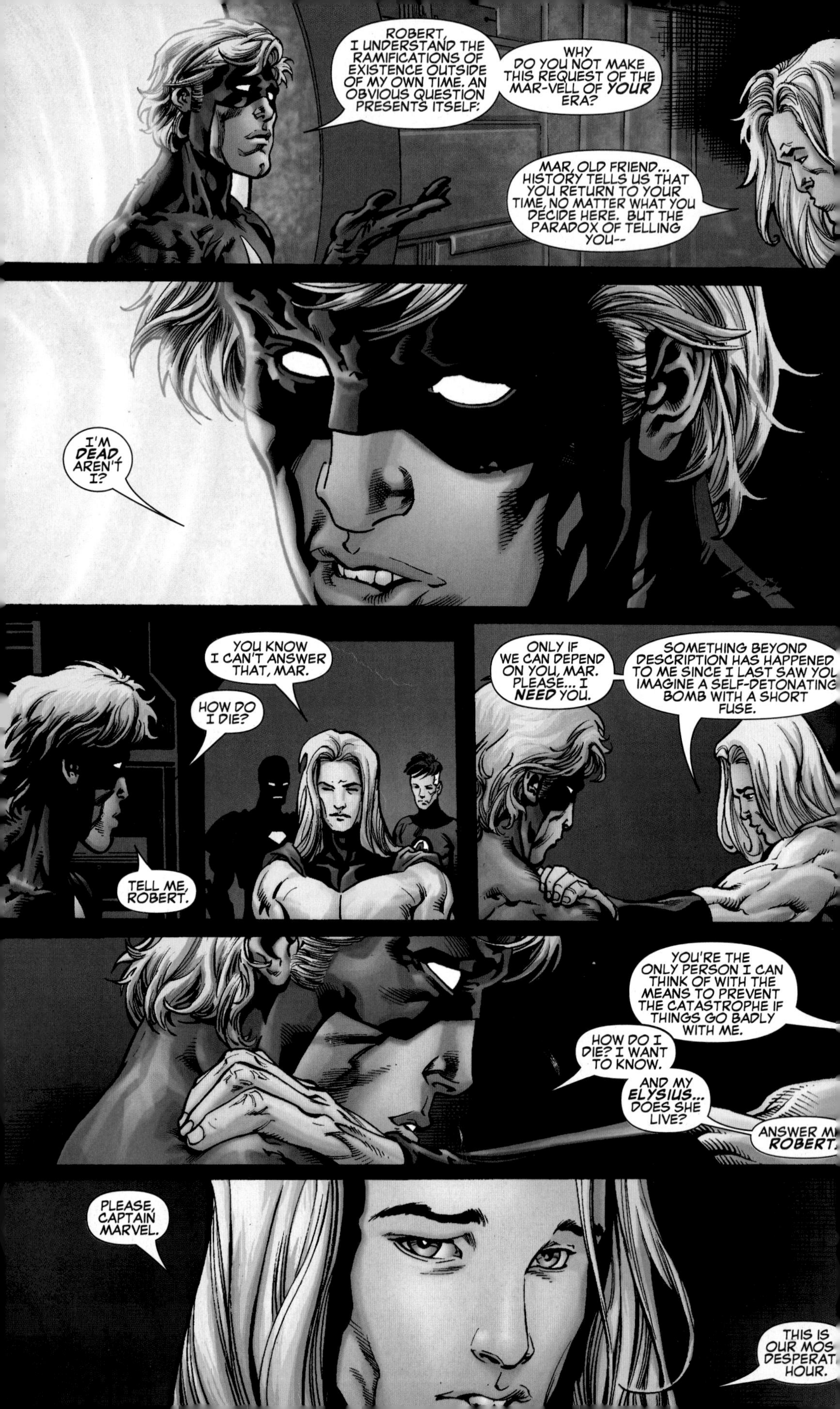

ROBERT, I UNDERSTAND THE RAMIFICATIONS OF EXISTENCE OUTSIDE OF MY OWN TIME. AN OBVIOUS QUESTION PRESENTS ITSELF:
WHY DO YOU NOT MAKE THIS REQUEST OF THE MAR-VELL OF YOUR ERA?
MAR, OLD FRIEND... HISTORY TELLS US THAT YOU RETURN TO YOUR TIME, NO MATTER WHAT YOU DECIDE HERE. BUT THE PARADOX OF TELLING YOU--
I'M DEAD, AREN'T I?
YOU KNOW I CAN'T ANSWER THAT, MAR.
HOW DO I DIE?
TELL ME, ROBERT.
ONLY IF WE CAN DEPEND ON YOU, MAR. PLEASE... I NEED YOU.
SOMETHING BEYOND DESCRIPTION HAS HAPPENED TO ME SINCE I LAST SAW YOU IMAGINE A SELF-DETONATING BOMB WITH A SHORT FUSE.
YOU'RE THE ONLY PERSON I CAN THINK OF WITH THE MEANS TO PREVENT THE CATASTROPHE IF THINGS GO BADLY WITH ME.
HOW DO I DIE? I WANT TO KNOW.
AND MY ELYSIUS... DOES SHE LIVE?
ANSWER ME ROBERT.
PLEASE, CAPTAIN MARVEL.
THIS IS OUR MOST DESPERATE HOUR.

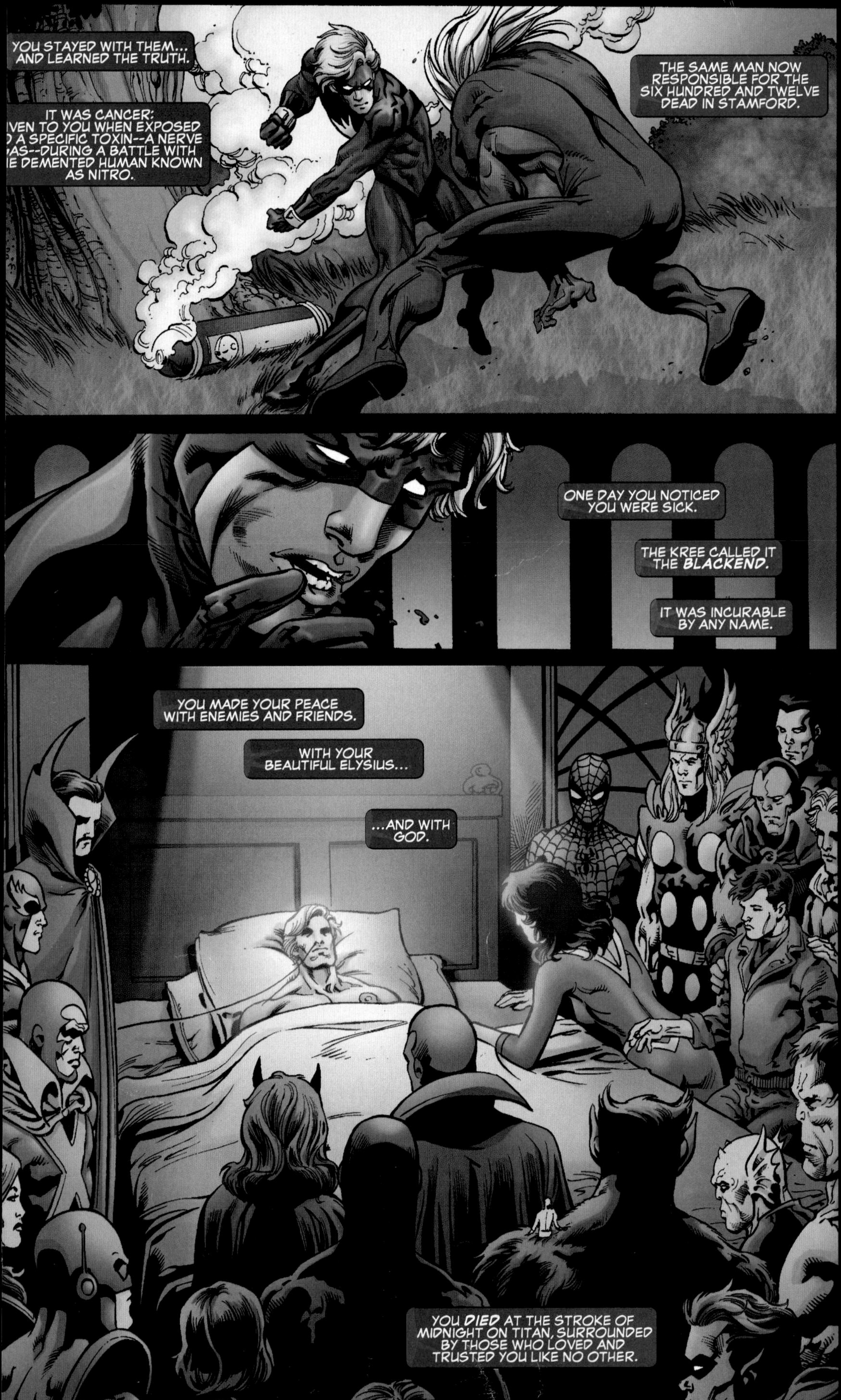
YOU STAYED WITH THEM... AND LEARNED THE TRUTH.
IT WAS CANCER: IVEN TO YOU WHEN EXPOSED D A SPECIFIC TOXIN--A NERVE GAS--DURING A BATTLE WITH E DEMENTED HUMAN KNOWN AS NITRO.
THE SAME MAN NOW RESPONSIBLE FOR THE SIX HUNDRED AND TWELVE DEAD IN STAMFORD.
ONE DAY YOU NOTICED YOU WERE SICK.
THE KREE CALLED IT THE *BLACKEND.*
IT WAS INCURABLE BY ANY NAME.
YOU MADE YOUR PEACE WITH ENEMIES AND FRIENDS.
WITH YOUR BEAUTIFUL ELYSIUS...
...AND WITH GOD.
YOU *DIED* AT THE STROKE OF MIDNIGHT ON TITAN, SURROUNDED BY THOSE WHO LOVED AND TRUSTED YOU LIKE NO OTHER.

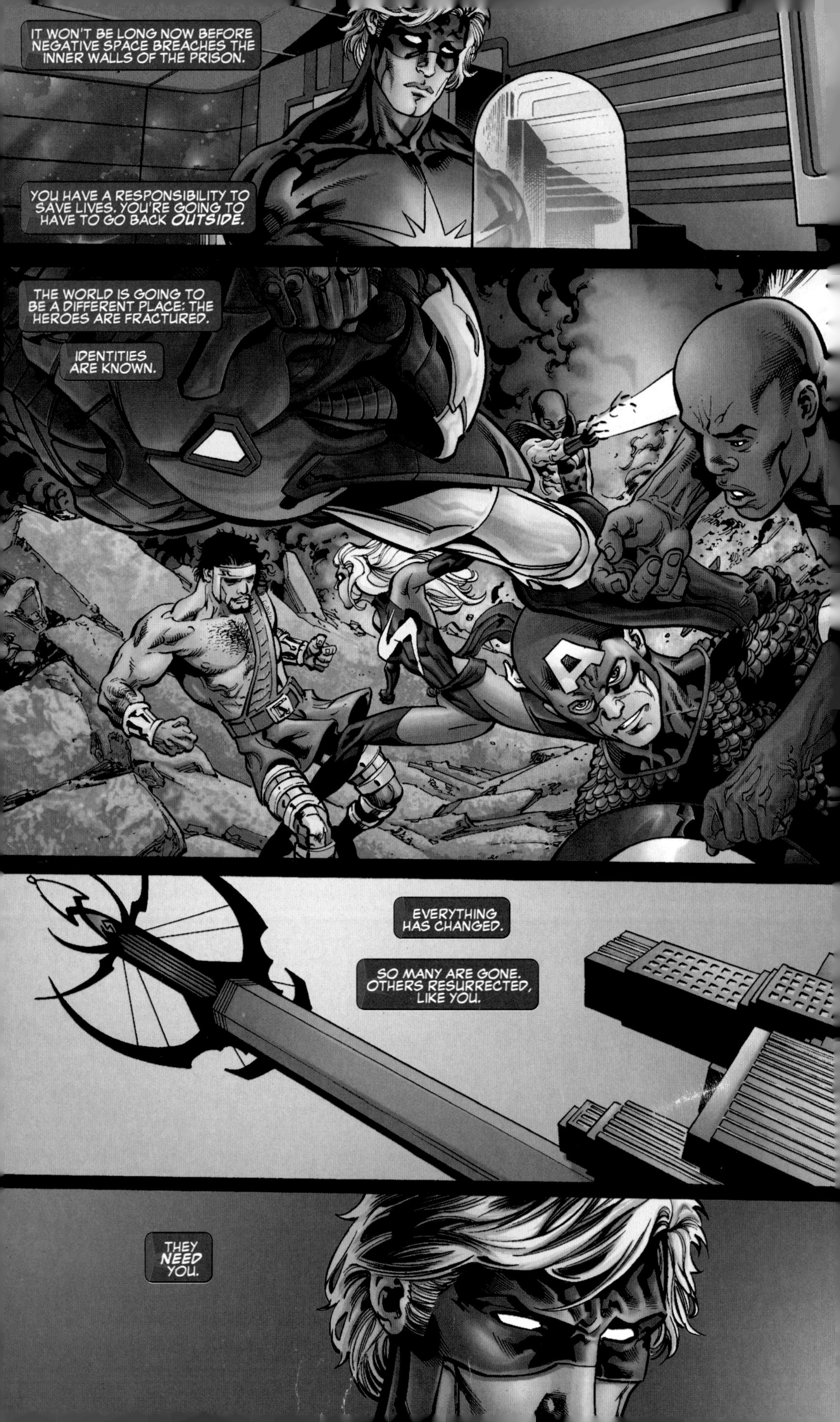
IT WON'T BE LONG NOW BEFORE NEGATIVE SPACE BREACHES THE INNER WALLS OF THE PRISON.
YOU HAVE A RESPONSIBILITY TO SAVE LIVES. YOU'RE GOING TO HAVE TO GO BACK *OUTSIDE.*
THE WORLD IS GOING TO BE A DIFFERENT PLACE: THE HEROES ARE FRACTURED.
IDENTITIES ARE KNOWN.
EVERYTHING HAS CHANGED.
SO MANY ARE GONE. OTHERS RESURRECTED, LIKE YOU.
THEY *NEED* YOU.

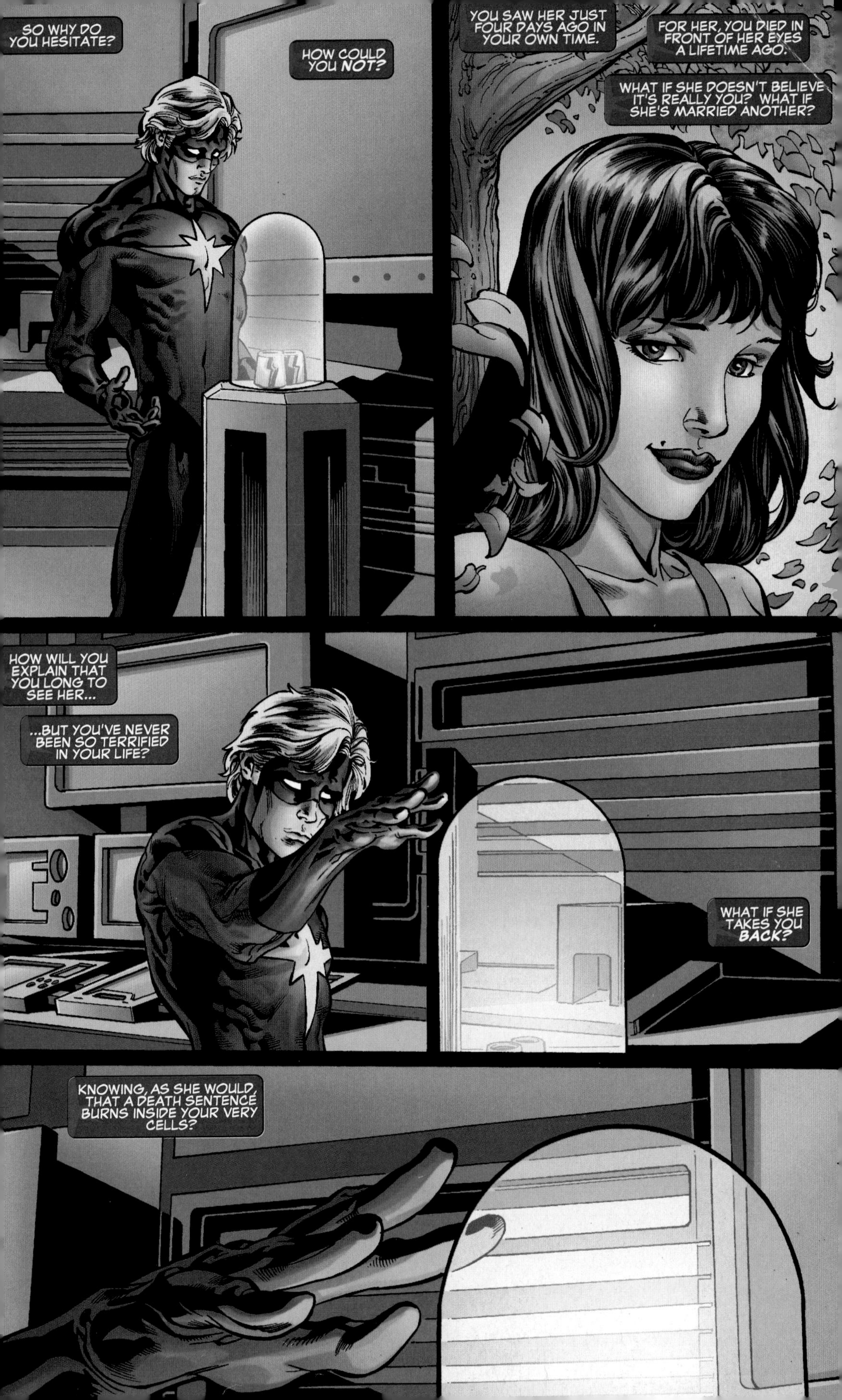

SO WHY DO YOU HESITATE?
HOW COULD YOU NOT?
YOU SAW HER JUST FOUR DAYS AGO IN YOUR OWN TIME.
FOR HER, YOU DIED IN FRONT OF HER EYES A LIFETIME AGO.
WHAT IF SHE DOESN'T BELIEVE IT'S REALLY YOU? WHAT IF SHE'S MARRIED ANOTHER?
HOW WILL YOU EXPLAIN THAT YOU LONG TO SEE HER...
...BUT YOU'VE NEVER BEEN SO TERRIFIED IN YOUR LIFE?
WHAT IF SHE TAKES YOU BACK?
KNOWING, AS SHE WOULD, THAT A DEATH SENTENCE BURNS INSIDE YOUR VERY CELLS?

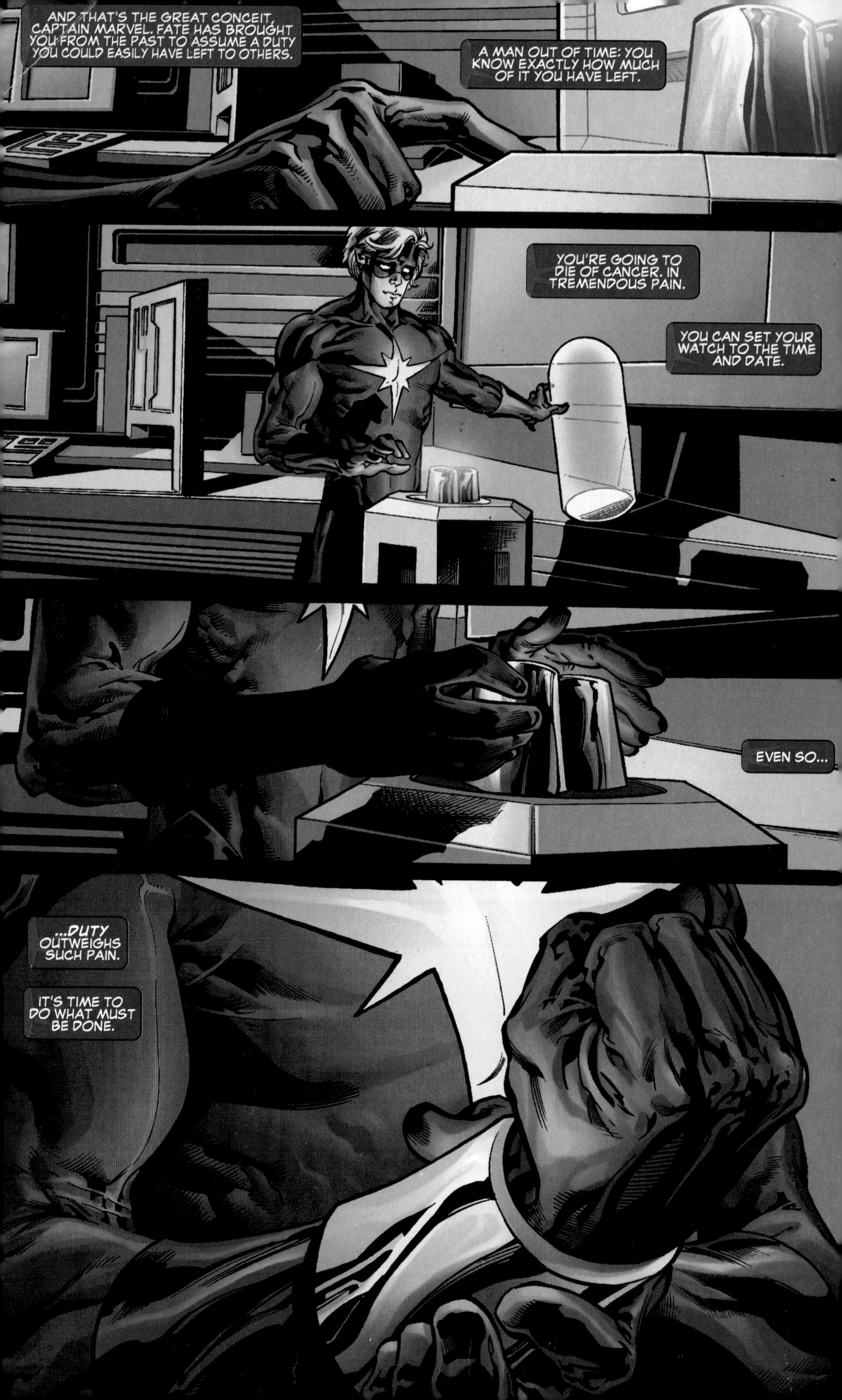
AND THAT'S THE GREAT CONCEIT, CAPTAIN MARVEL. FATE HAS BROUGHT YOU FROM THE PAST TO ASSUME A DUTY YOU COULD EASILY HAVE LEFT TO OTHERS.
A MAN OUT OF TIME: YOU KNOW EXACTLY HOW MUCH OF IT YOU HAVE LEFT.
YOU'RE GOING TO DIE OF CANCER. IN TREMENDOUS PAIN.
YOU CAN SET YOUR WATCH TO THE TIME AND DATE.
EVEN SO...
...DUTY OUTWEIGHS SUCH PAIN.
IT'S TIME TO DO WHAT MUST BE DONE.

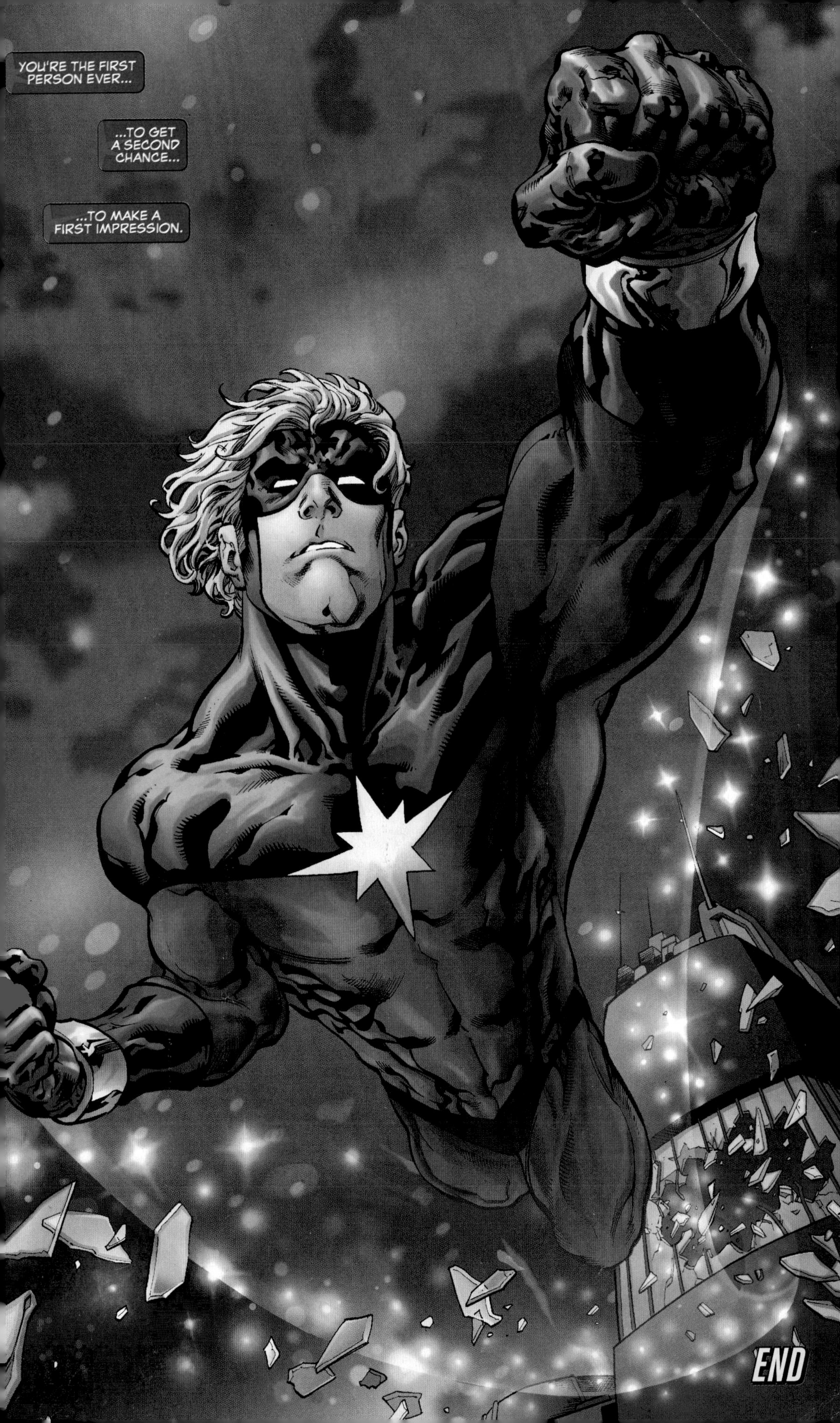
YOU'RE THE FIRST PERSON EVER...
...TO GET A SECOND CHANCE...
...TO MAKE A FIRST IMPRESSION.
END

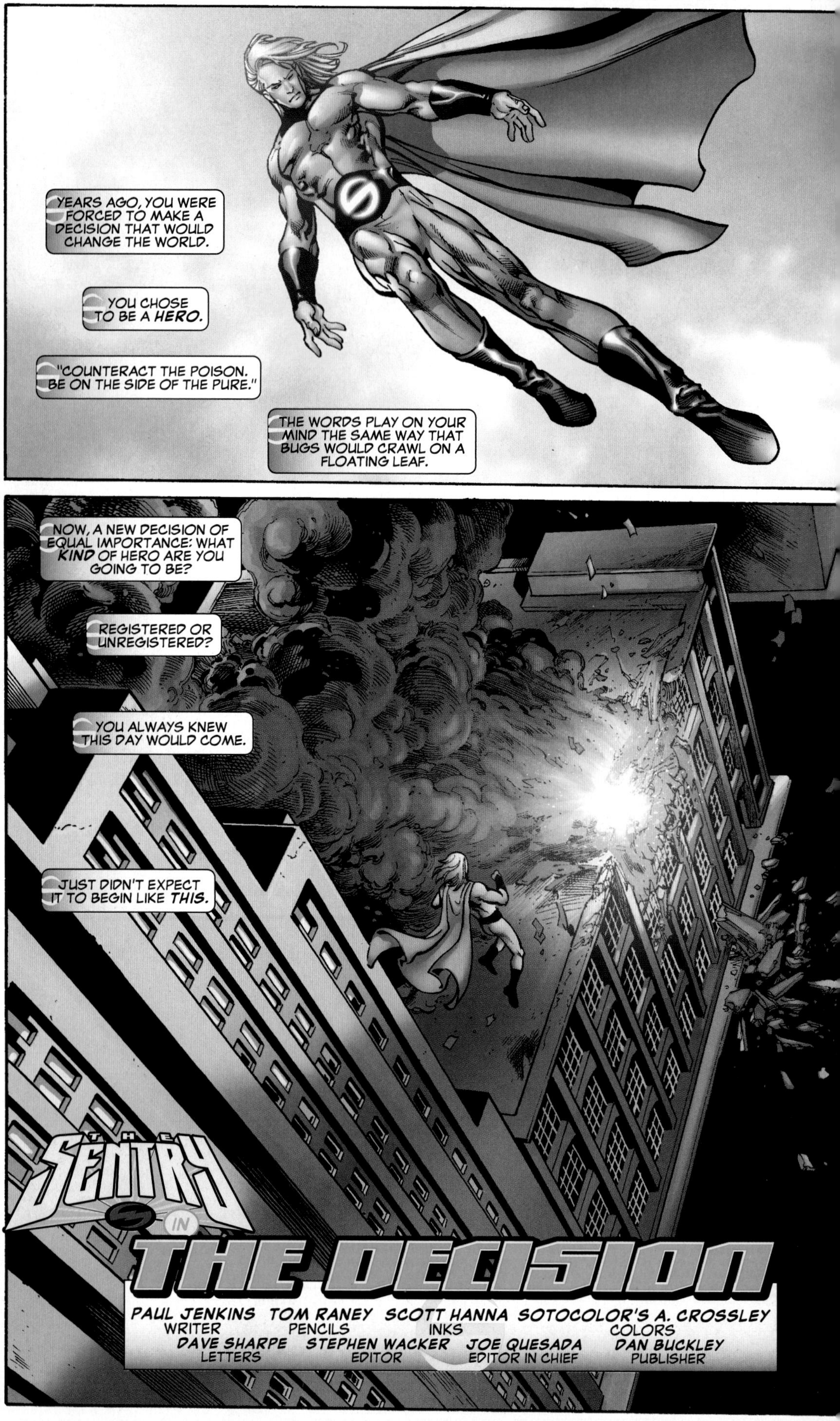
YEARS AGO, YOU WERE FORCED TO MAKE A DECISION THAT WOULD CHANGE THE WORLD.
YOU CHOSE TO BE A HERO.
"COUNTERACT THE POISON. BE ON THE SIDE OF THE PURE."
THE WORDS PLAY ON YOUR MIND THE SAME WAY THAT BUGS WOULD CRAWL ON A FLOATING LEAF.
NOW, A NEW DECISION OF EQUAL IMPORTANCE: WHAT KIND OF HERO ARE YOU GOING TO BE?
REGISTERED OR UNREGISTERED?
YOU ALWAYS KNEW THIS DAY WOULD COME.
JUST DIDN'T EXPECT IT TO BEGIN LIKE THIS.
THE SENTRY IN
THE DECISION
PAUL JENKINS WRITER
TOM RANEY PENCILS
SCOTT HANNA INKS
SOTOCOLOR'S A. CROSSLEY COLORS
DAVE SHARPE LETTERS
STEPHEN WACKER EDITOR
JOE QUESADA EDITOR IN CHIEF
DAN BUCKLEY PUBLISHER

CLOC: PINPOINT TARGET LOCATION AND IDENTIFY--

UNABLE TO COMPLY, SENTRY. TARGET REMAINS UNDETECTABLE.

ANALYZE AND SPECULATE.

SIR, MY PROBABILITY SUBROUTINES SUGGEST THE SUBJECT HAS STOLEN YOUR *OWN* ABILITY TO AVOID DETECTION BY DEFLECTING LIGHT AND RADIANT EMISSIONS--

SO HE'S *MIMICKING* ME?

THAT IS THE MOST LIKELY CONCLUSION.

IT'S TOO QUIET.

IN COMPARISON TO WHAT, SIR?

NOTHING. JUST THINKING OUT LOUD.

PLEASE RECHECK ALL EMISSION BANDWIDTHS.

I'M PRETTY SURE HE'S AROUND HERE SOME-WHERE.

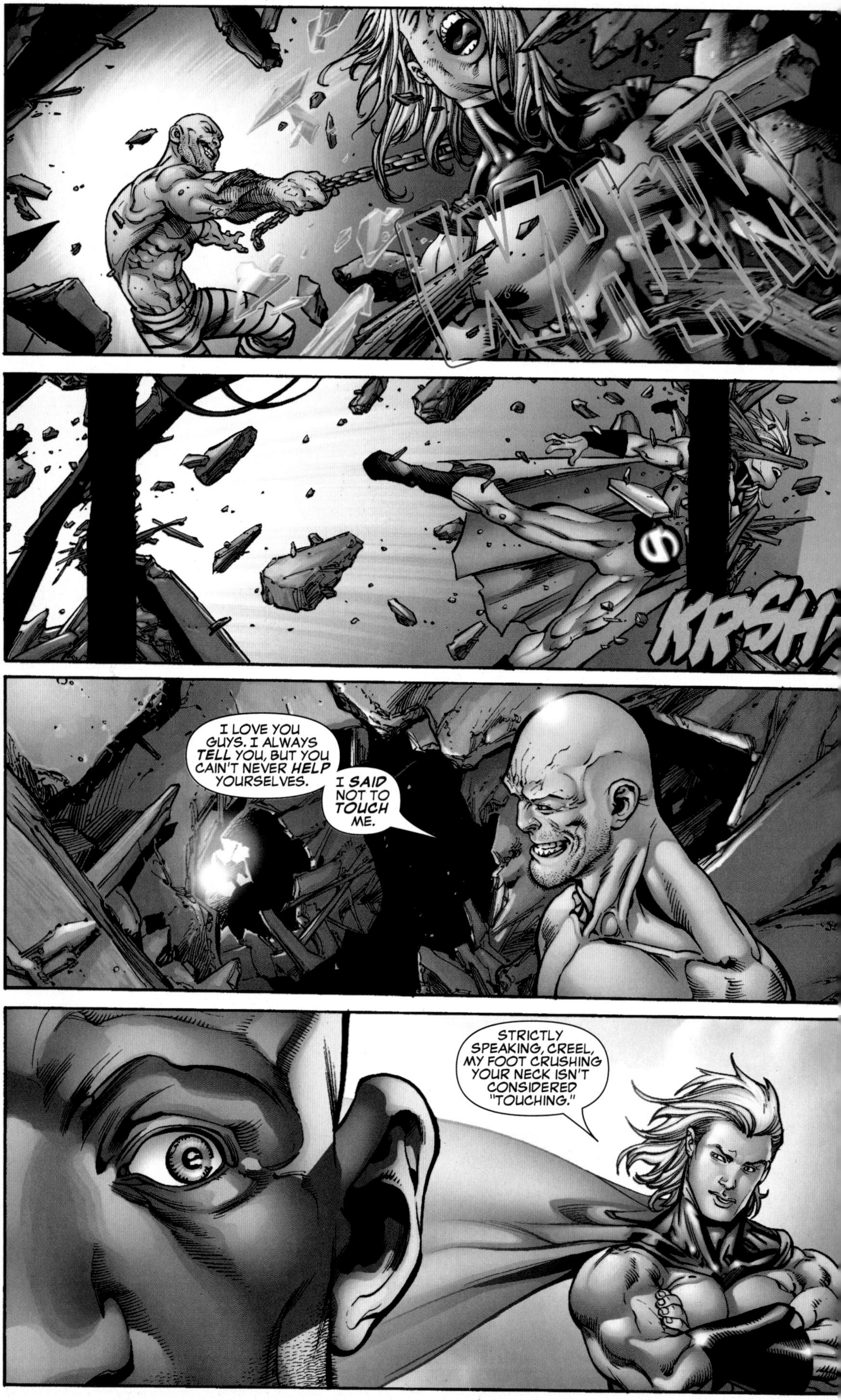
KRSH
I LOVE YOU GUYS. I ALWAYS TELL YOU, BUT YOU CAIN'T NEVER HELP YOURSELVES.
I SAID NOT TO TOUCH ME.
STRICTLY SPEAKING, CREEL, MY FOOT CRUSHING YOUR NECK ISN'T CONSIDERED "TOUCHING."

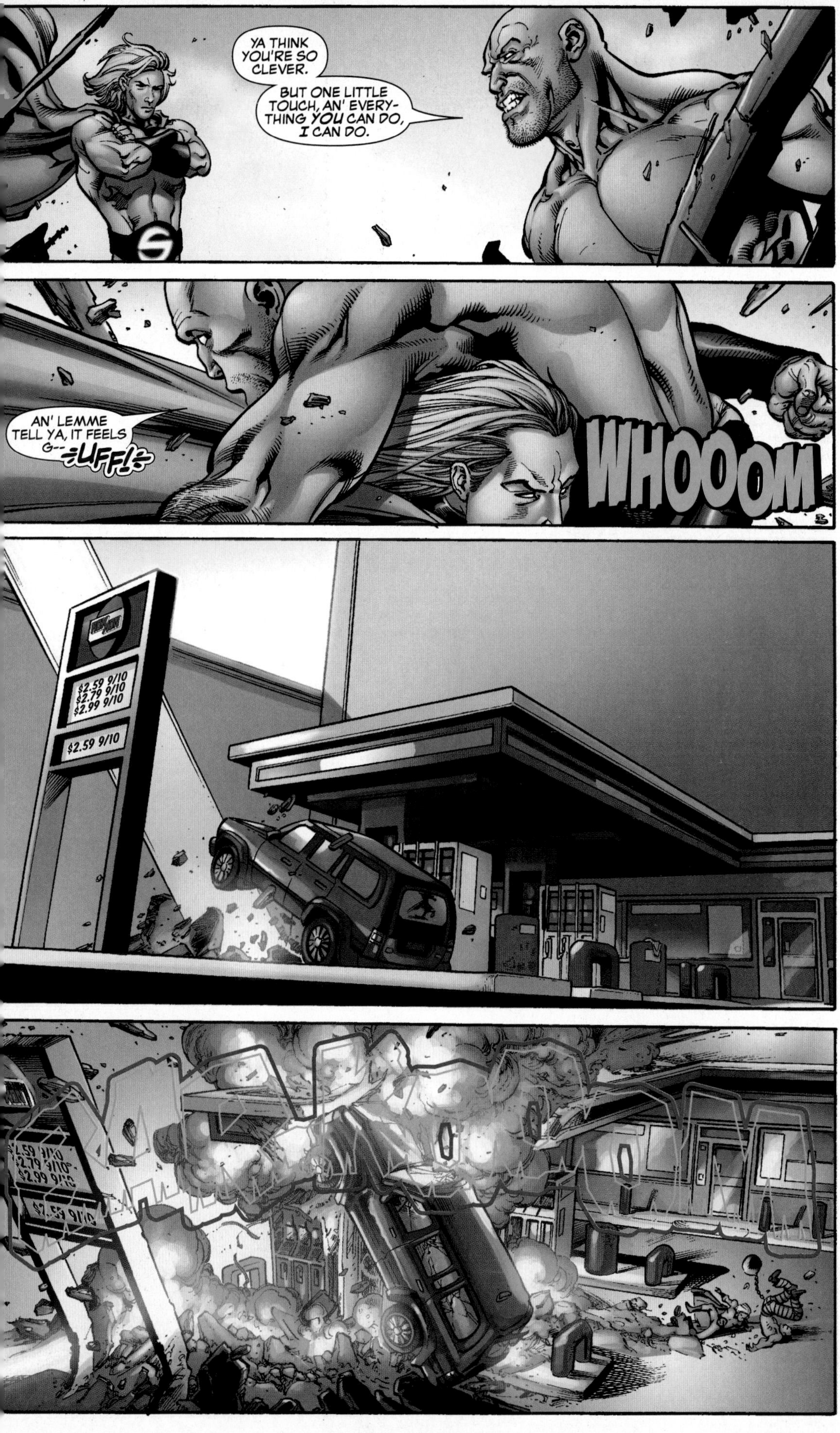
YA THINK YOU'RE SO CLEVER.
BUT ONE LITTLE TOUCH, AN' EVERY-THING YOU CAN DO, I CAN DO.
AN' LEMME TELL YA, IT FEELS G-- UFF!
WHOOOM
$2.59 9/10
$2.79 9/10
$2.99 9/10
$2.59 9/10

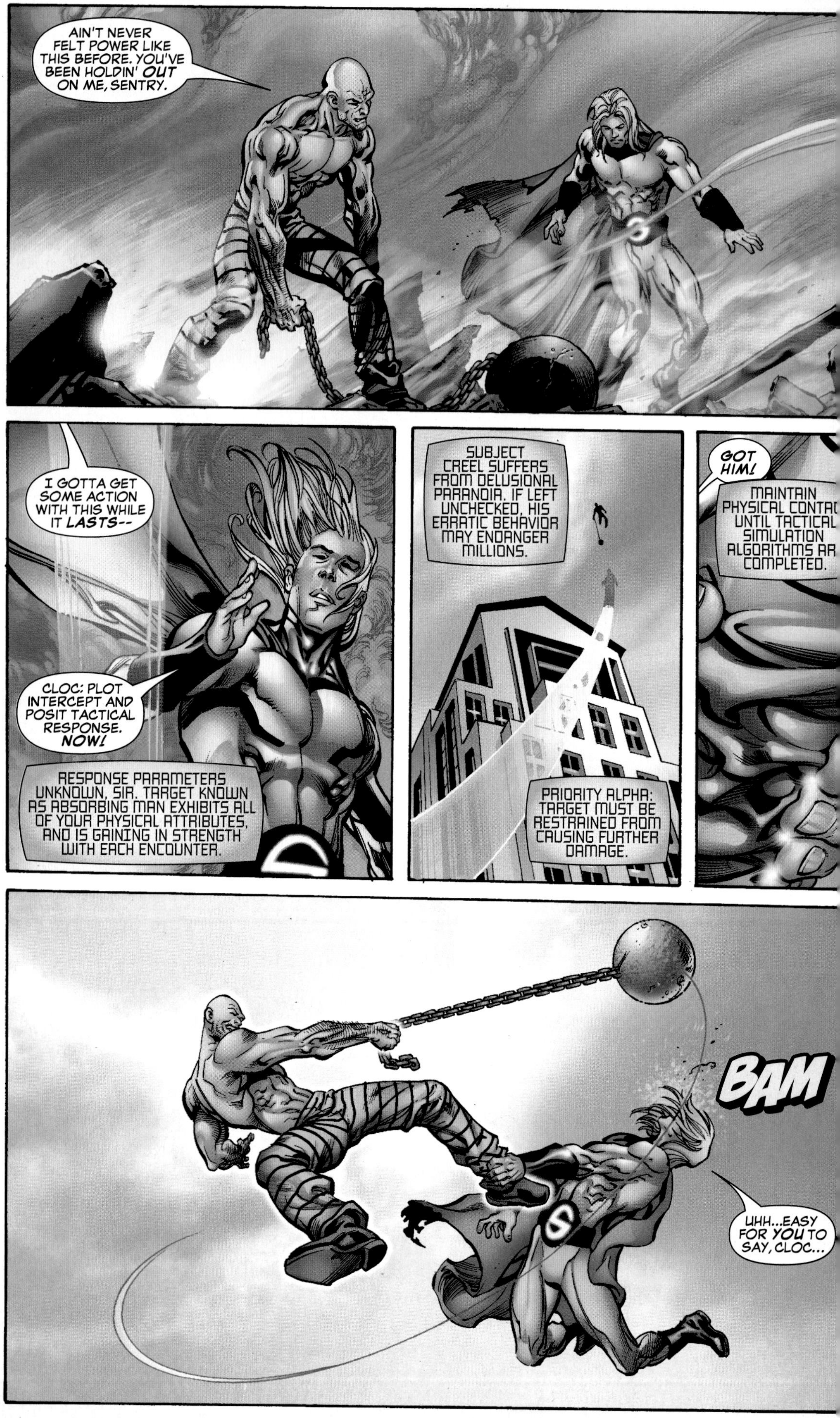
AIN'T NEVER FELT POWER LIKE THIS BEFORE. YOU'VE BEEN HOLDIN' OUT ON ME, SENTRY.
I GOTTA GET SOME ACTION WITH THIS WHILE IT LASTS--
CLOC: PLOT INTERCEPT AND POSIT TACTICAL RESPONSE. NOW!
RESPONSE PARAMETERS UNKNOWN, SIR. TARGET KNOWN AS ABSORBING MAN EXHIBITS ALL OF YOUR PHYSICAL ATTRIBUTES, AND IS GAINING IN STRENGTH WITH EACH ENCOUNTER.
SUBJECT CREEL SUFFERS FROM DELUSIONAL PARANOIA. IF LEFT UNCHECKED, HIS ERRATIC BEHAVIOR MAY ENDANGER MILLIONS.
PRIORITY ALPHA: TARGET MUST BE RESTRAINED FROM CAUSING FURTHER DAMAGE.
GOT HIM!
MAINTAIN PHYSICAL CONTRO UNTIL TACTICAL SIMULATION ALGORITHMS AR COMPLETED.
BAM
UHH...EASY FOR YOU TO SAY, CLOC...

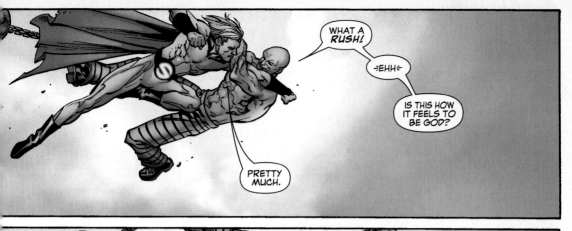

WHAT A *RUSH!*

⸗EHH⸗

IS THIS HOW IT FEELS TO BE GOD?

PRETTY MUCH.

IMAGINE THIS *DAY* IN, *DAY* OUT.

ALL THE DAMAGE YOU COULD DO...TELL ME SOMETHIN'--

HOW'D YOU EVER GIVE UP A DRUG LIKE THIS?

TRUE POWER URTS, CREEL. IT'S OMETHING YOU'D NEVER UNDER-STAND.

⸗MFF⸗

IT'S WHAT *SEPARATES* US.

POWER *RULES,* DUDE. IF YOU GOT IT, *FLAUNT* IT.

LET LOOSE... YOU KNOW YOU *WANT* TO.

THIS IS YOUR LAST WARNING.

⸗HUFF⸗

SUBMIT NOW, OR SUFFER THE CONSEQUENCES.

YOU CALL THAT BABY TAP A *WARNING?*

HA! HEHH... YOU CAN'T *HURT* ME, IDIOT. NOT WHEN I'M *YOU.*

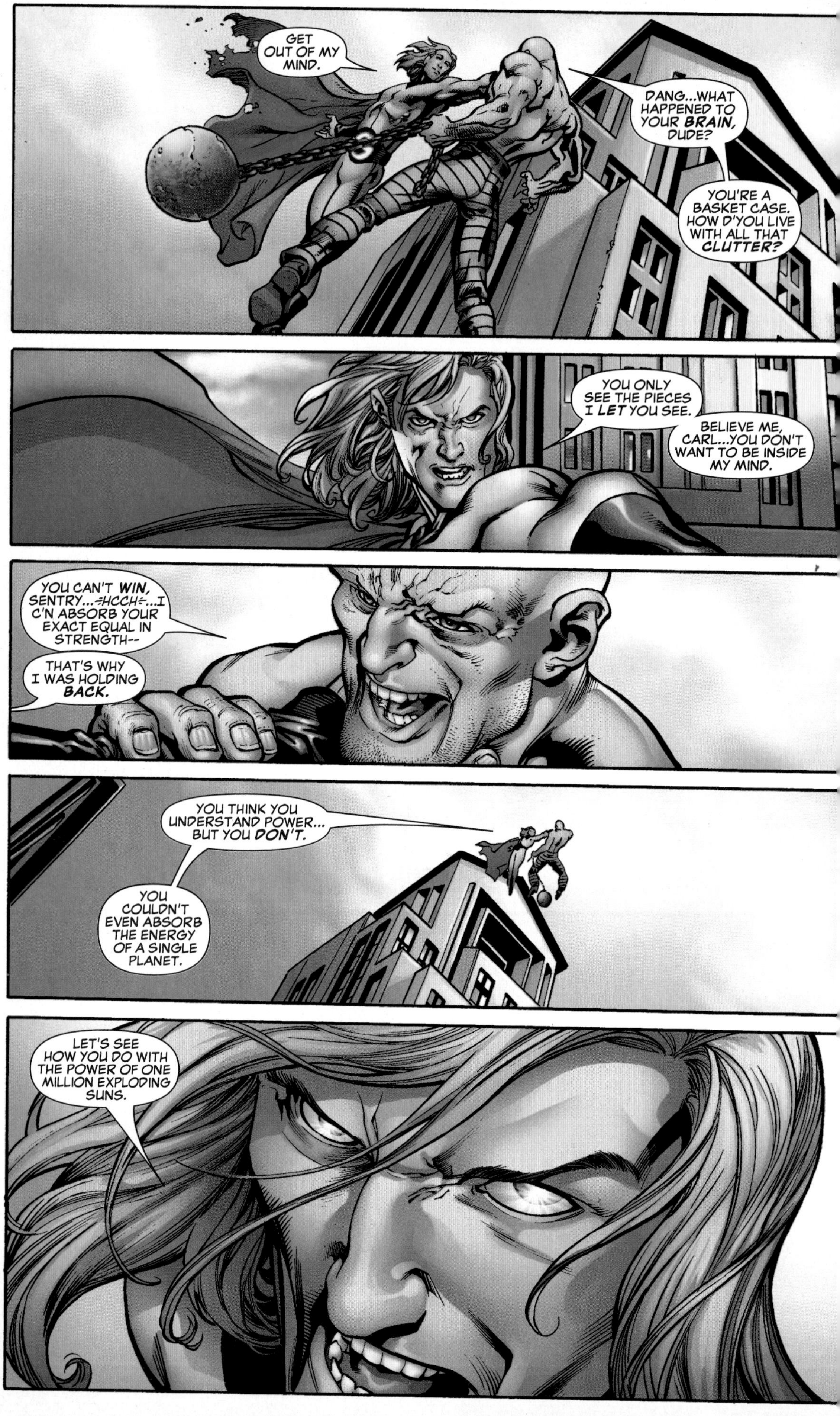
GET OUT OF MY MIND.
DANG...WHAT HAPPENED TO YOUR **BRAIN,** DUDE?
YOU'RE A BASKET CASE. HOW D'YOU LIVE WITH ALL THAT **CLUTTER?**
YOU ONLY SEE THE PIECES I **LET** YOU SEE.
BELIEVE ME, CARL...YOU DON'T WANT TO BE INSIDE MY MIND.
YOU CAN'T **WIN,** SENTRY...⇌HCCH⇌...I C'N ABSORB YOUR EXACT EQUAL IN STRENGTH--
THAT'S WHY I WAS HOLDING **BACK.**
YOU THINK YOU UNDERSTAND POWER... BUT YOU **DON'T.**
YOU COULDN'T EVEN ABSORB THE ENERGY OF A SINGLE PLANET.
LET'S SEE HOW YOU DO WITH THE POWER OF ONE MILLION EXPLODING SUNS.

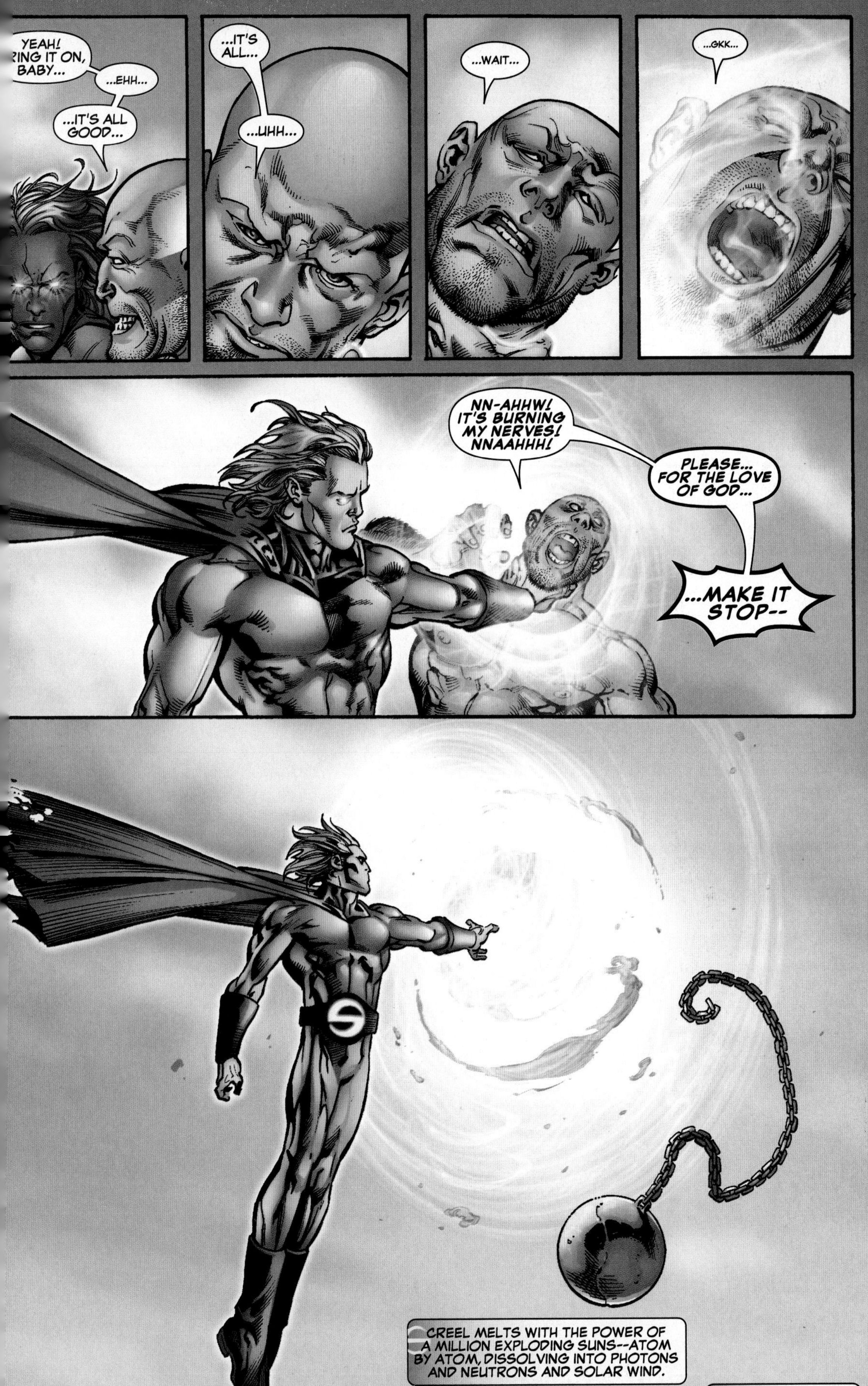

YEAH! BRING IT ON, BABY...
...EHH...
...IT'S ALL GOOD...
...IT'S ALL...
...UHH...
...WAIT...
...GKK...
NN-AHHW! IT'S BURNING MY NERVES! NNAAHHH!
PLEASE... FOR THE LOVE OF GOD...
...MAKE IT STOP--
CREEL MELTS WITH THE POWER OF A MILLION EXPLODING SUNS--ATOM BY ATOM, DISSOLVING INTO PHOTONS AND NEUTRONS AND SOLAR WIND.
YOU ALREADY KNOW HE'LL BE BACK.

AND WHEN HE COMES BACK, WHAT KIND OF WORLD WILL BE WAITING?

WHAT ABOUT YOU, SENTRY? WHERE WILL YOU FIT IN?

HOW MANY TIMES WILL YOU HAVE SAVED THE WORLD?

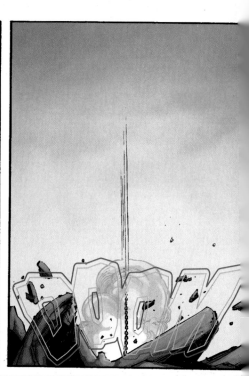

WHO'S TO SAY YOU WON'T BE THE ONE TO *DESTROY* IT?

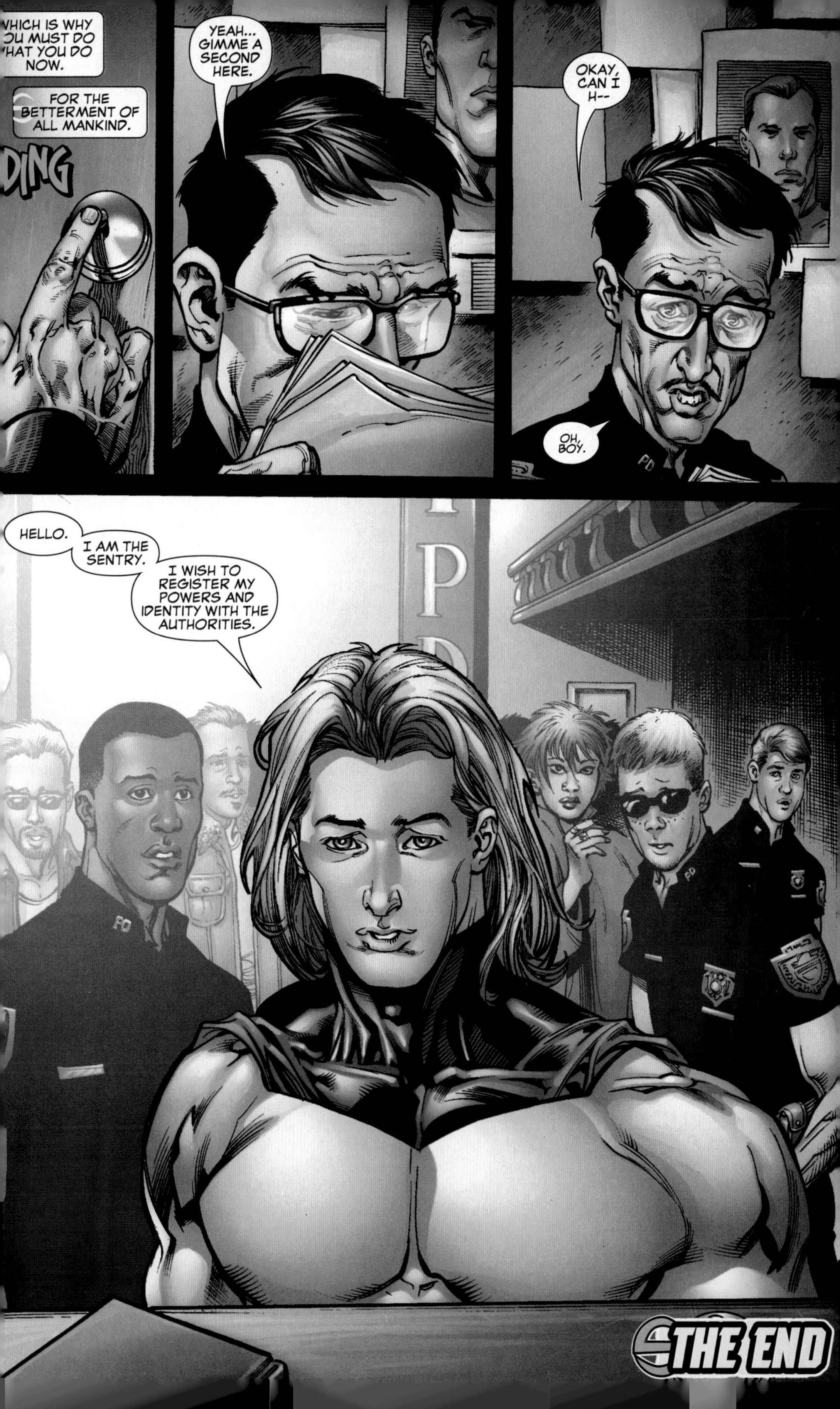
WHICH IS WHY
OU MUST DO
WHAT YOU DO
NOW.
FOR THE BETTERMENT OF ALL MANKIND.
DING
YEAH... GIMME A SECOND HERE.
OKAY, CAN I H--
OH, BOY.
HELLO.
I AM THE SENTRY.
I WISH TO REGISTER MY POWERS AND IDENTITY WITH THE AUTHORITIES.
THE END

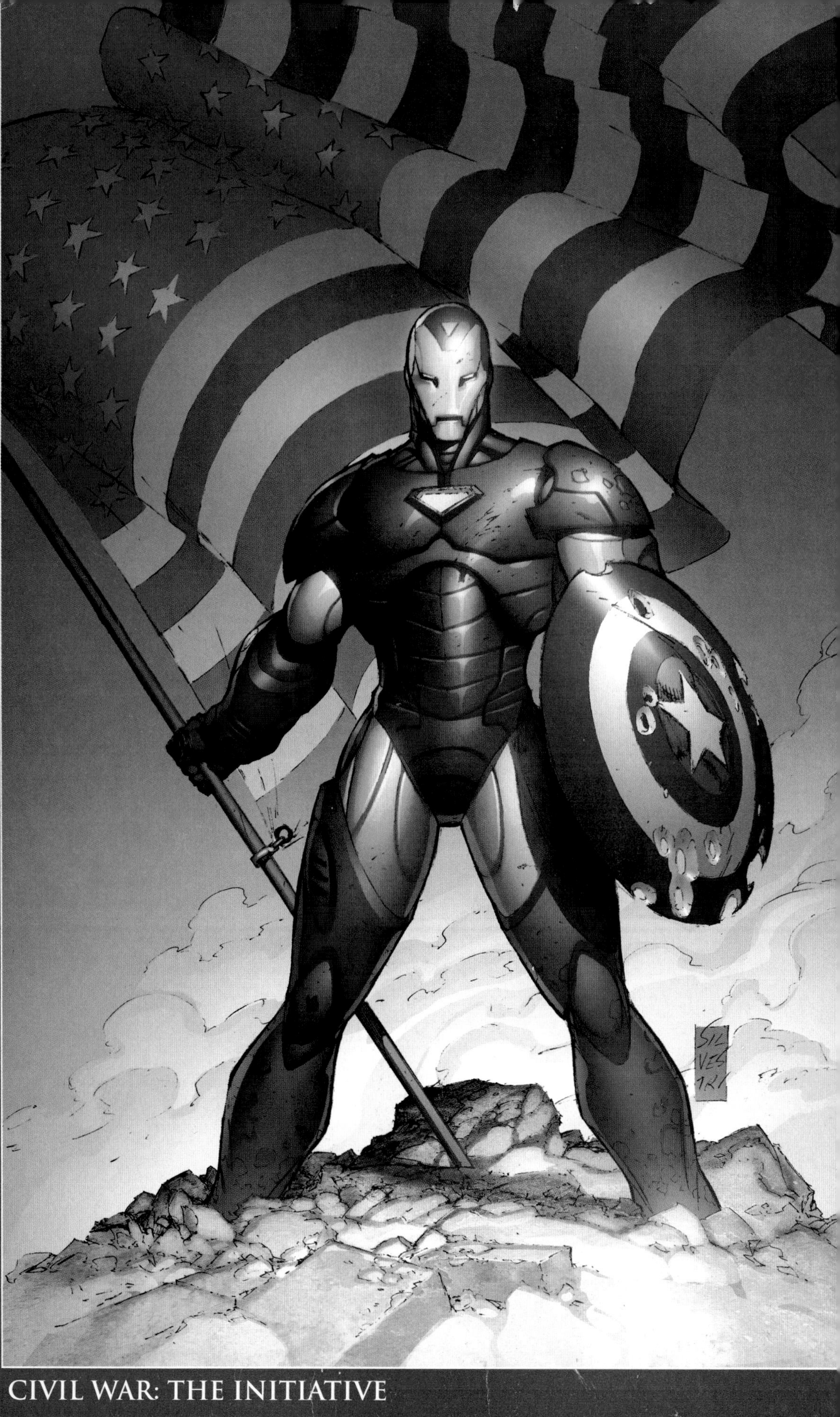

SIL
VES
TRI

CIVIL WAR: THE INITIATIVE

CIVIL WAR
THE INITIATIVE

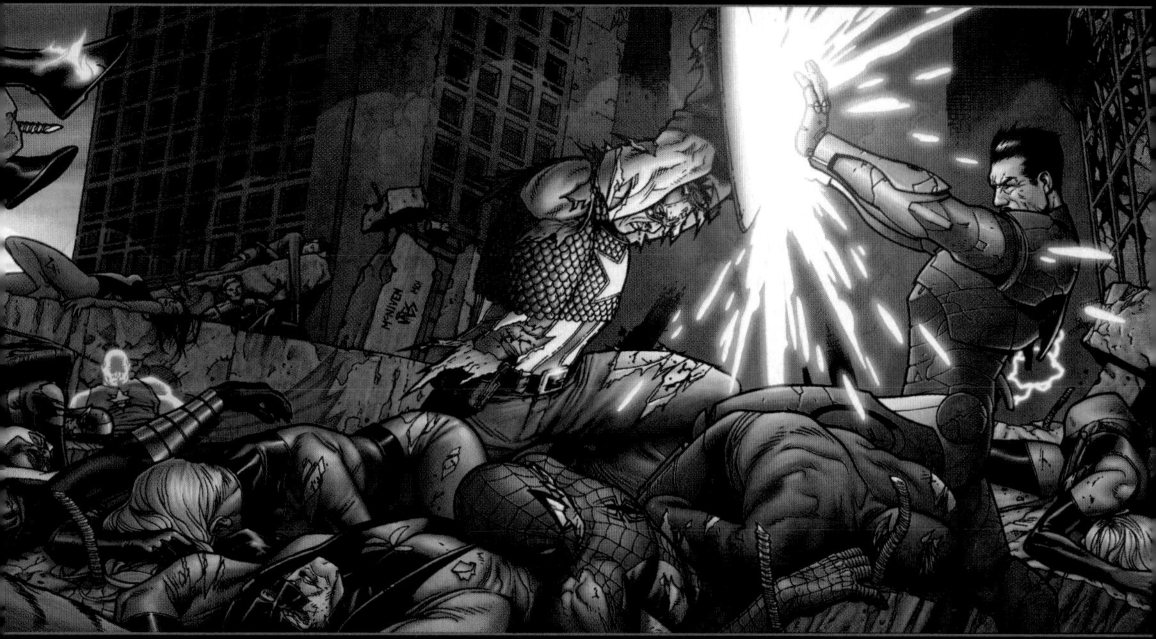

McNIVEN

Superhuman Registration Act has been passed, requiring all individuals possessing anormal abilities to register their powers and identities with the government. Disagreement the Act split the super hero community in two, with Tony Stark, Iron Man, as the figurehead the pro-registration faction, and Steve Rogers, Captain America, leading the anti-registration ellion. The conflict erupted into violence, only ending with the surrender and arrest—and eventual assassination—of Captain America.

v, the Civil War is over, and Tony Stark has been named the Director of S.H.I.E.L.D., the rnational peacekeeping force. He has set into motion THE INITIATIVE, a plan for training and policing super heroes in this brave new world.

BRIAN BENDIS (PAGES 1-12, 22-34) WRITER

WARREN ELLIS (PAGES 13-21) WRITER

MARC SILVESTRI PENCILS

TOP COW PRODUCTIONS
ART & LETTERS

MICHAEL BROUSSARD & ERIC BASALDUA BACKGROUND ARTISTS

JOE WEEMS WITH MARCO GALLI & RICK BASALDUA INKS

TROY PETERI LETTERS

ROB LEVIN FOR TOP COW

FRANK D'ARMATA COLORS

RICH GINTER PRODUCTION

MOLLY LAZER & AUBREY SITTERSON

TOM BREVOORT

JOE QUESADA

DAN BUCKLEY

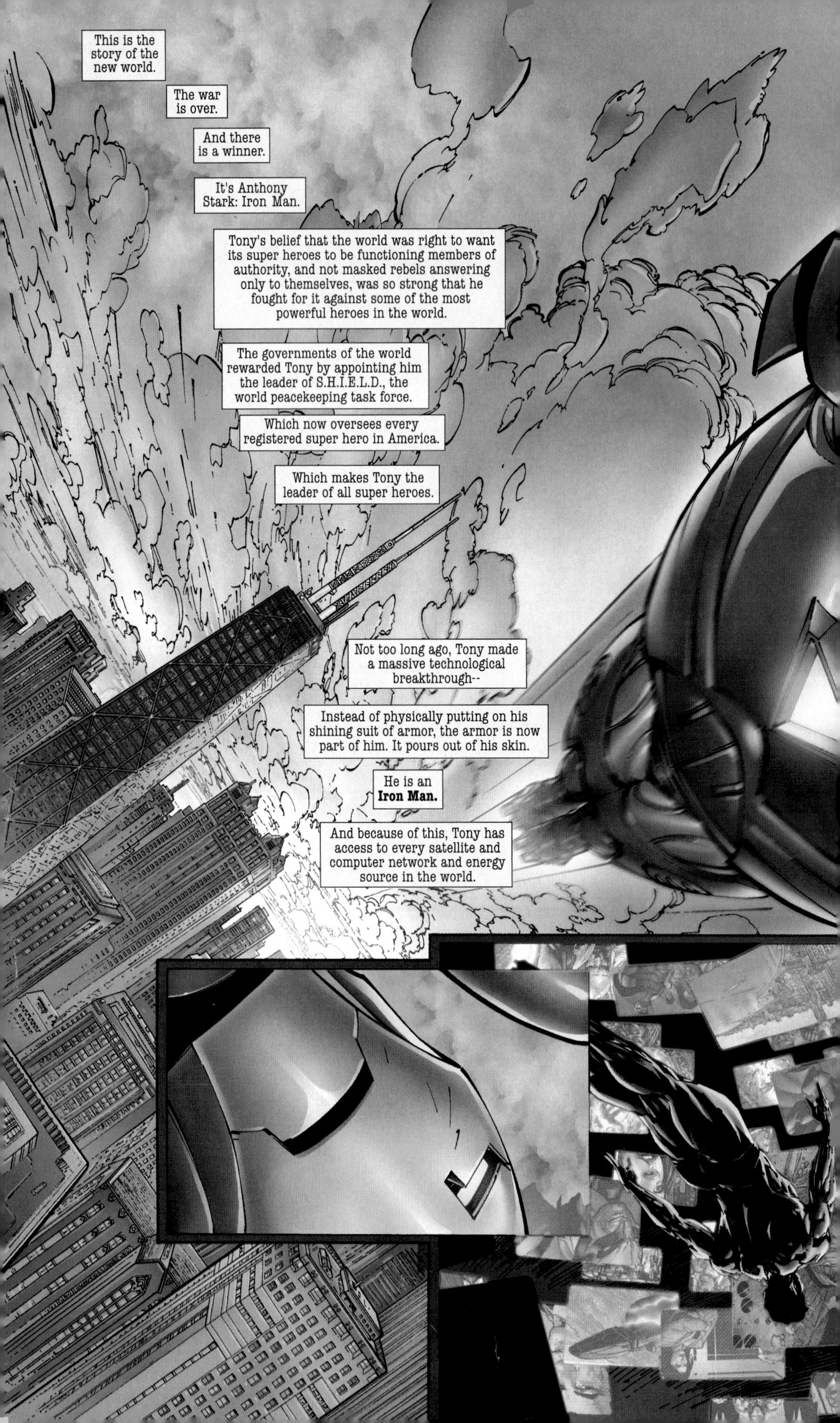
This is the story of the new world.
The war is over.
And there is a winner.
It's Anthony Stark: Iron Man.
Tony's belief that the world was right to want its super heroes to be functioning members of authority, and not masked rebels answering only to themselves, was so strong that he fought for it against some of the most powerful heroes in the world.
The governments of the world rewarded Tony by appointing him the leader of S.H.I.E.L.D., the world peacekeeping task force.
Which now oversees every registered super hero in America.
Which makes Tony the leader of all super heroes.
Not too long ago, Tony made a massive technological breakthrough--
Instead of physically putting on his shining suit of armor, the armor is now part of him. It pours out of his skin.
He is an **Iron Man.**
And because of this, Tony has access to every satellite and computer network and energy source in the world.

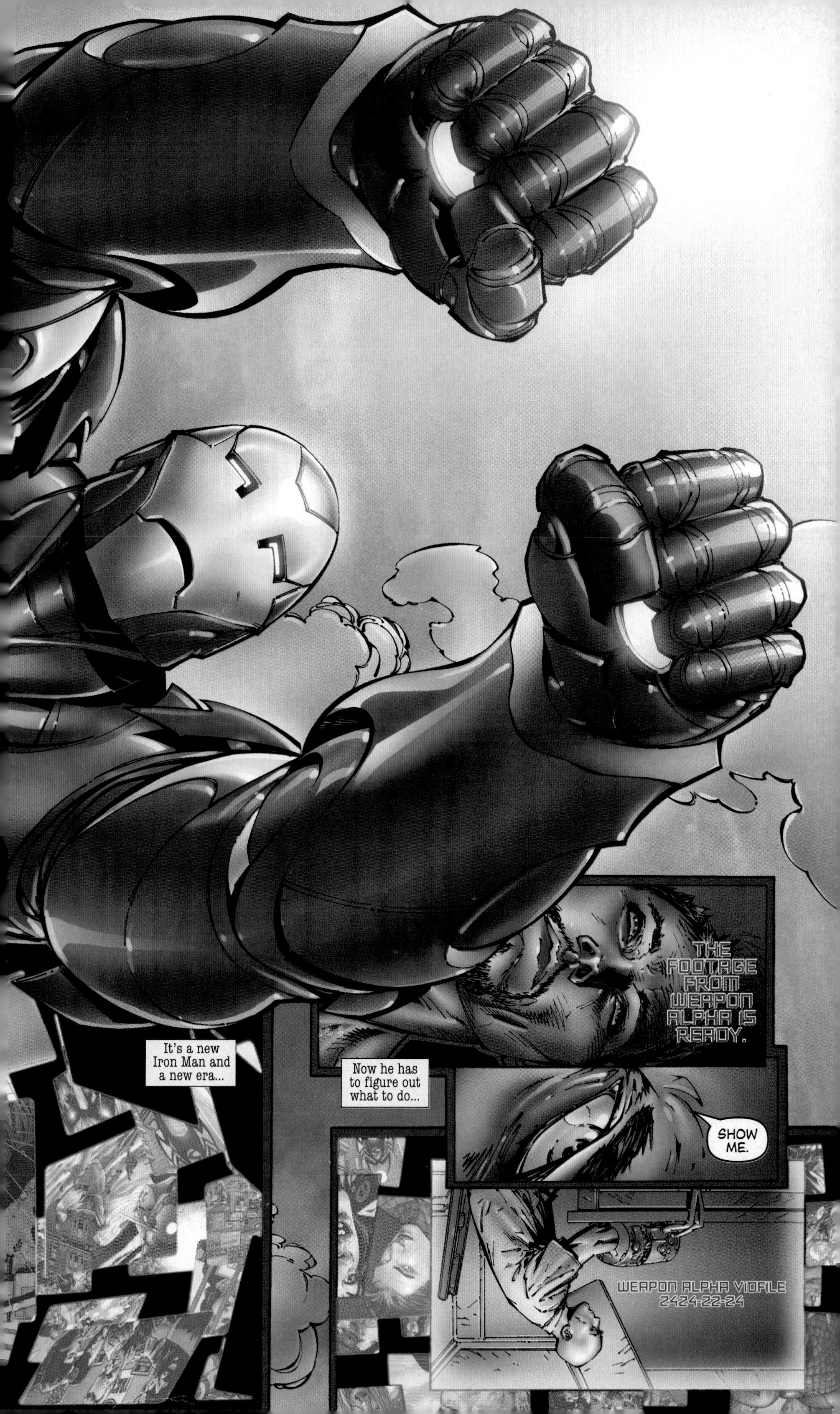
THE FOOTAGE FROM WEAPON ALPHA IS READY.
It's a new Iron Man and a new era...
Now he has to figure out what to do...
SHOW ME.
WEAPON ALPHA VIDFILE 2424-22-24

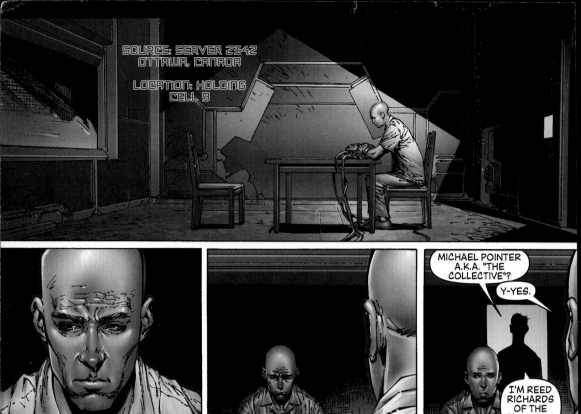

MICHAEL POINTER A.K.A. "THE COLLECTIVE"?

Y-YES.

I'M REED RICHARDS OF THE FANTASTIC FOUR.

OH MY GOD.

HAVE YOU EVER HAD POLIO?

UH, WHAT?

HAVE YOU EVER HAD POLIO?

NO.

SMALLPOX.

NO.

HERPES?

NO. (HERPES?)

YOU USED TO WORK FOR THE POST OFFICE IN NORTH POLE, ALASKA. IS YOUR GOVERNMENT MEDICAL RECORD FROM YOUR LAST PHYSICAL CORRECT?

YEAH, I GUESS.

UM, WHAT IS--?

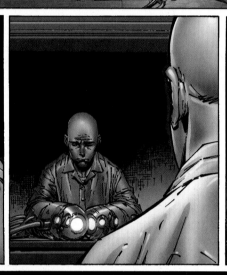

DO YOU DRINK?

NO.

SMOKE?

NO.

DID YOU EVER AT ONE TIME?

NO.

IS THAT YOUR NATURAL HAIR COLOR?

YES, I- I MEAN, WAS.

UM, WHAT IS THIS ALL--?

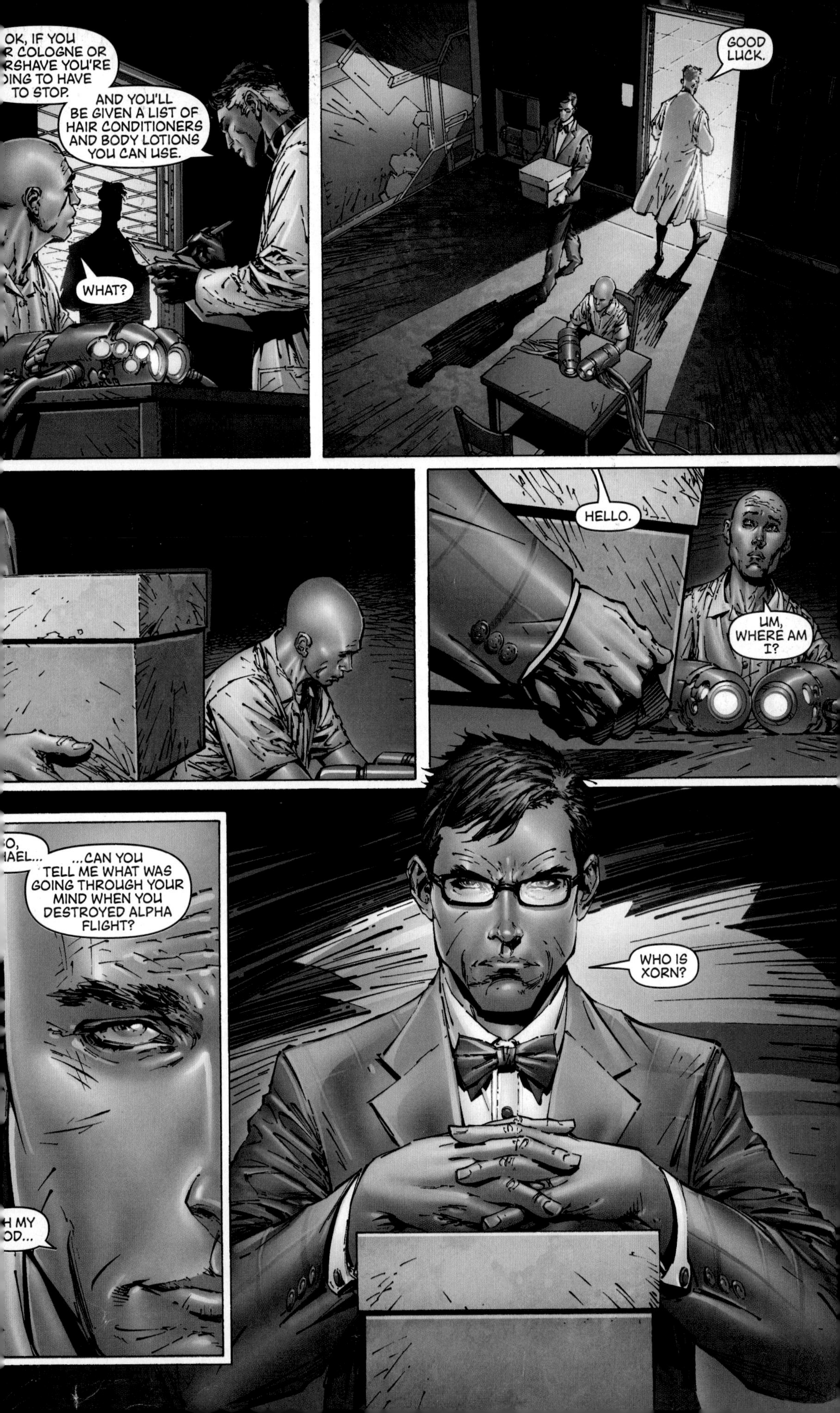
OK, IF YOU
R COLOGNE OR
RSHAVE YOU'RE
OING TO HAVE
TO STOP.
AND YOU'LL BE GIVEN A LIST OF HAIR CONDITIONERS AND BODY LOTIONS YOU CAN USE.
WHAT?
GOOD LUCK.
HELLO.
UM, WHERE AM I?
O, HAEL...
...CAN YOU TELL ME WHAT WAS GOING THROUGH YOUR MIND WHEN YOU DESTROYED ALPHA FLIGHT?
WHO IS XORN?
H MY OD...

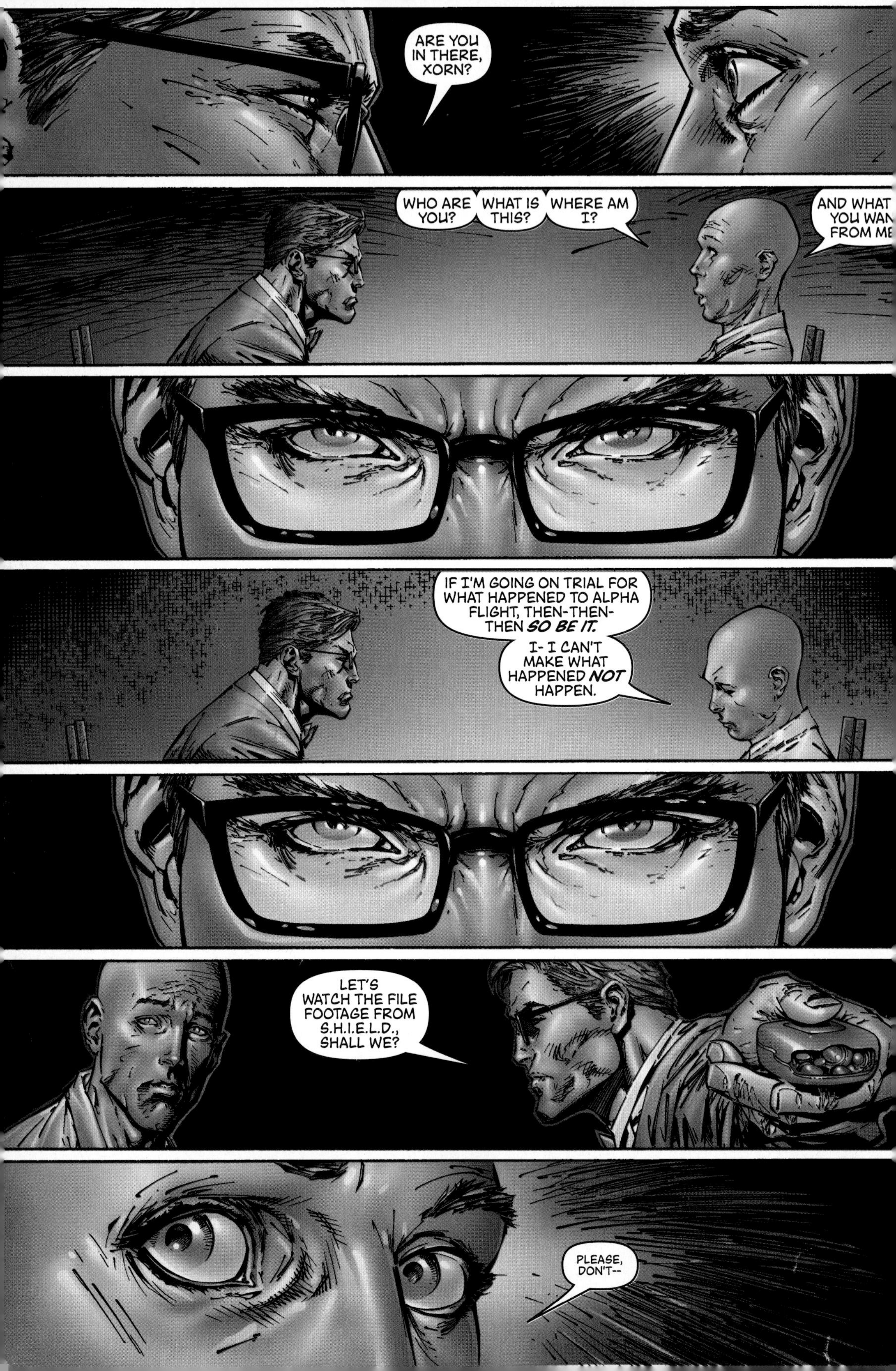
ARE YOU IN THERE, XORN?
WHO ARE YOU?
WHAT IS THIS?
WHERE AM I?
AND WHAT YOU WAN FROM ME
IF I'M GOING ON TRIAL FOR WHAT HAPPENED TO ALPHA FLIGHT, THEN-THEN-THEN *SO BE IT.*
I- I CAN'T MAKE WHAT HAPPENED *NOT* HAPPEN.
LET'S WATCH THE FILE FOOTAGE FROM S.H.I.E.L.D., SHALL WE?
PLEASE, DON'T--

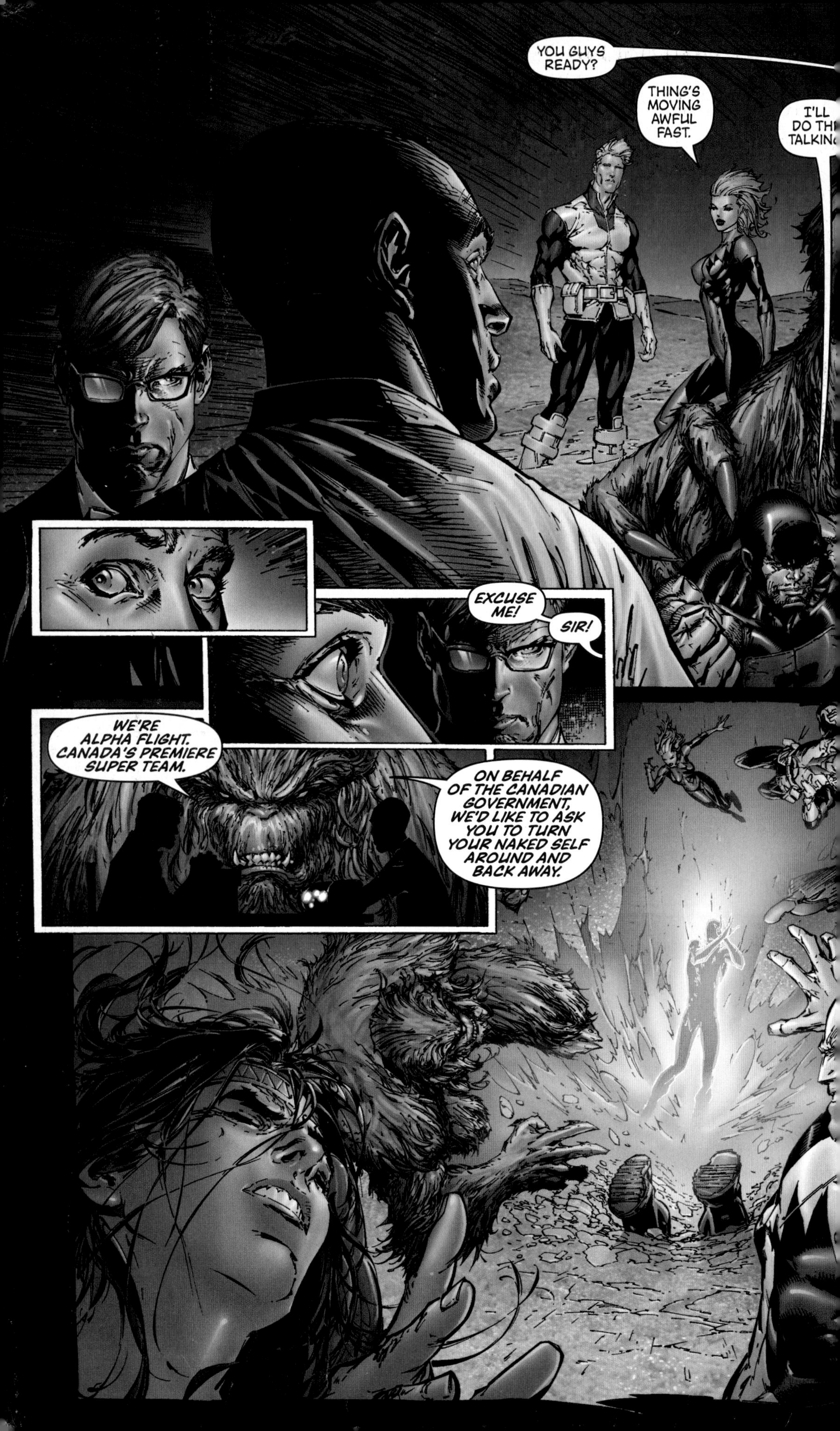
YOU GUYS READY?
THING'S MOVING AWFUL FAST.
I'LL DO TH TALKING
EXCUSE ME!
SIR!
WE'RE ALPHA FLIGHT. CANADA'S PREMIERE SUPER TEAM.
ON BEHALF OF THE CANADIAN GOVERNMENT, WE'D LIKE TO ASK YOU TO TURN YOUR NAKED SELF AROUND AND BACK AWAY.

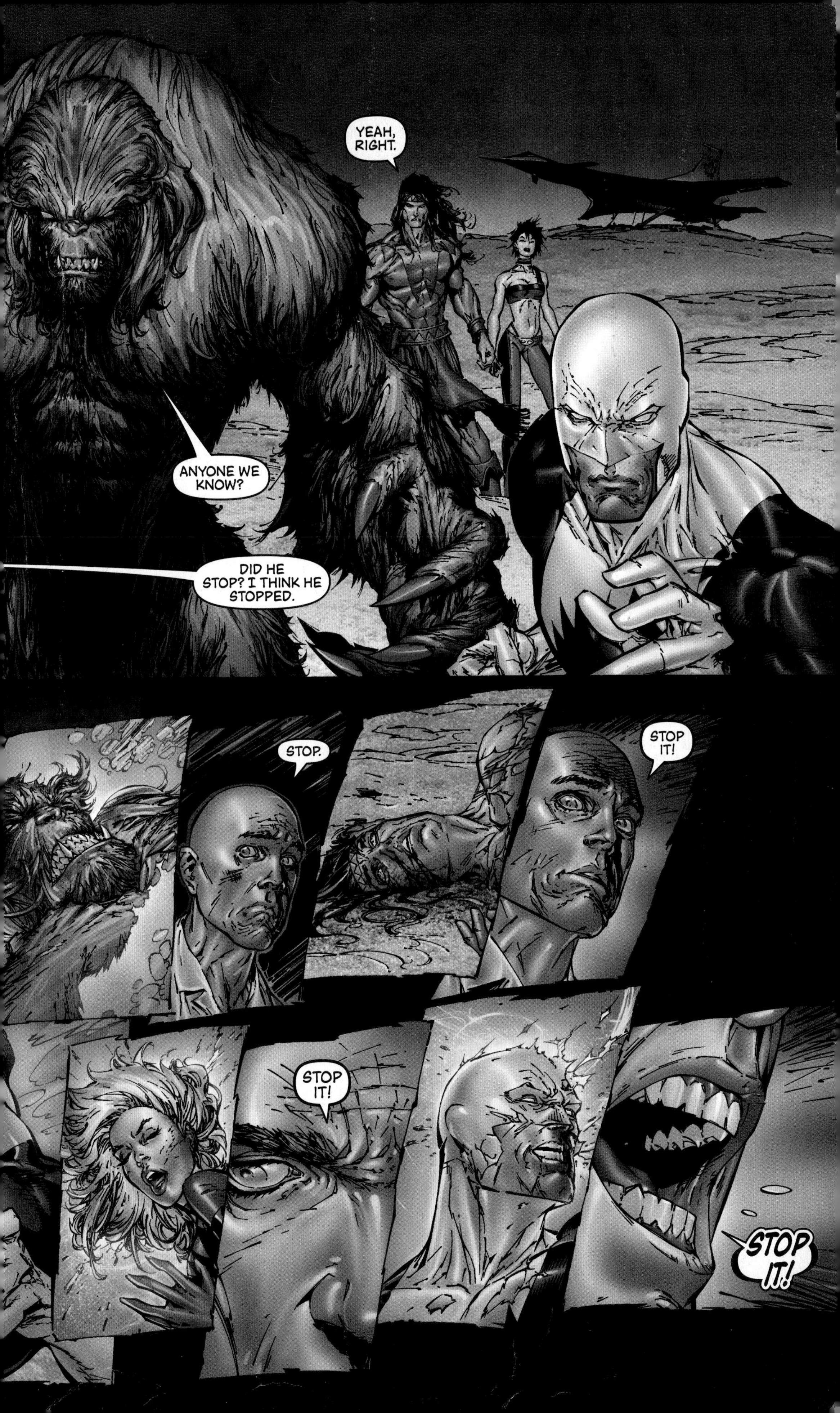
YEAH, RIGHT.
ANYONE WE KNOW?
DID HE STOP? I THINK HE STOPPED.
STOP.
STOP IT!
STOP IT!
STOP IT!

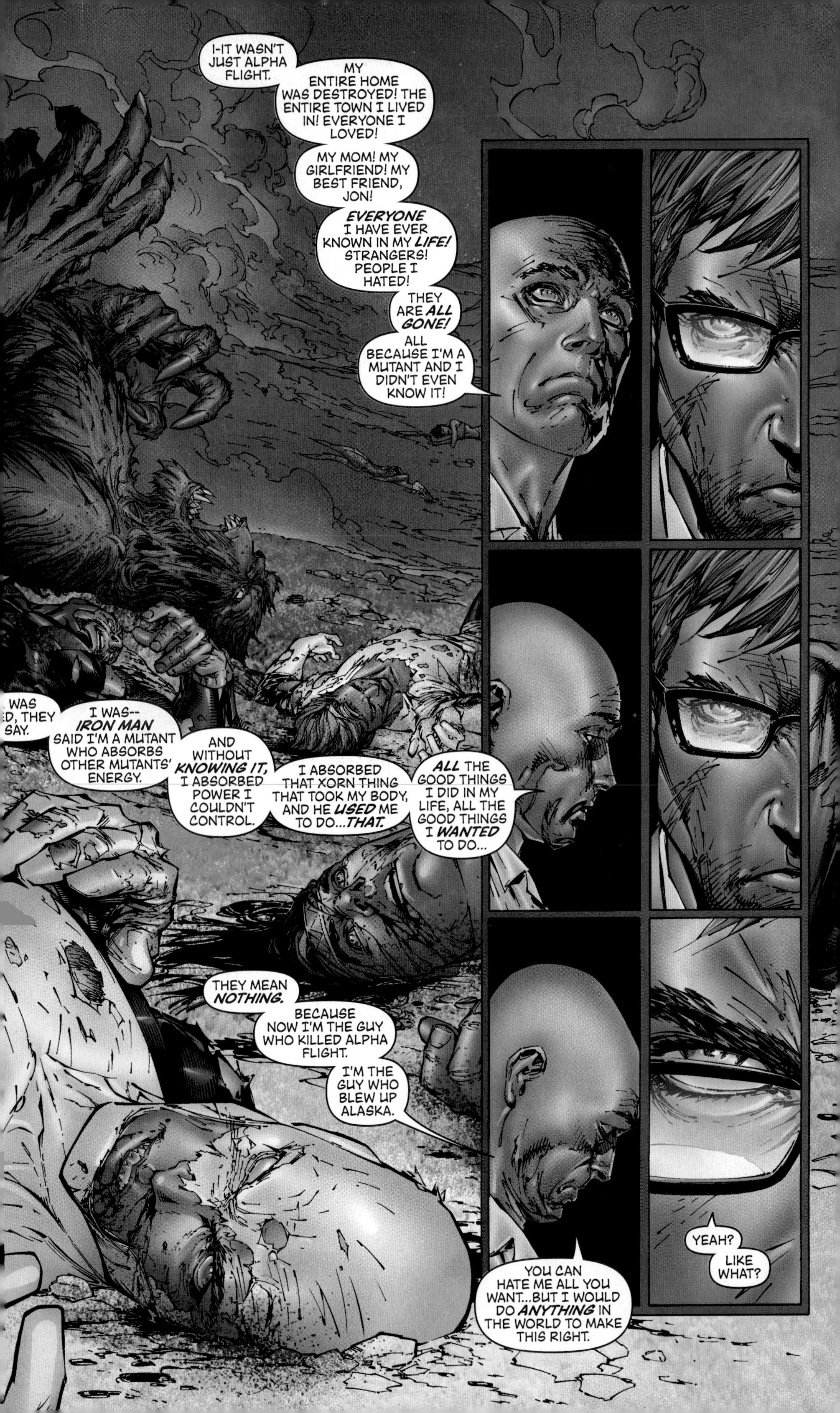

I-IT WASN'T JUST ALPHA FLIGHT.
MY ENTIRE HOME WAS DESTROYED! THE ENTIRE TOWN I LIVED IN! EVERYONE I LOVED!
MY MOM! MY GIRLFRIEND! MY BEST FRIEND, JON!
EVERYONE I HAVE EVER KNOWN IN MY LIFE! STRANGERS! PEOPLE I HATED!
THEY ARE ALL GONE!
ALL BECAUSE I'M A MUTANT AND I DIDN'T EVEN KNOW IT!
WAS D, THEY SAY.
I WAS-- IRON MAN SAID I'M A MUTANT WHO ABSORBS OTHER MUTANTS' ENERGY.
AND WITHOUT KNOWING IT, I ABSORBED POWER I COULDN'T CONTROL.
I ABSORBED THAT XORN THING THAT TOOK MY BODY, AND HE USED ME TO DO...THAT.
ALL THE GOOD THINGS I DID IN MY LIFE, ALL THE GOOD THINGS I WANTED TO DO...
THEY MEAN NOTHING.
BECAUSE NOW I'M THE GUY WHO KILLED ALPHA FLIGHT.
I'M THE GUY WHO BLEW UP ALASKA.
YOU CAN HATE ME ALL YOU WANT...BUT I WOULD DO ANYTHING IN THE WORLD TO MAKE THIS RIGHT.
YEAH?
LIKE WHAT?

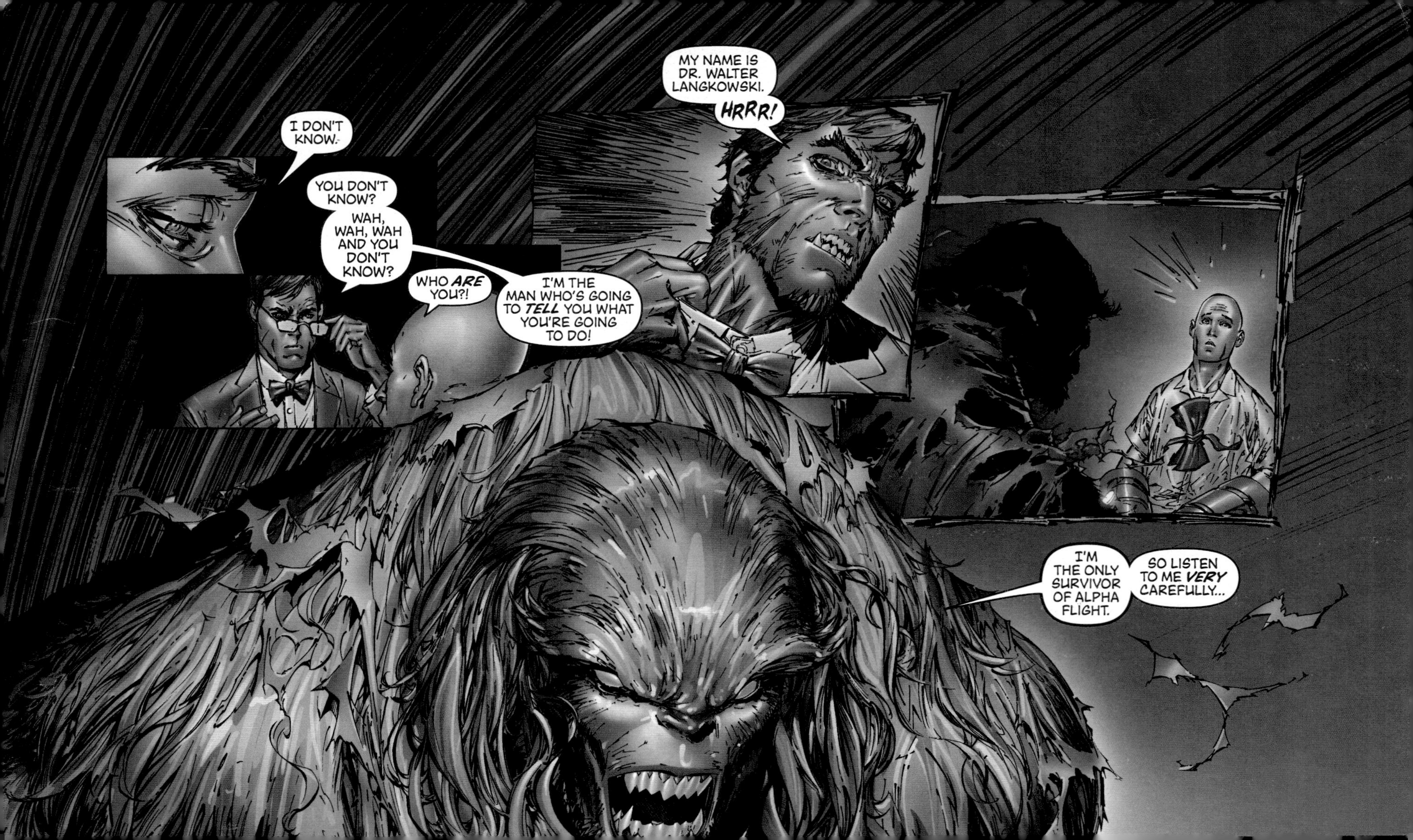
I DON'T KNOW.
YOU DON'T KNOW?
WAH, WAH, WAH AND YOU DON'T KNOW?
WHO ARE YOU?!
I'M THE MAN WHO'S GOING TO TELL YOU WHAT YOU'RE GOING TO DO!
MY NAME IS DR. WALTER LANGKOWSKI.
HRRR!
I'M THE ONLY SURVIVOR OF ALPHA FLIGHT.
SO LISTEN TO ME VERY CAREFULLY...

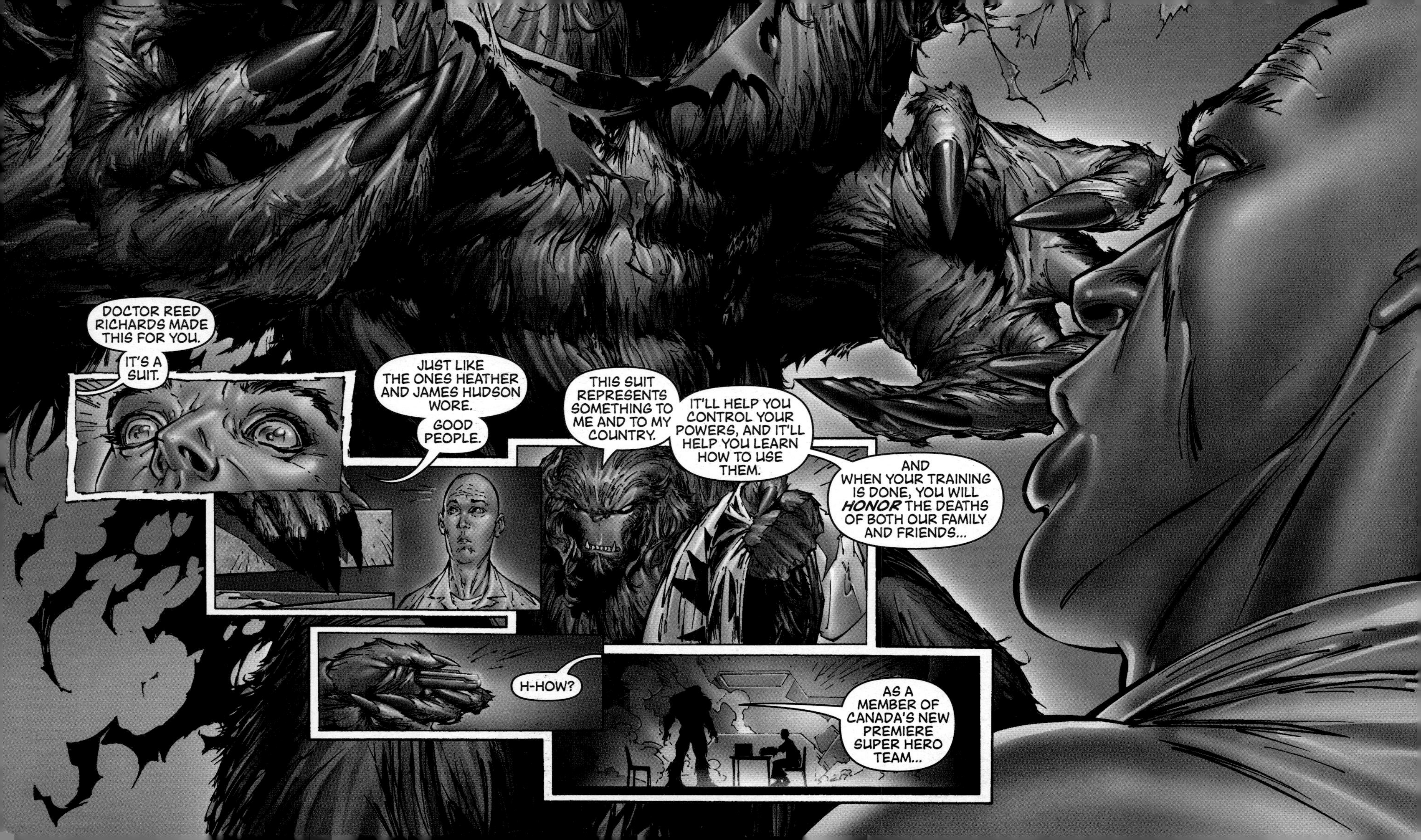
DOCTOR REED RICHARDS MADE THIS FOR YOU.
IT'S A SUIT.
JUST LIKE THE ONES HEATHER AND JAMES HUDSON WORE.
GOOD PEOPLE.
THIS SUIT REPRESENTS SOMETHING TO ME AND TO MY COUNTRY.
IT'LL HELP YOU CONTROL YOUR POWERS, AND IT'LL HELP YOU LEARN HOW TO USE THEM.
AND WHEN YOUR TRAINING IS DONE, YOU WILL *HONOR* THE DEATHS OF BOTH OUR FAMILY AND FRIENDS...
H-HOW?
AS A MEMBER OF CANADA'S NEW PREMIERE SUPER HERO TEAM...

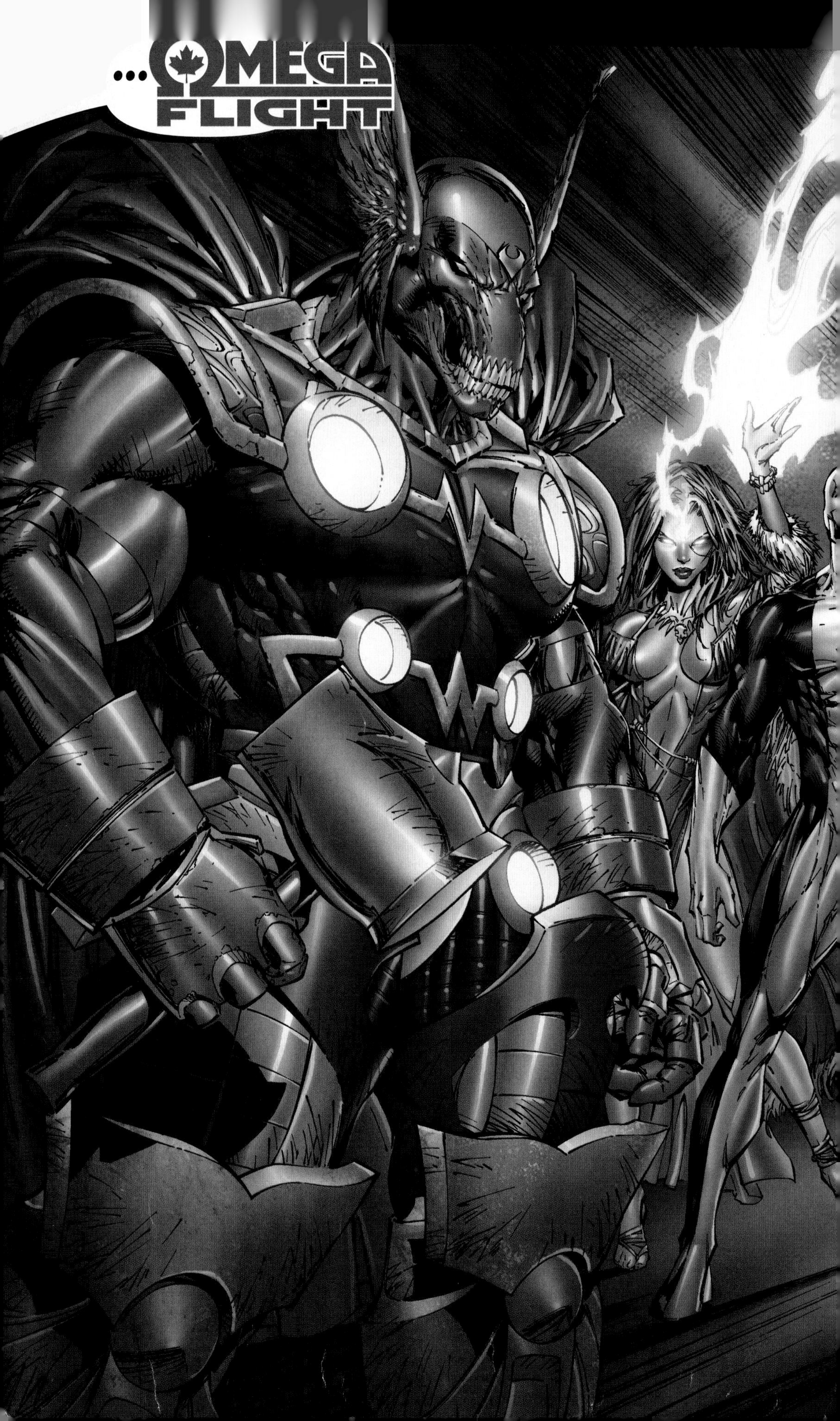
...OMEGA FLIGHT

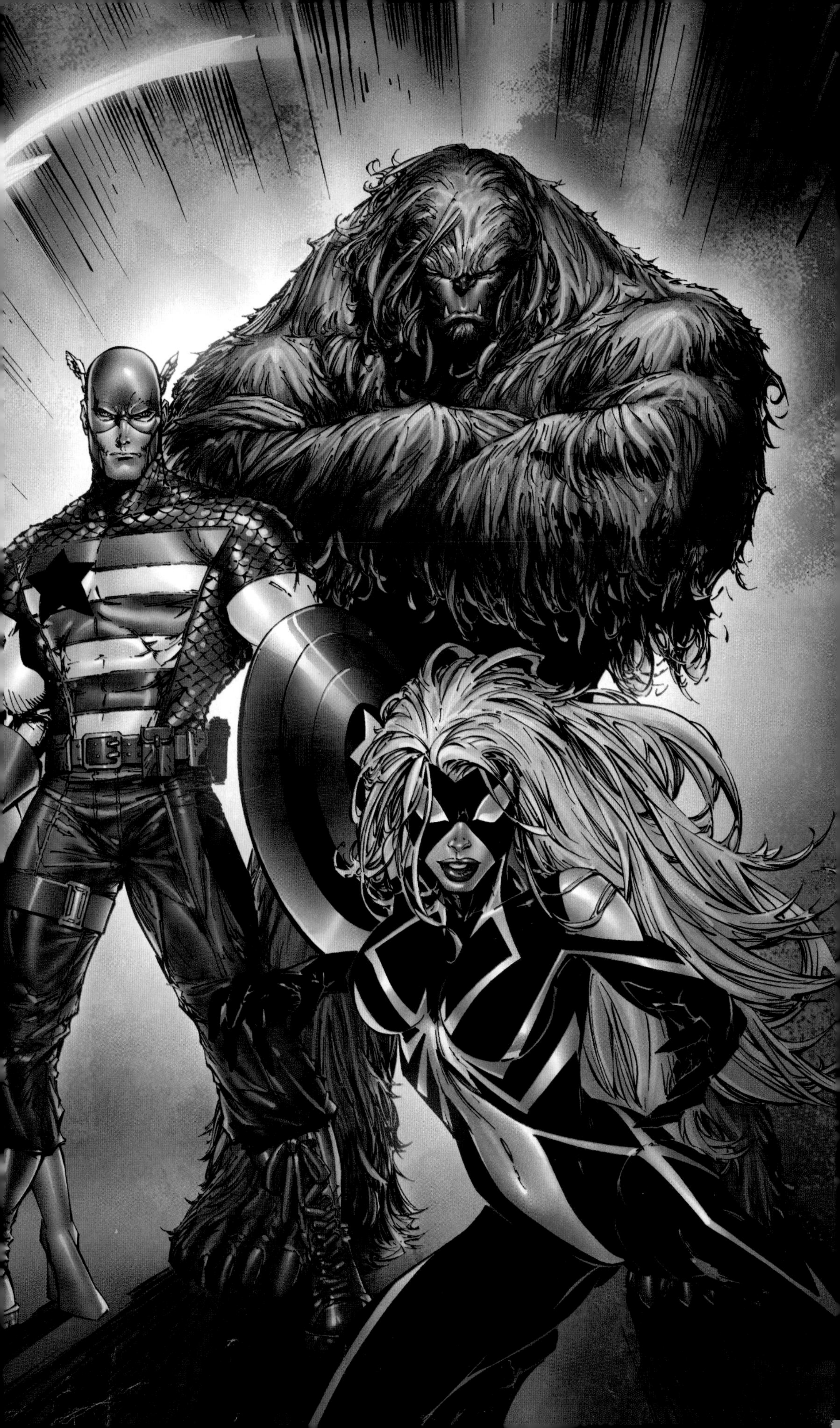

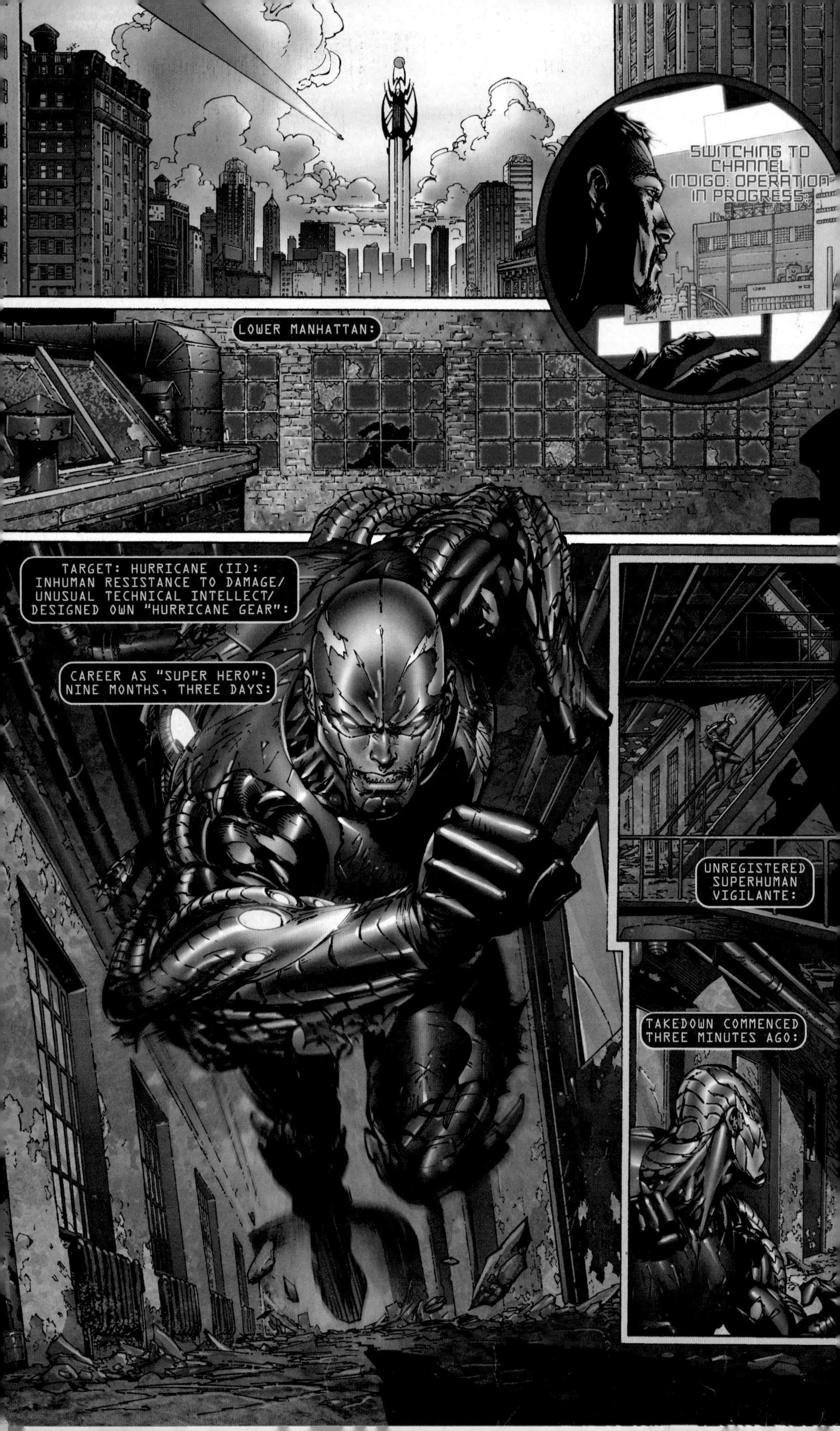
SWITCHING TO CHANNEL INDIGO: OPERATION IN PROGRESS:
LOWER MANHATTAN:
TARGET: HURRICANE (II): INHUMAN RESISTANCE TO DAMAGE/ UNUSUAL TECHNICAL INTELLECT/ DESIGNED OWN "HURRICANE GEAR":
CAREER AS "SUPER HERO": NINE MONTHS, THREE DAYS:
UNREGISTERED SUPERHUMAN VIGILANTE:
TAKEDOWN COMMENCED THREE MINUTES AGO:

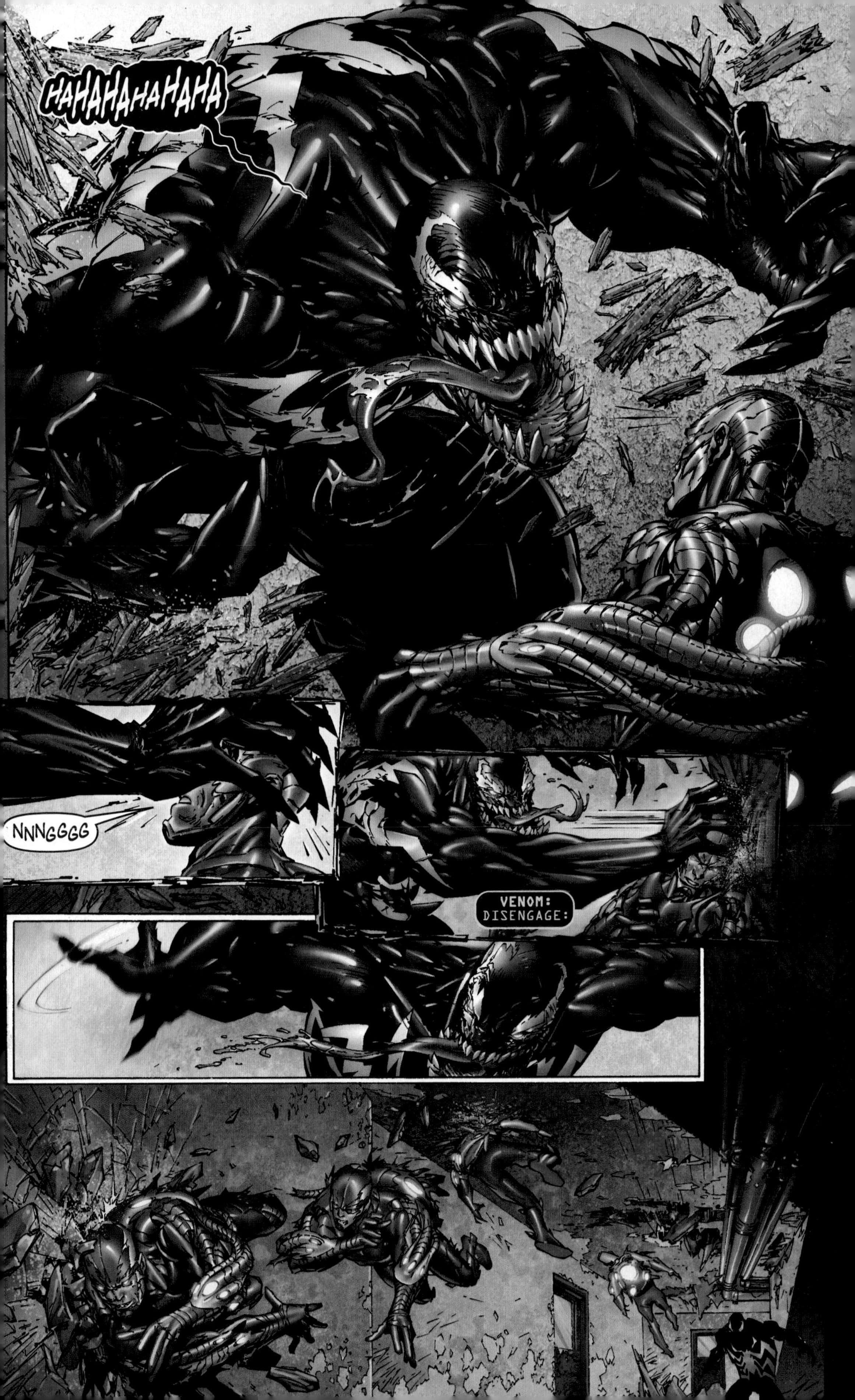
HAHAHAHAHAHA
NNNGGGG
VENOM:
DISENGAGE:

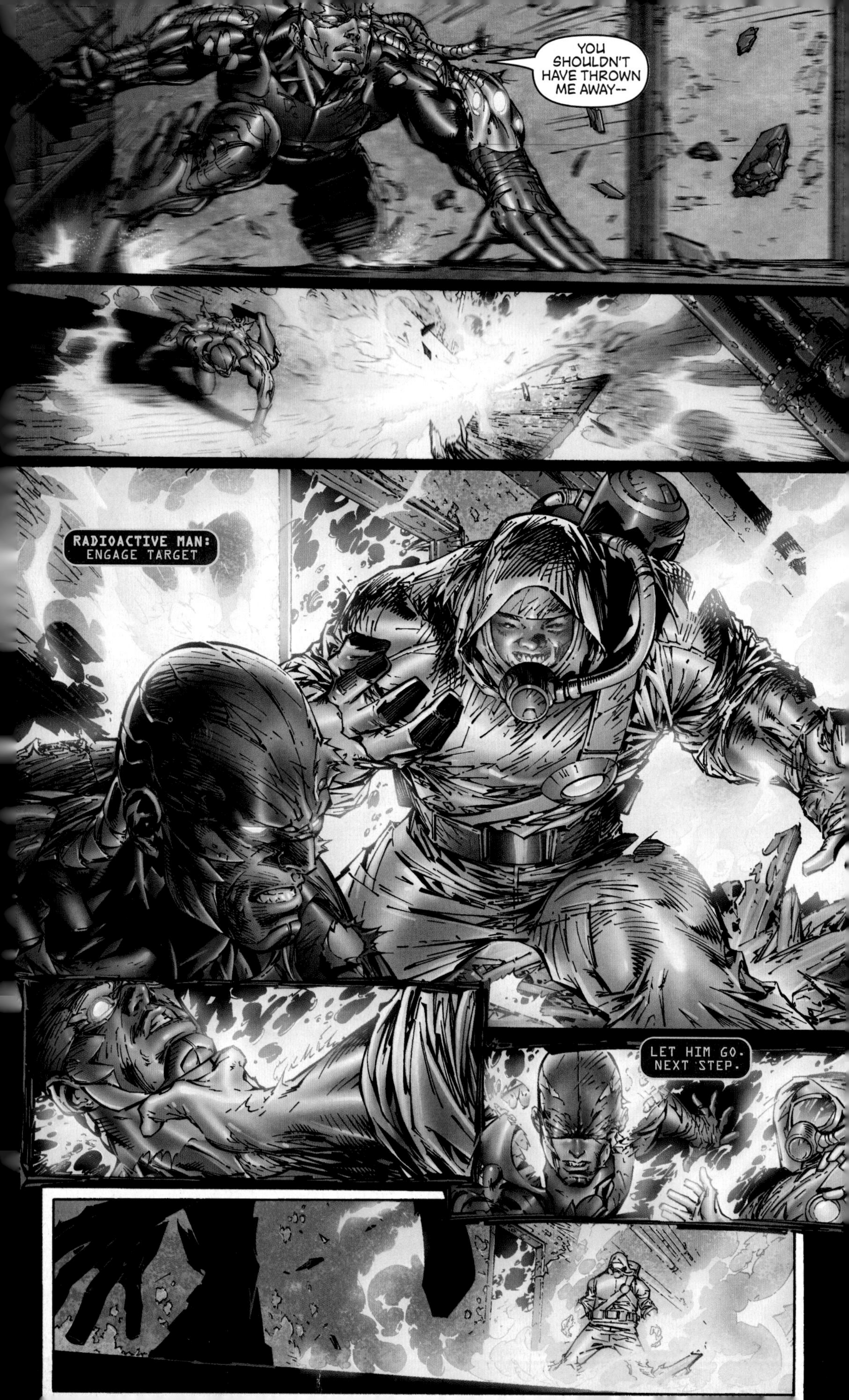
YOU SHOULDN'T HAVE THROWN ME AWAY--
RADIOACTIVE MAN: ENGAGE TARGET
LET HIM GO. NEXT STEP.

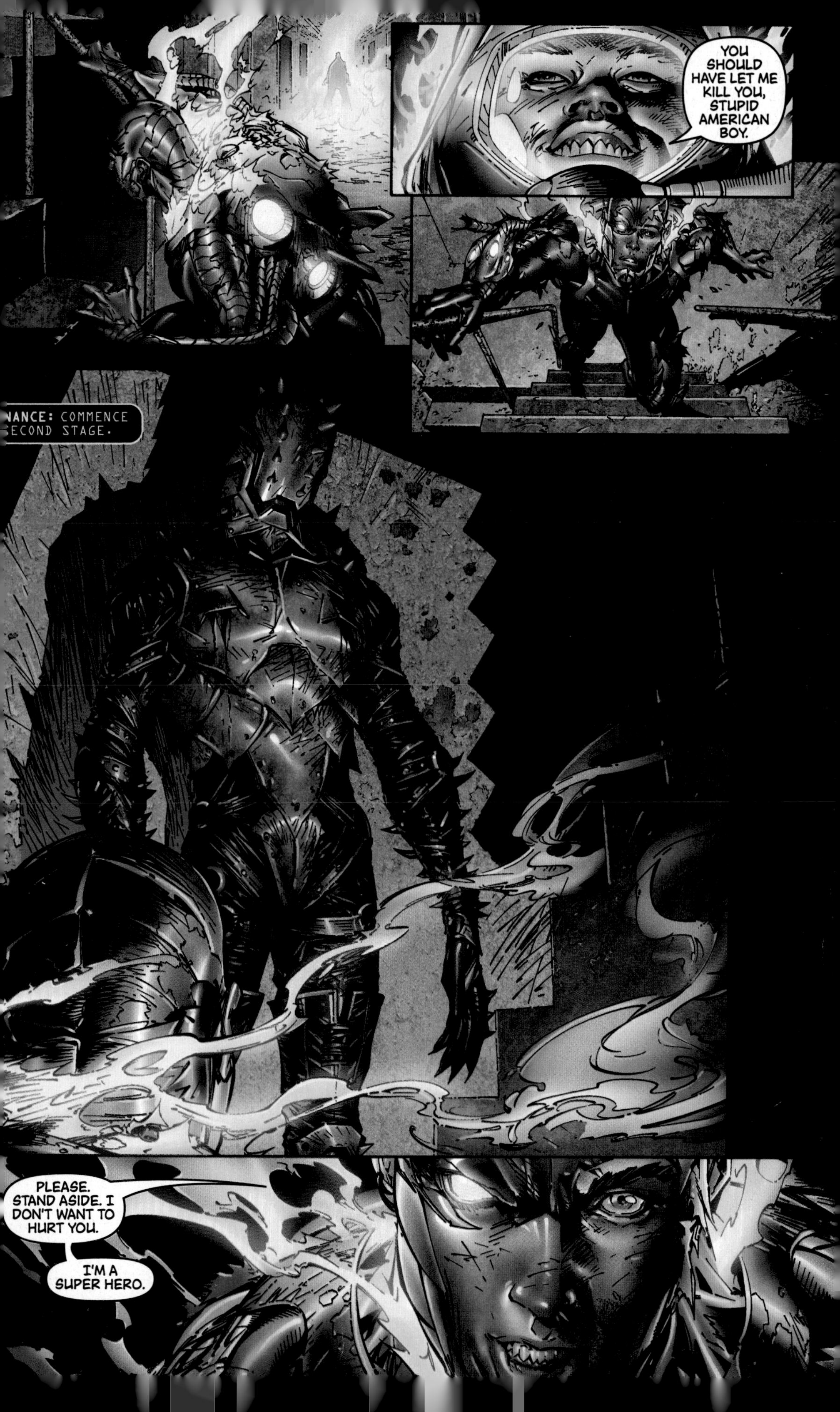
YOU SHOULD HAVE LET ME KILL YOU, STUPID AMERICAN BOY.
NANCE: COMMENCE
ECOND STAGE.
PLEASE. STAND ASIDE. I DON'T WANT TO HURT YOU.
I'M A SUPER HERO.

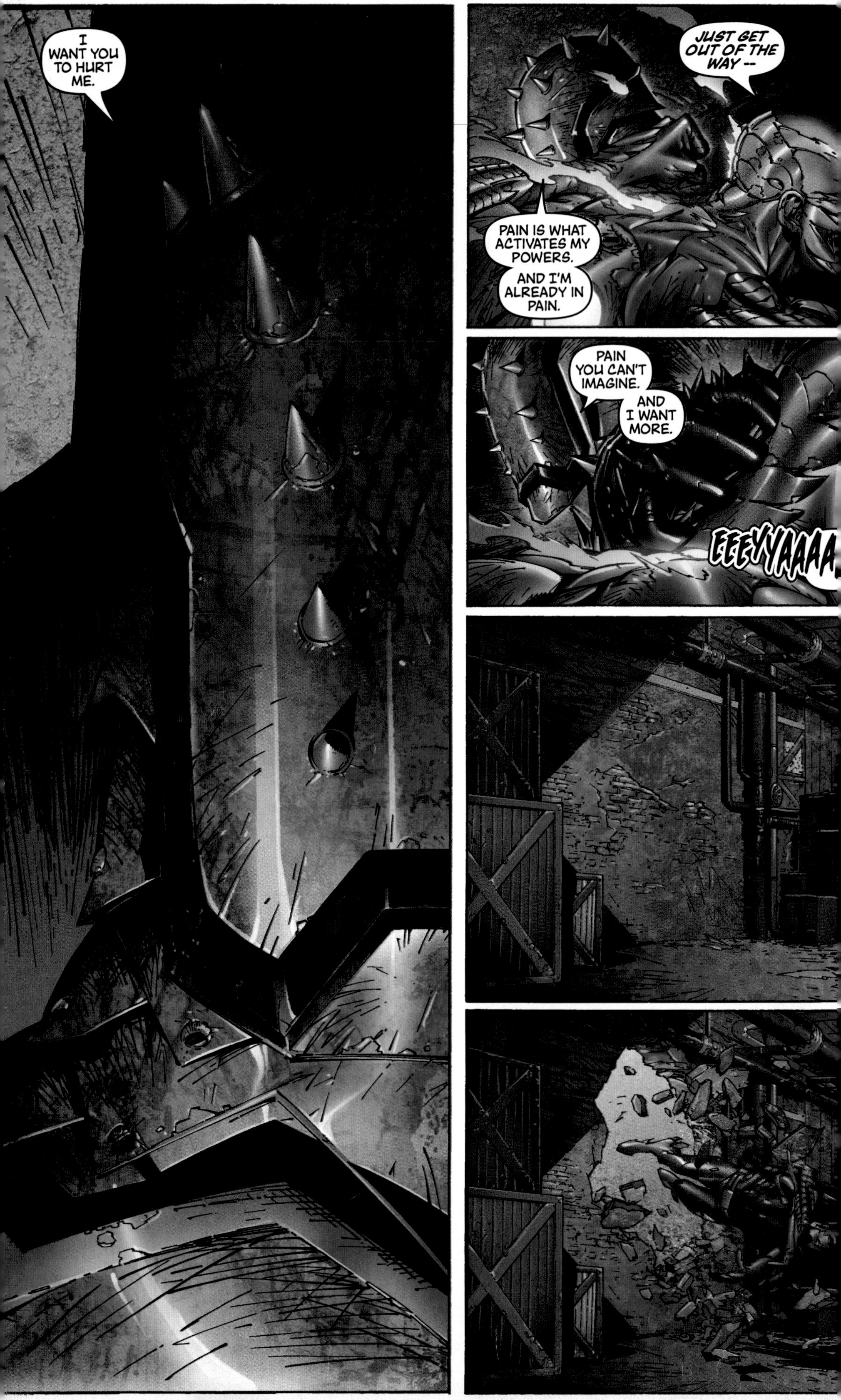
I WANT YOU TO HURT ME.
JUST GET OUT OF THE WAY --
PAIN IS WHAT ACTIVATES MY POWERS.
AND I'M ALREADY IN PAIN.
PAIN YOU CAN'T IMAGINE.
AND I WANT MORE.
EEEYYAAAA

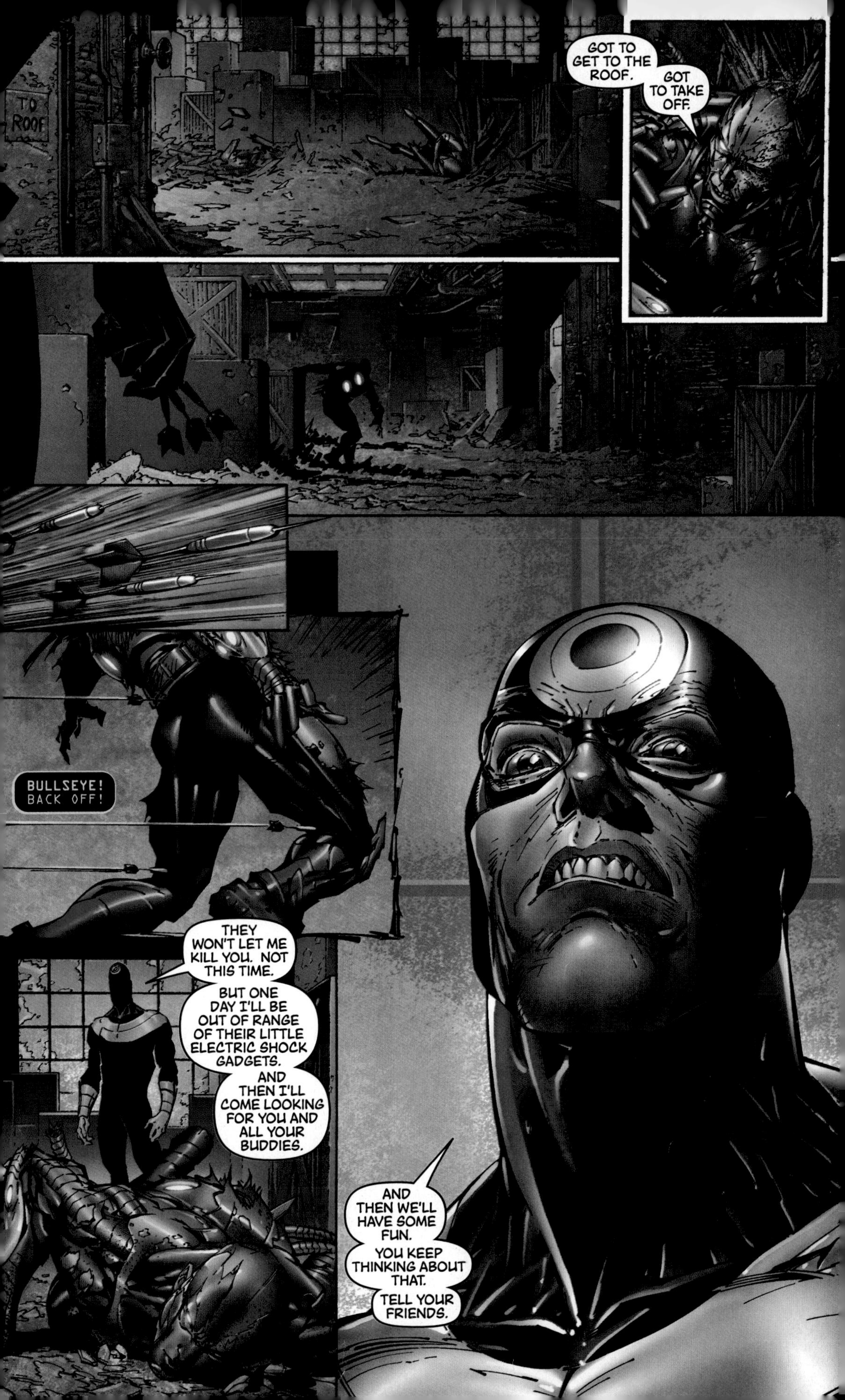
TO ROOF
GOT TO GET TO THE ROOF.
GOT TO TAKE OFF.
BULLSEYE! BACK OFF!
THEY WON'T LET ME KILL YOU. NOT THIS TIME.
BUT ONE DAY I'LL BE OUT OF RANGE OF THEIR LITTLE ELECTRIC SHOCK GADGETS.
AND THEN I'LL COME LOOKING FOR YOU AND ALL YOUR BUDDIES.
AND THEN WE'LL HAVE SOME FUN.
YOU KEEP THINKING ABOUT THAT.
TELL YOUR FRIENDS.

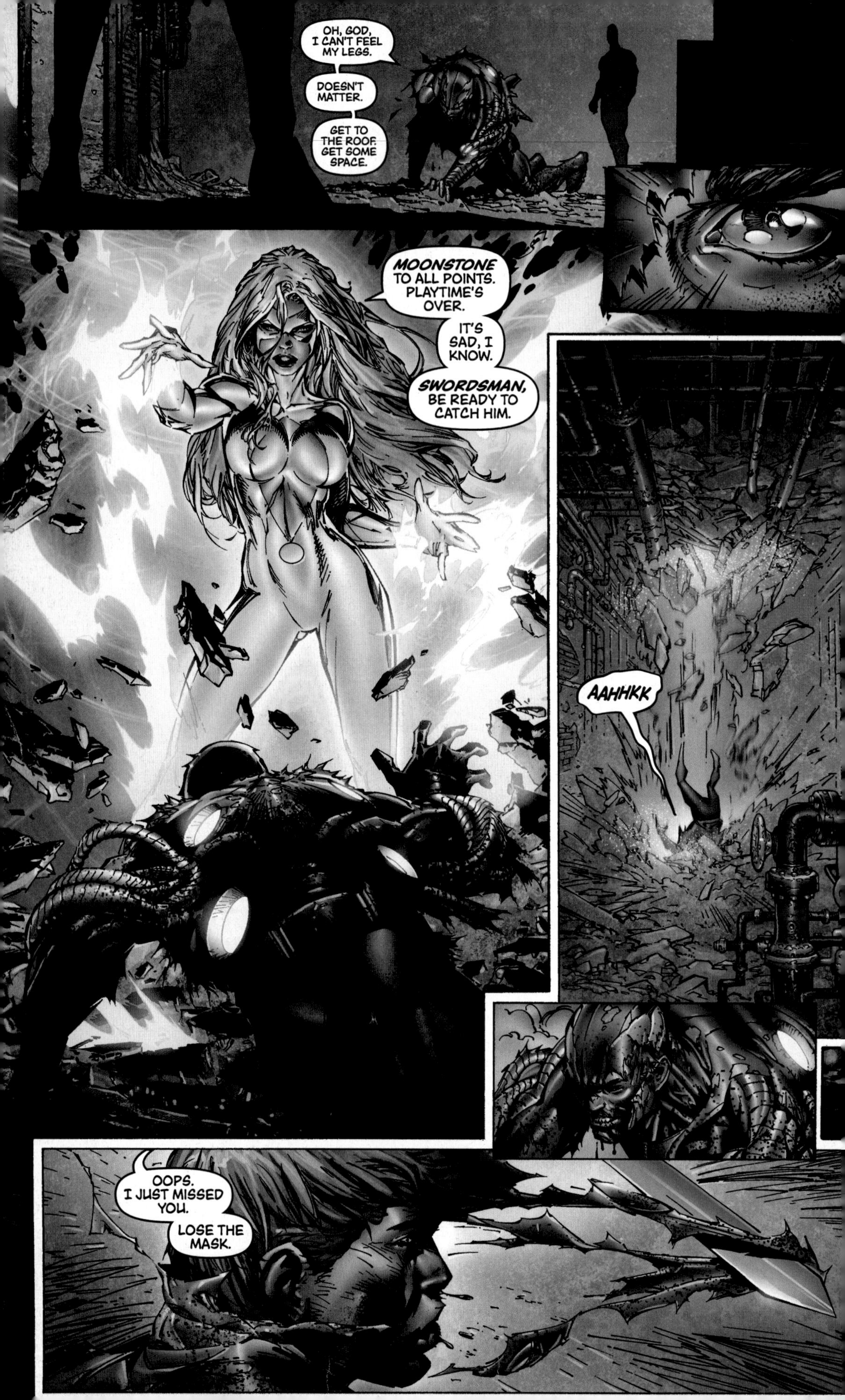
OH, GOD, I CAN'T FEEL MY LEGS.
DOESN'T MATTER.
GET TO THE ROOF. GET SOME SPACE.
MOONSTONE TO ALL POINTS. PLAYTIME'S OVER.
IT'S SAD, I KNOW.
SWORDSMAN, BE READY TO CATCH HIM.
AAHHKK
OOPS. I JUST MISSED YOU.
LOSE THE MASK.

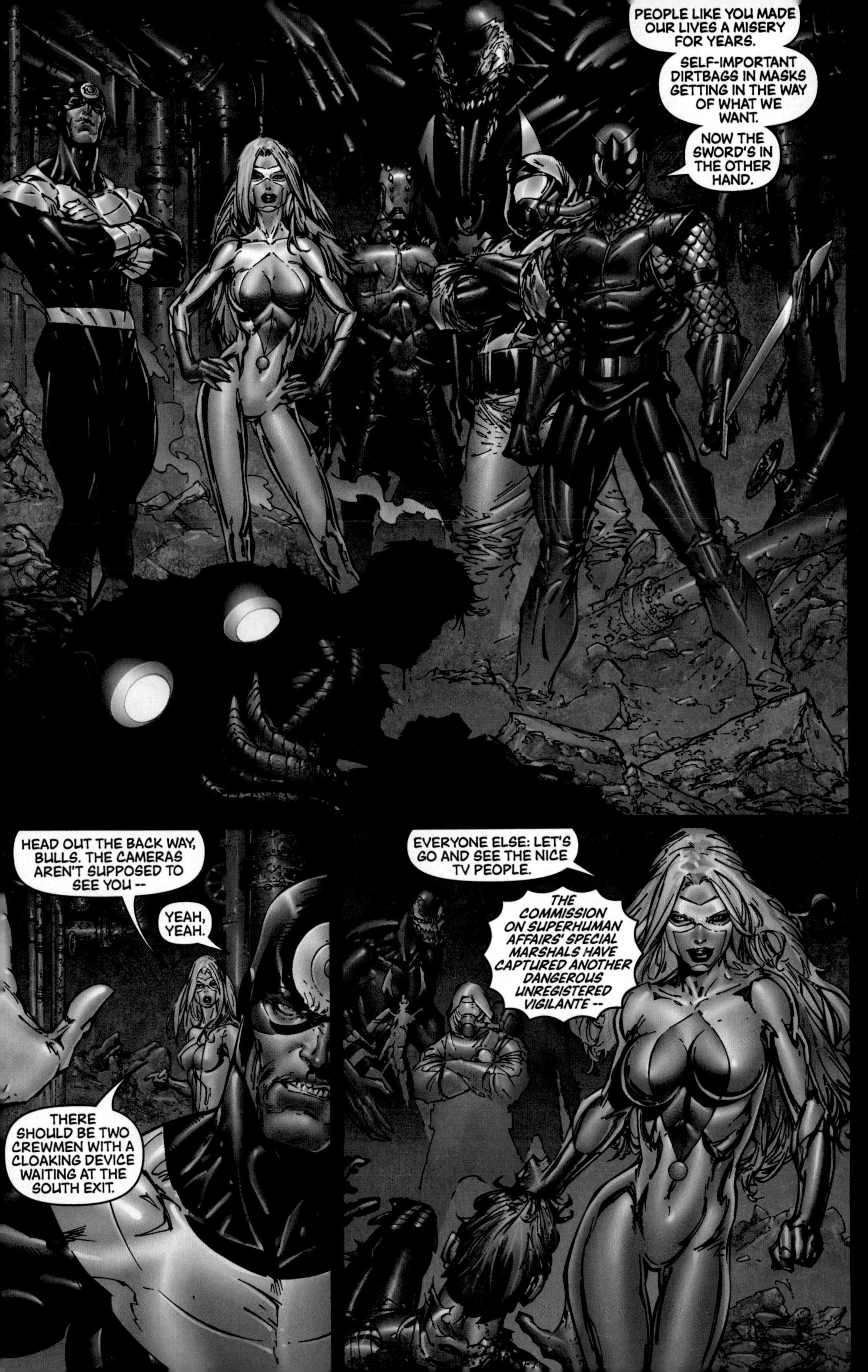
PEOPLE LIKE YOU MADE OUR LIVES A MISERY FOR YEARS.
SELF-IMPORTANT DIRTBAGS IN MASKS GETTING IN THE WAY OF WHAT WE WANT.
NOW THE SWORD'S IN THE OTHER HAND.
HEAD OUT THE BACK WAY, BULLS. THE CAMERAS AREN'T SUPPOSED TO SEE YOU --
YEAH, YEAH.
THERE SHOULD BE TWO CREWMEN WITH A CLOAKING DEVICE WAITING AT THE SOUTH EXIT.
EVERYONE ELSE: LET'S GO AND SEE THE NICE TV PEOPLE.
THE COMMISSION ON SUPERHUMAN AFFAIRS' SPECIAL MARSHALS HAVE CAPTURED ANOTHER DANGEROUS UNREGISTERED VIGILANTE --

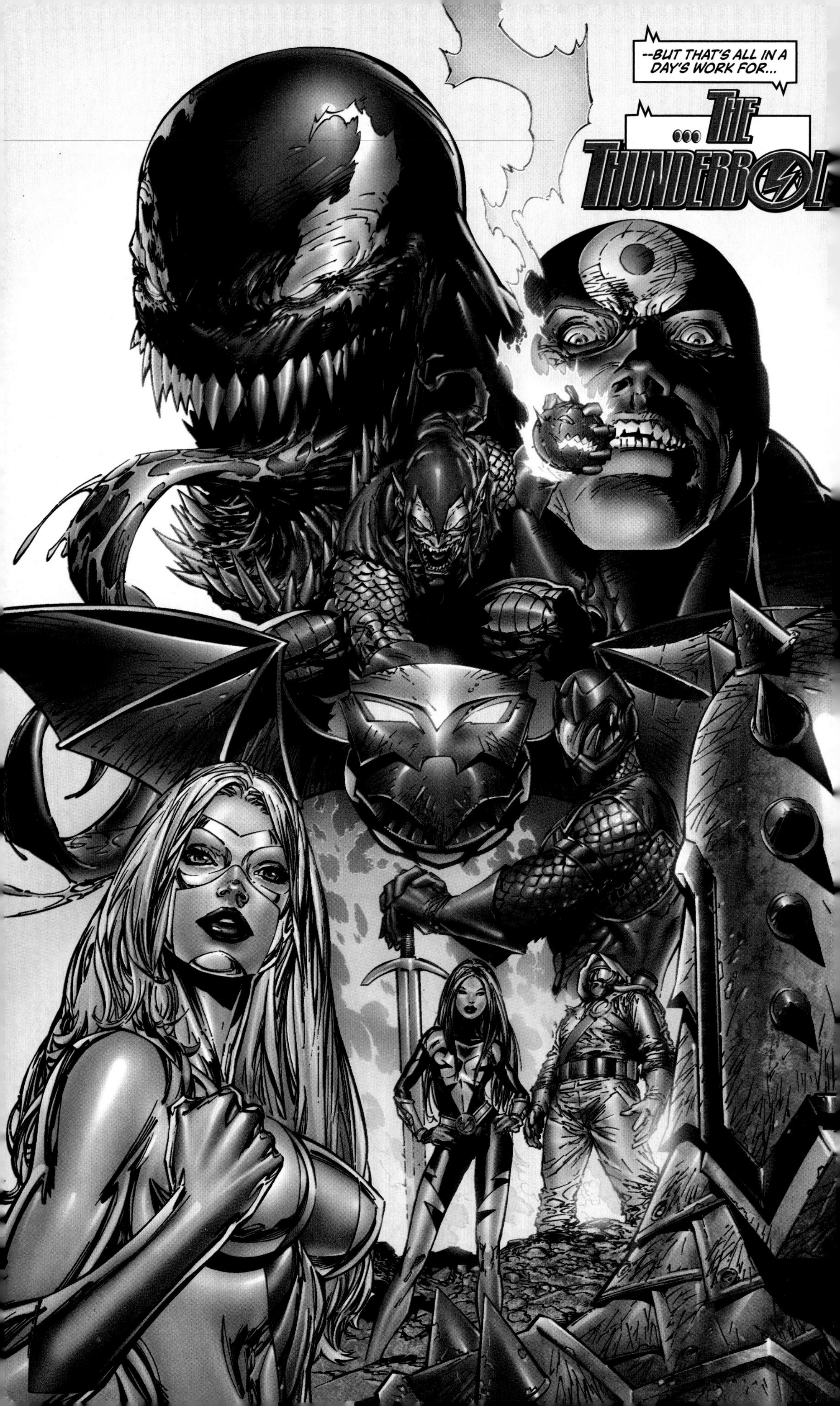
--BUT THAT'S ALL IN A DAY'S WORK FOR...
...THE THUNDERBOL

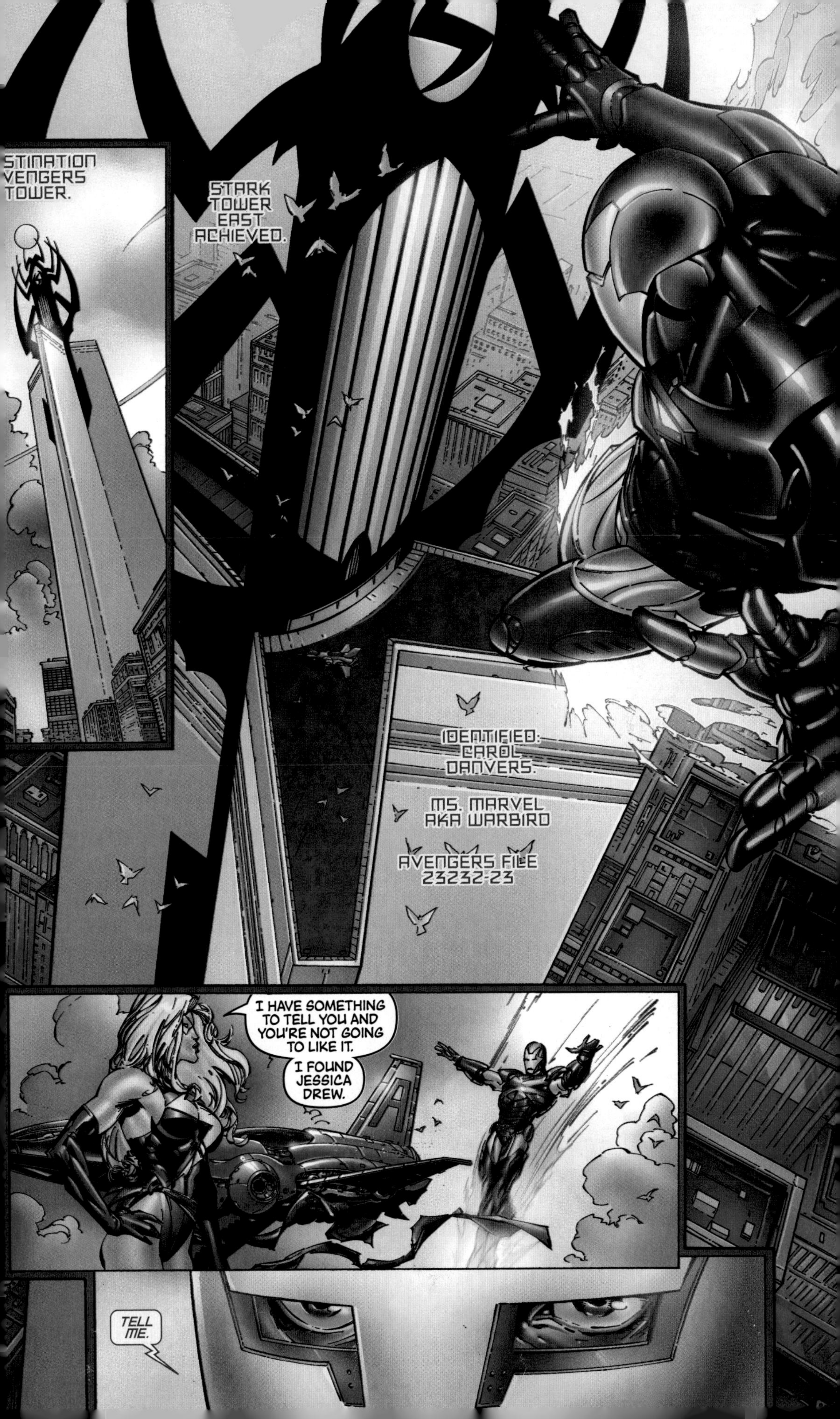
STINATION
VENGERS
TOWER.
STARK
TOWER
EAST
ACHIEVED.
IDENTIFIED:
CAROL
DANVERS.
MS. MARVEL
AKA WARBIRD
AVENGERS FILE
23232-23
I HAVE SOMETHING TO TELL YOU AND YOU'RE NOT GOING TO LIKE IT.
I FOUND JESSICA DREW.
TELL ME.

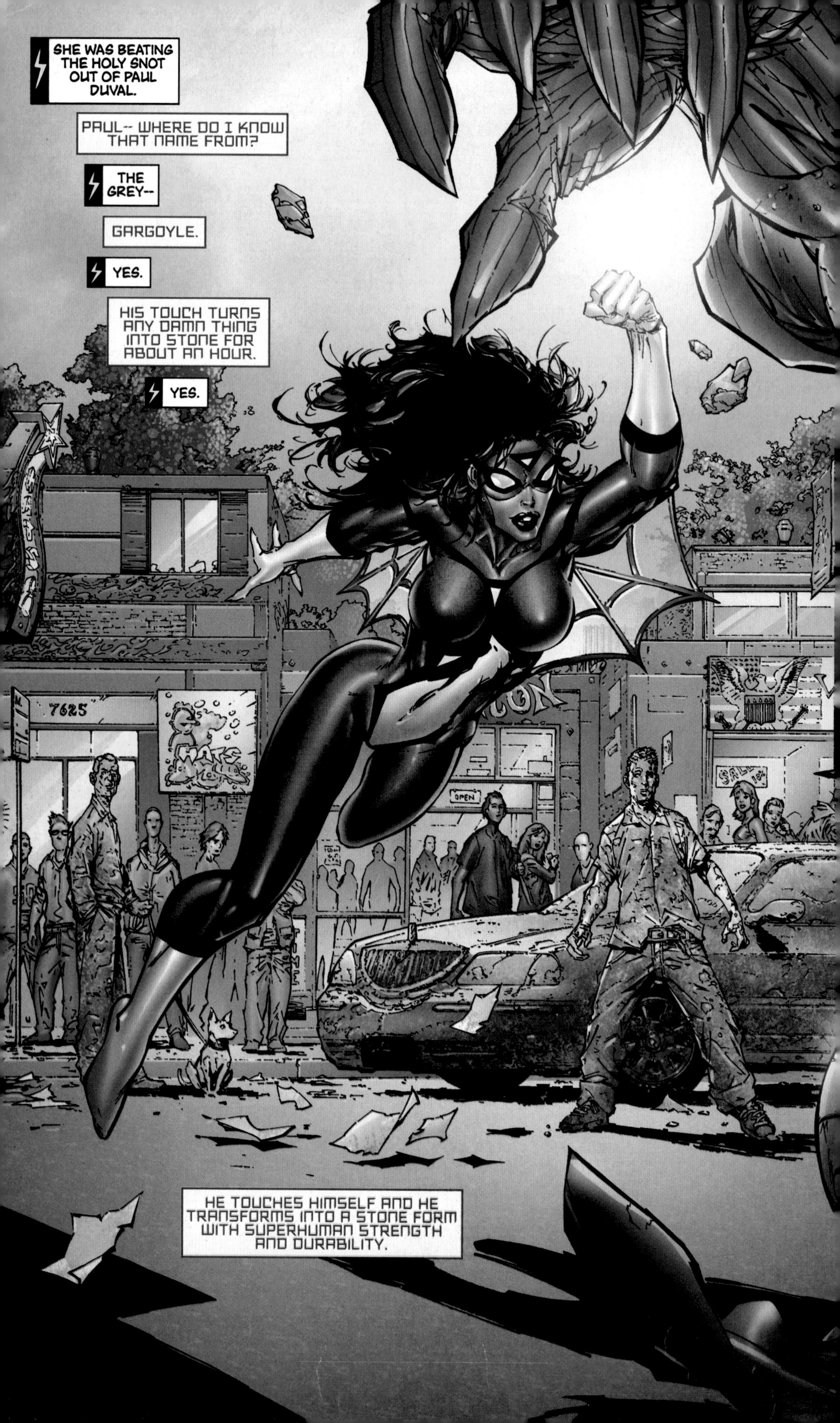

SHE WAS BEATING THE HOLY SNOT OUT OF PAUL DUVAL.
PAUL-- WHERE DO I KNOW THAT NAME FROM?
THE GREY--
GARGOYLE.
YES.
HIS TOUCH TURNS ANY DAMN THING INTO STONE FOR ABOUT AN HOUR.
YES.
7625
OPEN
HE TOUCHES HIMSELF AND HE TRANSFORMS INTO A STONE FORM WITH SUPERHUMAN STRENGTH AND DURABILITY.

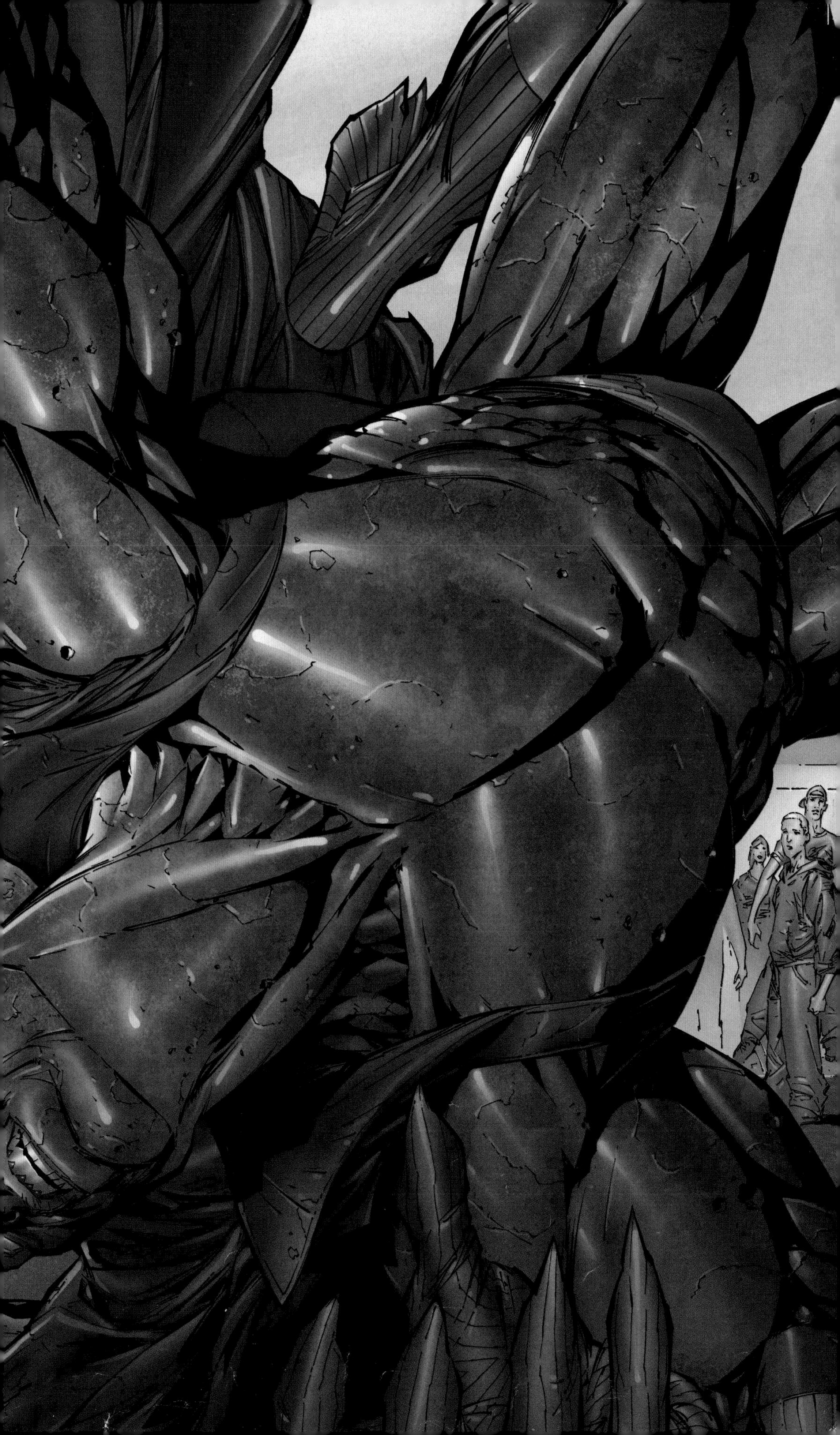

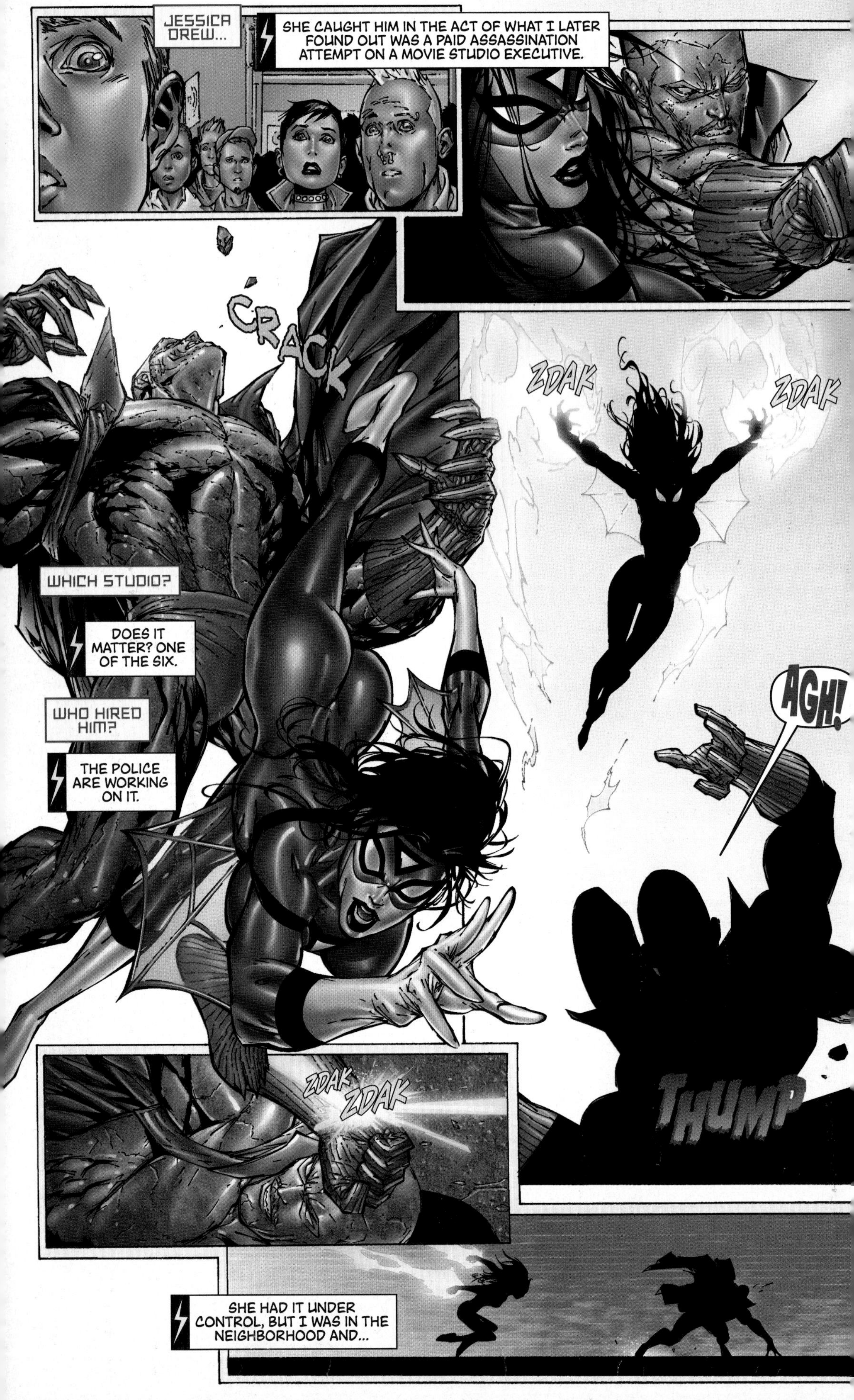

JESSICA DREW...
SHE CAUGHT HIM IN THE ACT OF WHAT I LATER FOUND OUT WAS A PAID ASSASSINATION ATTEMPT ON A MOVIE STUDIO EXECUTIVE.
CRACK
WHICH STUDIO?
DOES IT MATTER? ONE OF THE SIX.
WHO HIRED HIM?
THE POLICE ARE WORKING ON IT.
ZDAK
ZDAK
AGH!
ZDAK
ZDAK
THUMP
SHE HAD IT UNDER CONTROL, BUT I WAS IN THE NEIGHBORHOOD AND...

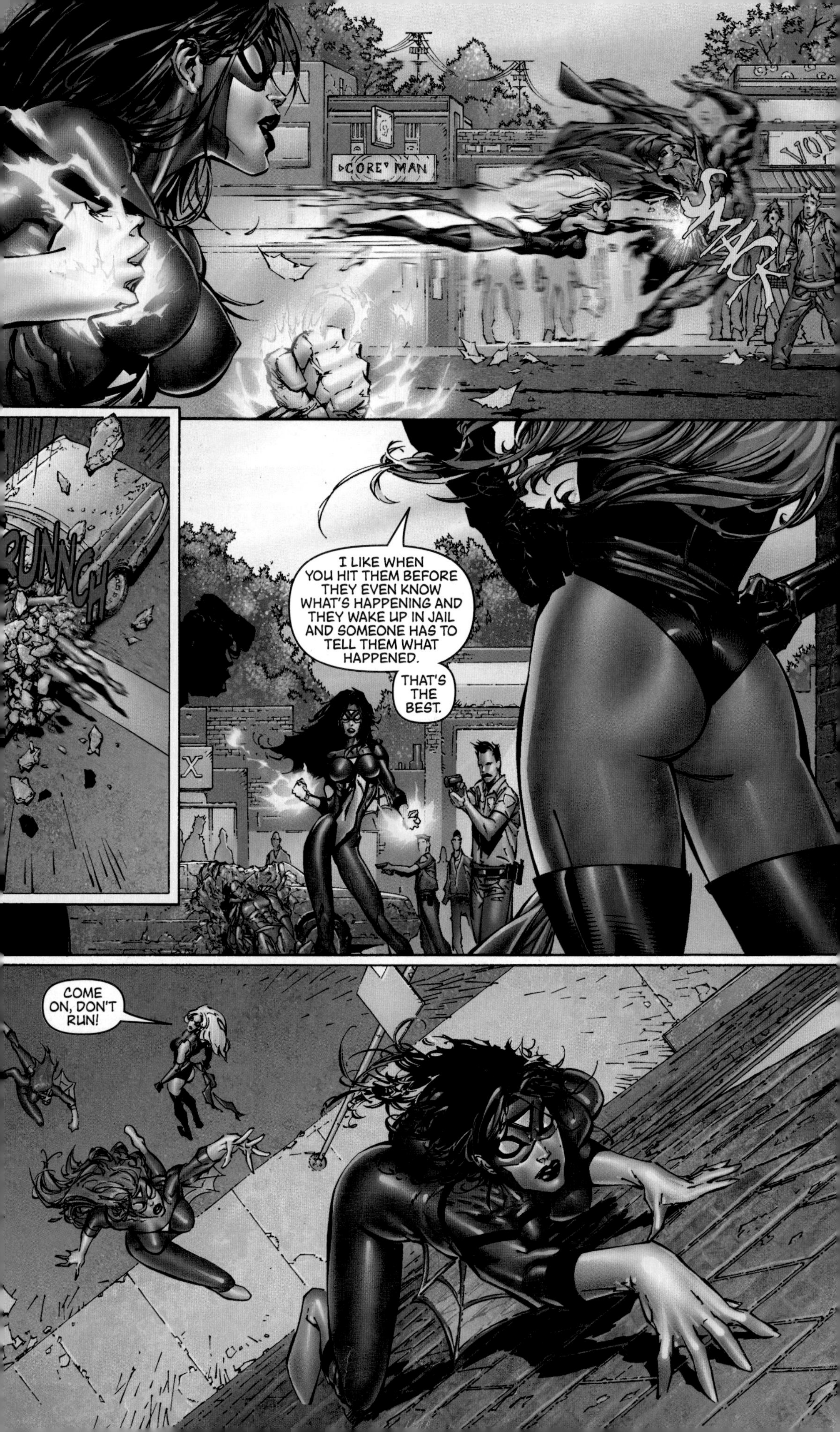
CORE' MAN
SMACK
RUNNCH
I LIKE WHEN YOU HIT THEM BEFORE THEY EVEN KNOW WHAT'S HAPPENING AND THEY WAKE UP IN JAIL AND SOMEONE HAS TO TELL THEM WHAT HAPPENED.
THAT'S THE BEST.
COME ON, DON'T RUN!

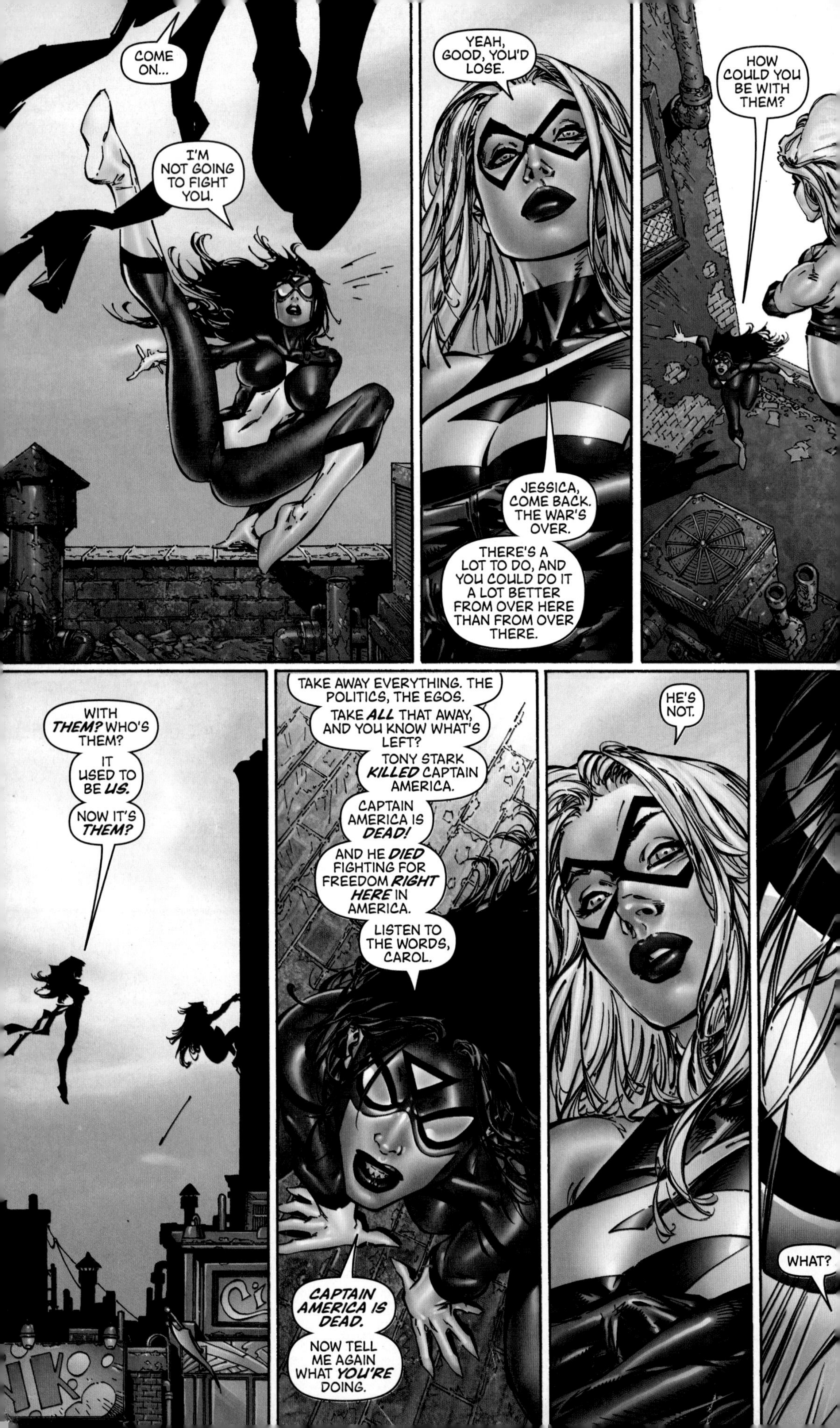
COME ON...
I'M NOT GOING TO FIGHT YOU.
YEAH, GOOD, YOU'D LOSE.
JESSICA, COME BACK. THE WAR'S OVER.
THERE'S A LOT TO DO, AND YOU COULD DO IT A LOT BETTER FROM OVER HERE THAN FROM OVER THERE.
HOW COULD YOU BE WITH THEM?
WITH *THEM?* WHO'S THEM?
IT USED TO BE *US.*
NOW IT'S *THEM?*
TAKE AWAY EVERYTHING. THE POLITICS, THE EGOS.
TAKE *ALL* THAT AWAY, AND YOU KNOW WHAT'S LEFT?
TONY STARK *KILLED* CAPTAIN AMERICA.
CAPTAIN AMERICA IS *DEAD!*
AND HE *DIED* FIGHTING FOR FREEDOM *RIGHT HERE* IN AMERICA.
LISTEN TO THE WORDS, CAROL.
CAPTAIN AMERICA IS DEAD.
NOW TELL ME AGAIN WHAT *YOU'RE* DOING.
HE'S NOT.
WHAT?

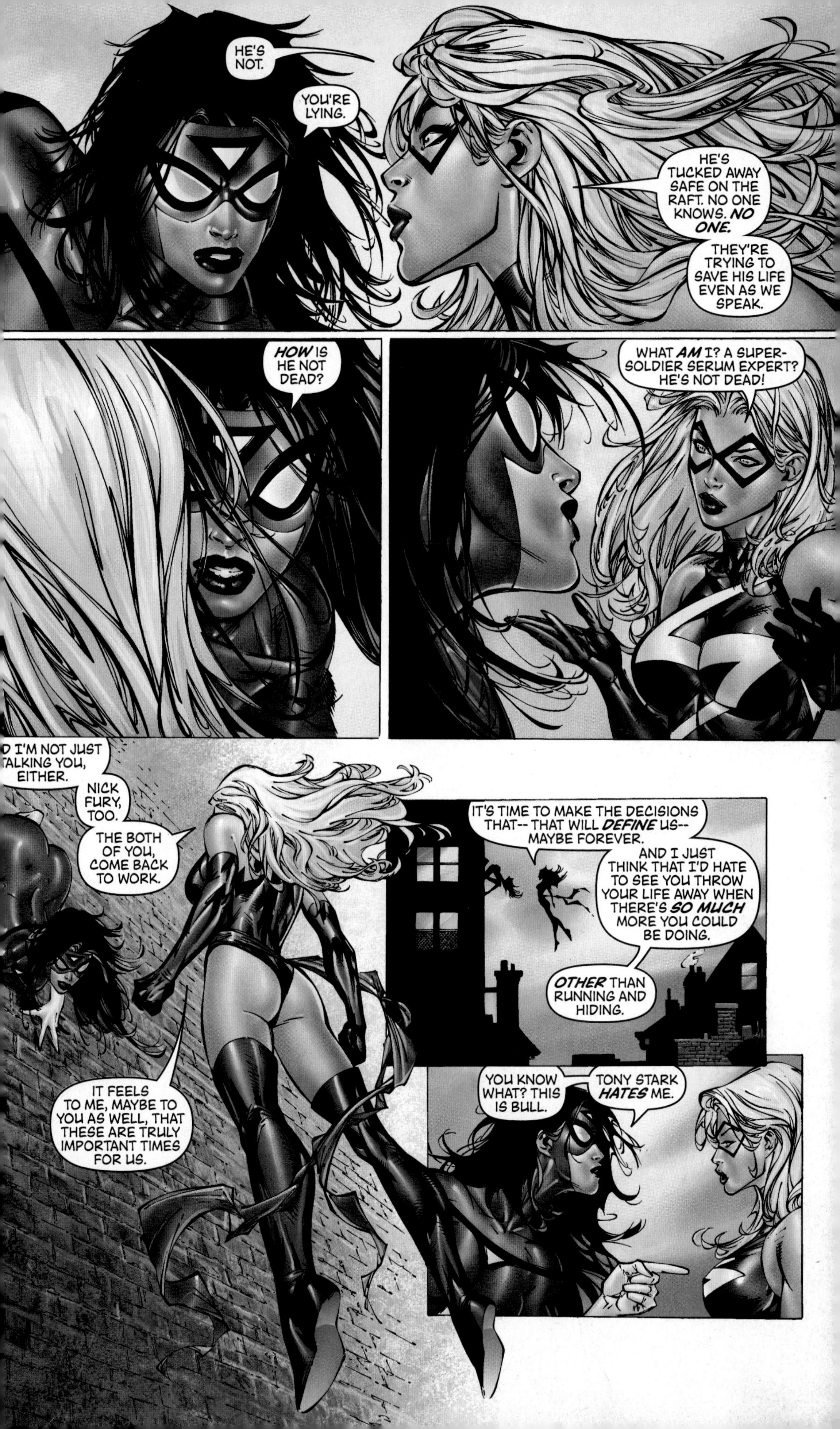

HE'S NOT.
YOU'RE LYING.
HE'S TUCKED AWAY SAFE ON THE RAFT. NO ONE KNOWS. ***NO ONE.***
THEY'RE TRYING TO SAVE HIS LIFE EVEN AS WE SPEAK.
HOW IS HE NOT DEAD?
WHAT ***AM*** I? A SUPER-SOLDIER SERUM EXPERT? HE'S NOT DEAD!
D I'M NOT JUST TALKING YOU, EITHER.
NICK FURY, TOO.
THE BOTH OF YOU, COME BACK TO WORK.
IT FEELS TO ME, MAYBE TO YOU AS WELL, THAT THESE ARE TRULY IMPORTANT TIMES FOR US.
IT'S TIME TO MAKE THE DECISIONS THAT-- THAT WILL ***DEFINE*** US-- MAYBE FOREVER.
AND I JUST THINK THAT I'D HATE TO SEE YOU THROW YOUR LIFE AWAY WHEN THERE'S ***SO MUCH*** MORE YOU COULD BE DOING.
OTHER THAN RUNNING AND HIDING.
YOU KNOW WHAT? THIS IS BULL.
TONY STARK ***HATES*** ME.

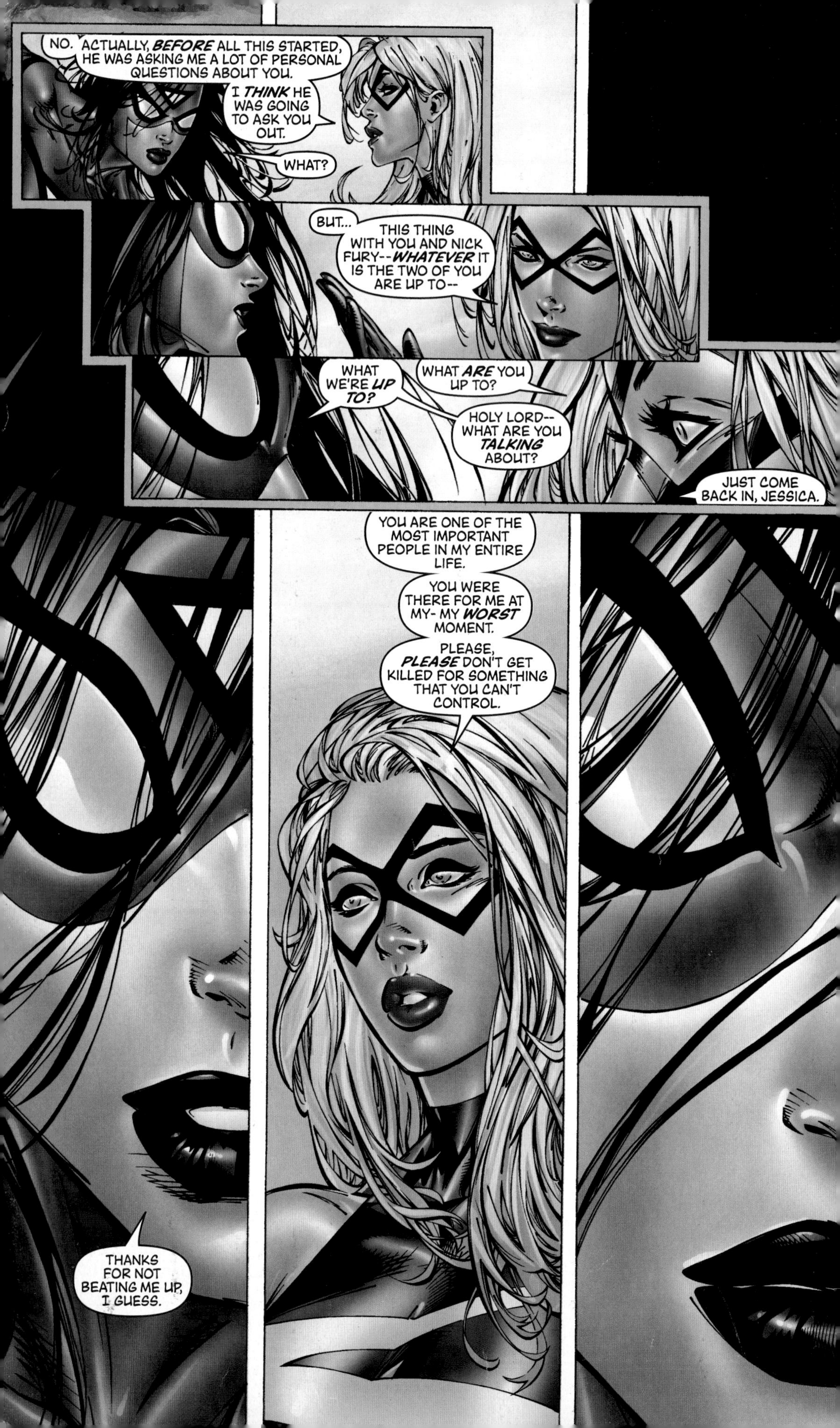
NO.
ACTUALLY, BEFORE ALL THIS STARTED, HE WAS ASKING ME A LOT OF PERSONAL QUESTIONS ABOUT YOU.
I THINK HE WAS GOING TO ASK YOU OUT.
WHAT?
BUT...
THIS THING WITH YOU AND NICK FURY--WHATEVER IT IS THE TWO OF YOU ARE UP TO--
WHAT WE'RE UP TO?
WHAT ARE YOU UP TO?
HOLY LORD-- WHAT ARE YOU TALKING ABOUT?
JUST COME BACK IN, JESSICA.
YOU ARE ONE OF THE MOST IMPORTANT PEOPLE IN MY ENTIRE LIFE.
YOU WERE THERE FOR ME AT MY- MY WORST MOMENT.
PLEASE, PLEASE DON'T GET KILLED FOR SOMETHING THAT YOU CAN'T CONTROL.
THANKS FOR NOT BEATING ME UP, I GUESS.

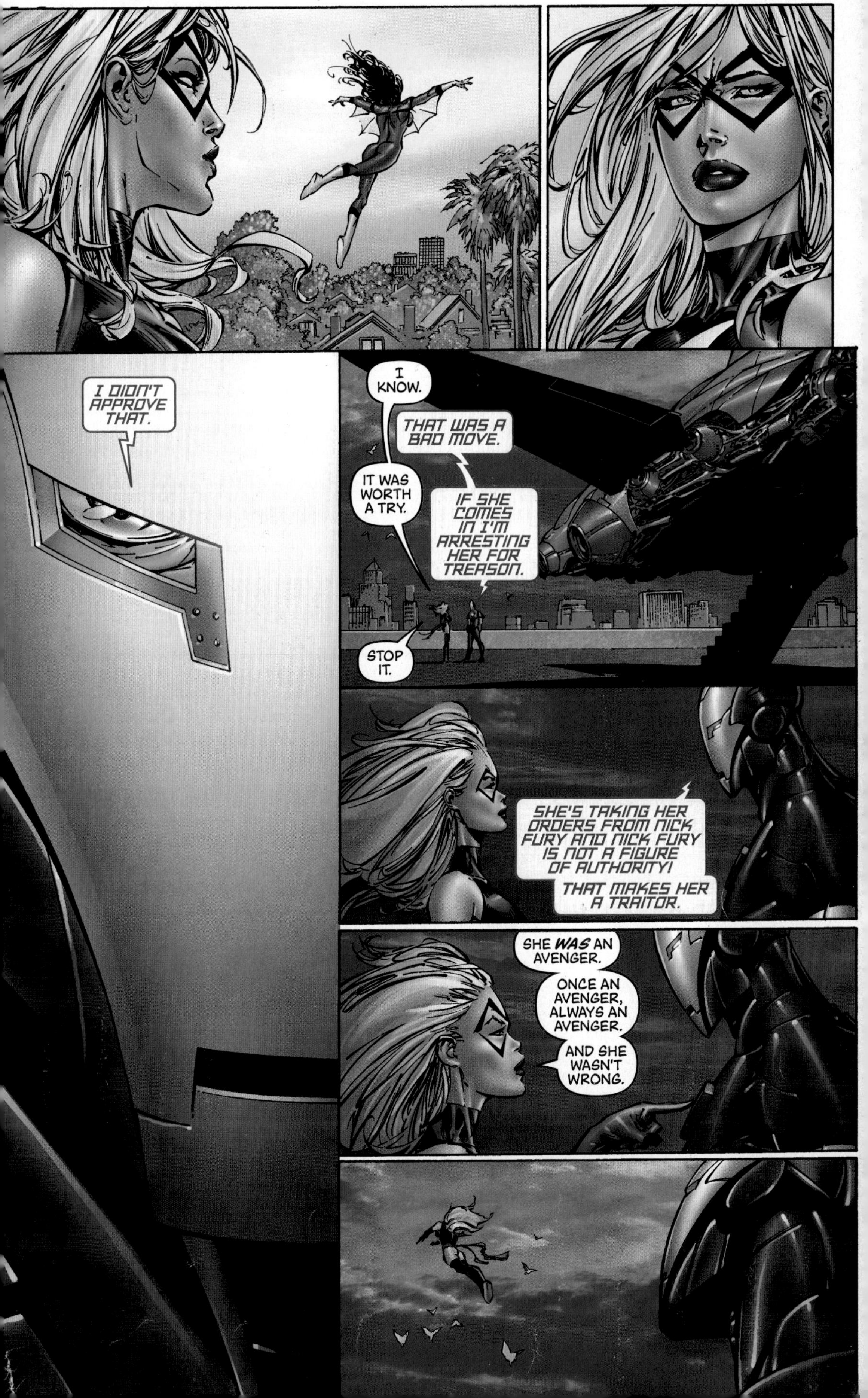

I DIDN'T APPROVE THAT.
I KNOW.
THAT WAS A BAD MOVE.
IT WAS WORTH A TRY.
IF SHE COMES IN I'M ARRESTING HER FOR TREASON.
STOP IT.
SHE'S TAKING HER ORDERS FROM NICK FURY AND NICK FURY IS NOT A FIGURE OF AUTHORITY!
THAT MAKES HER A TRAITOR.
SHE *WAS* AN AVENGER.
ONCE AN AVENGER, ALWAYS AN AVENGER.
AND SHE WASN'T WRONG.

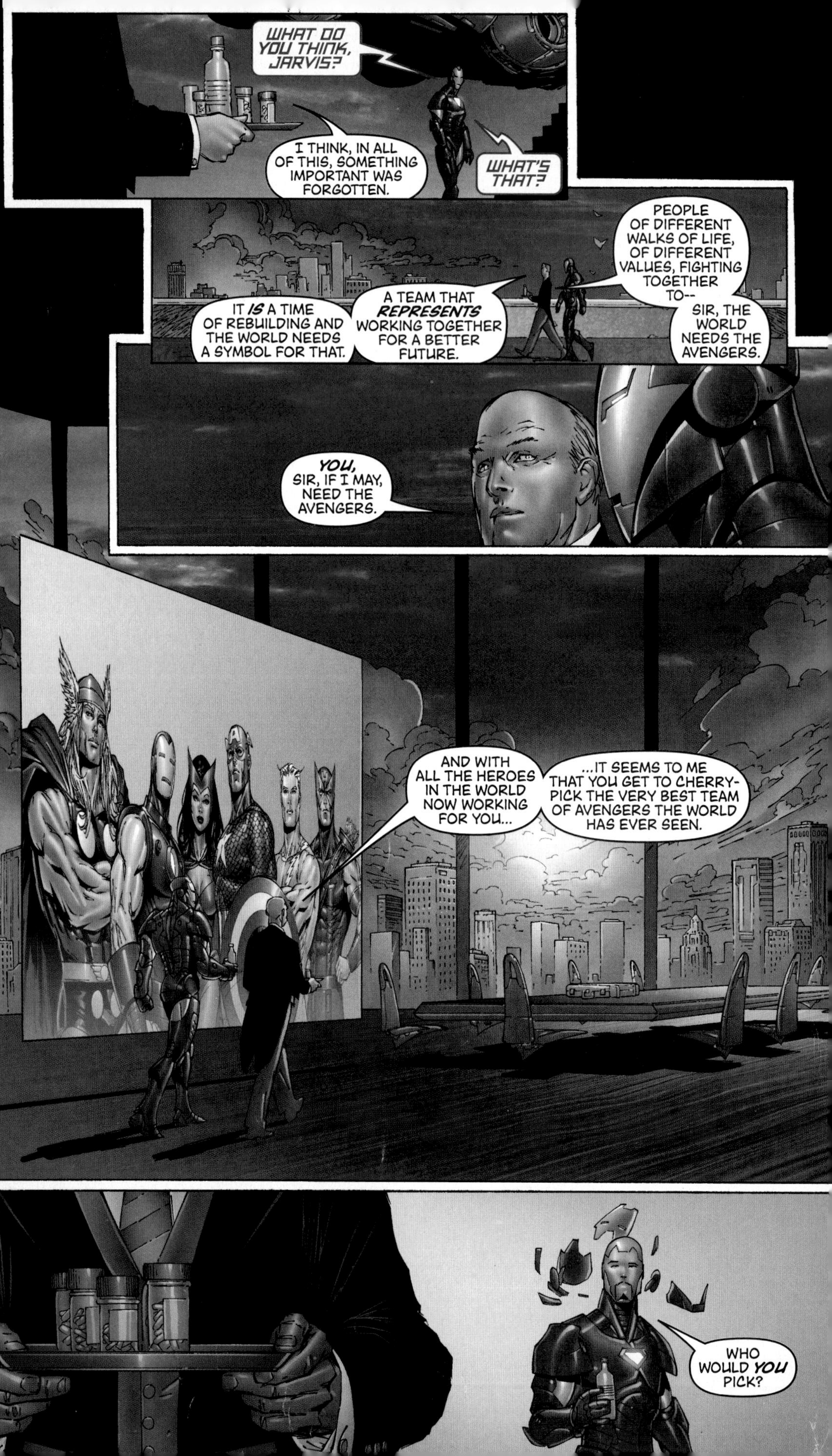
WHAT DO YOU THINK, JARVIS?
I THINK, IN ALL OF THIS, SOMETHING IMPORTANT WAS FORGOTTEN.
WHAT'S THAT?
IT *IS* A TIME OF REBUILDING AND THE WORLD NEEDS A SYMBOL FOR THAT.
A TEAM THAT *REPRESENTS* WORKING TOGETHER FOR A BETTER FUTURE.
PEOPLE OF DIFFERENT WALKS OF LIFE, OF DIFFERENT VALUES, FIGHTING TOGETHER TO--
SIR, THE WORLD NEEDS THE AVENGERS.
YOU, SIR, IF I MAY, NEED THE AVENGERS.
AND WITH ALL THE HEROES IN THE WORLD NOW WORKING FOR YOU...
...IT SEEMS TO ME THAT YOU GET TO CHERRY-PICK THE VERY BEST TEAM OF AVENGERS THE WORLD HAS EVER SEEN.
WHO WOULD *YOU* PICK?

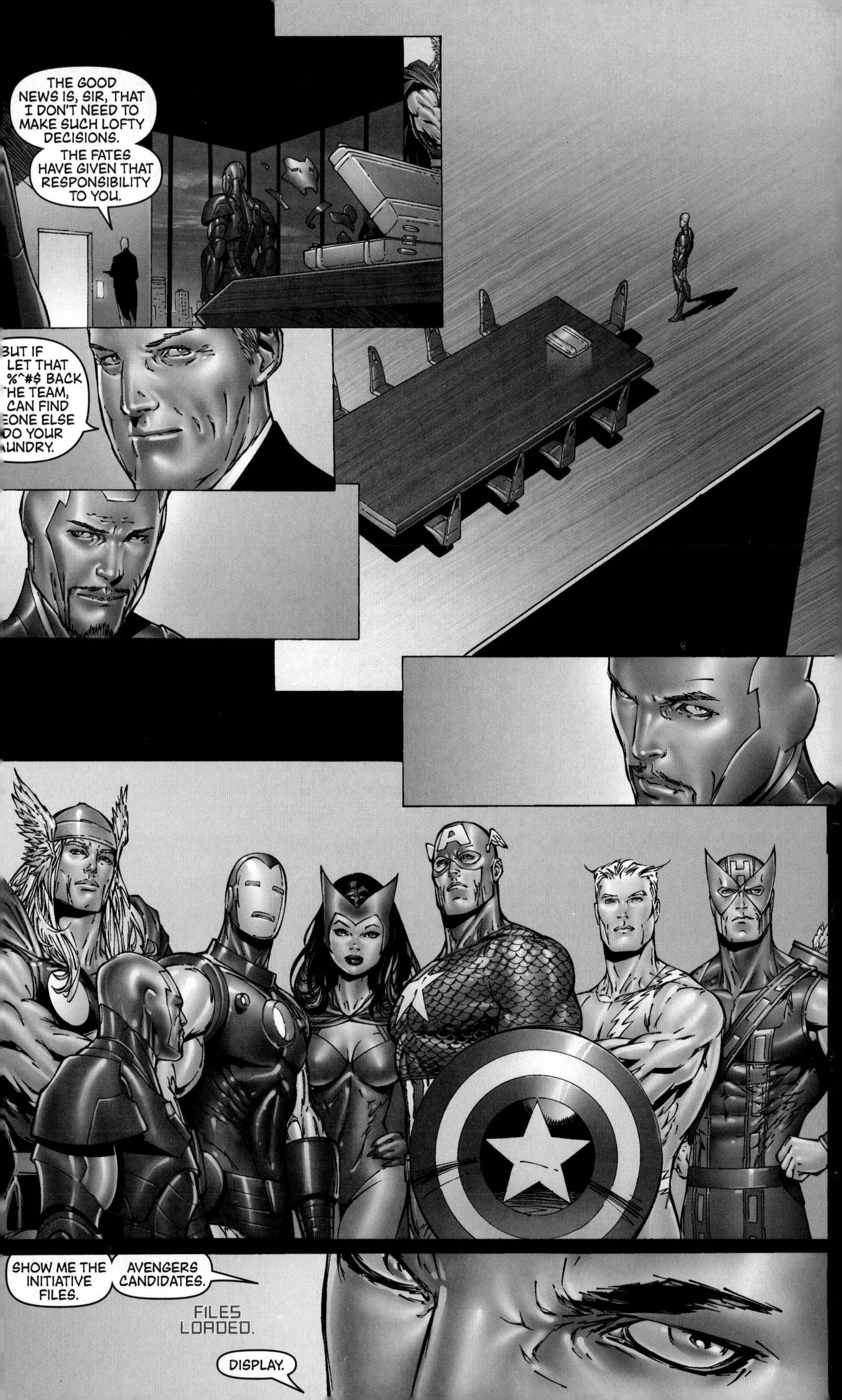
THE GOOD NEWS IS, SIR, THAT I DON'T NEED TO MAKE SUCH LOFTY DECISIONS.
THE FATES HAVE GIVEN THAT RESPONSIBILITY TO YOU.
BUT IF LET THAT %^#$ BACK HE TEAM, CAN FIND EONE ELSE DO YOUR UNDRY.
SHOW ME THE INITIATIVE FILES.
AVENGERS CANDIDATES.
FILES LOADED.
DISPLAY.

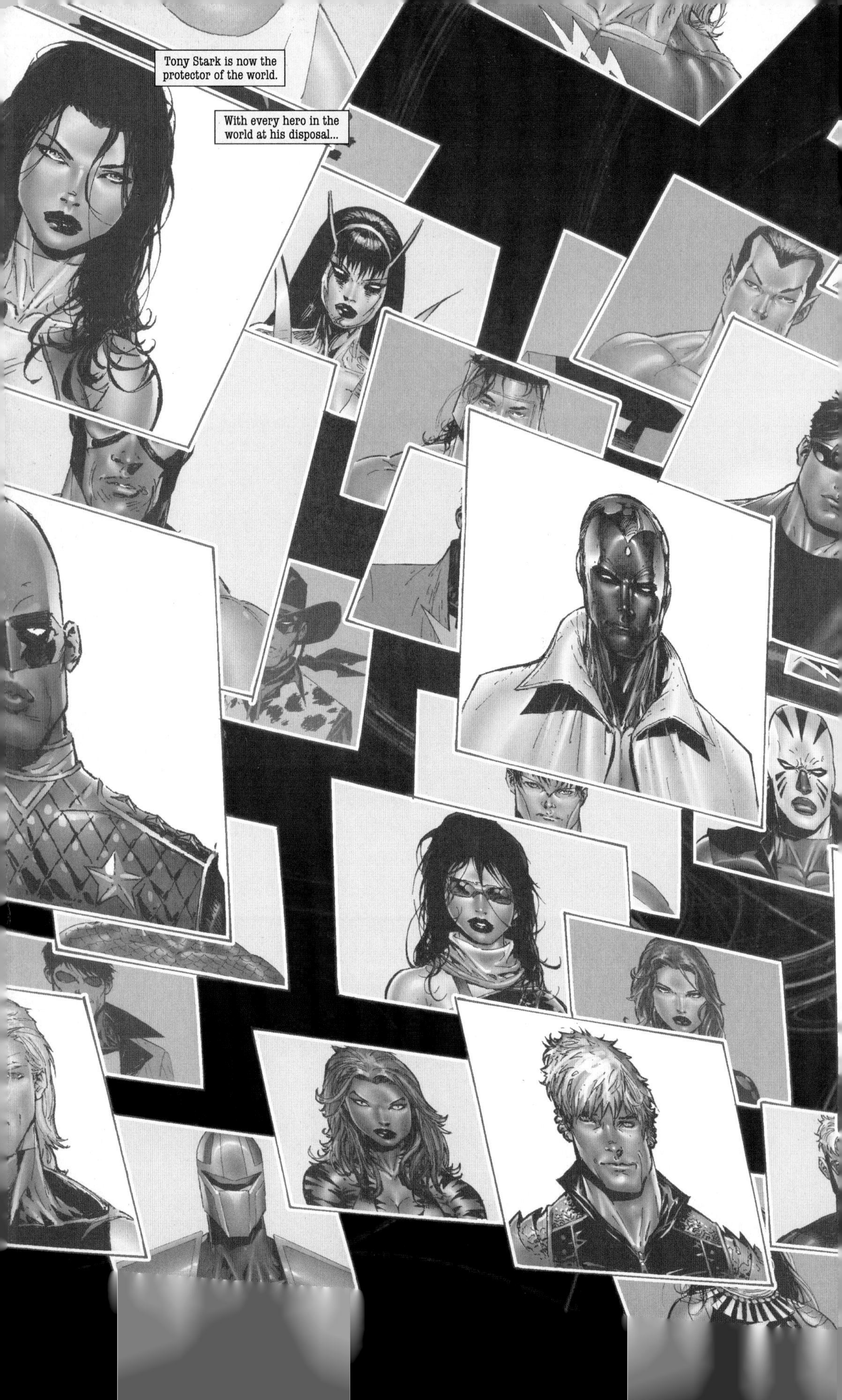
Tony Stark is now the protector of the world.
With every hero in the world at his disposal...

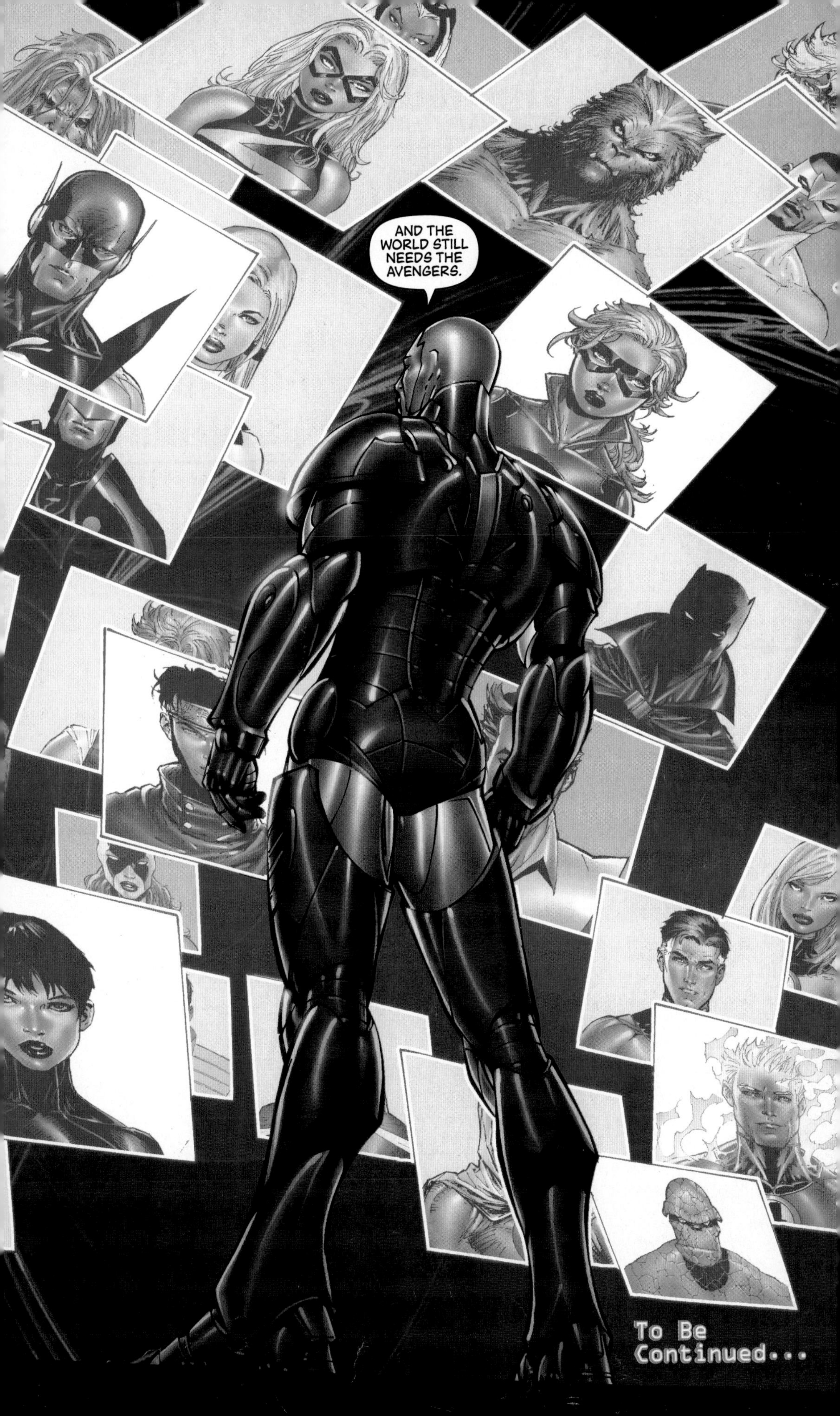
AND THE WORLD STILL NEEDS THE AVENGERS.
To Be Continued...

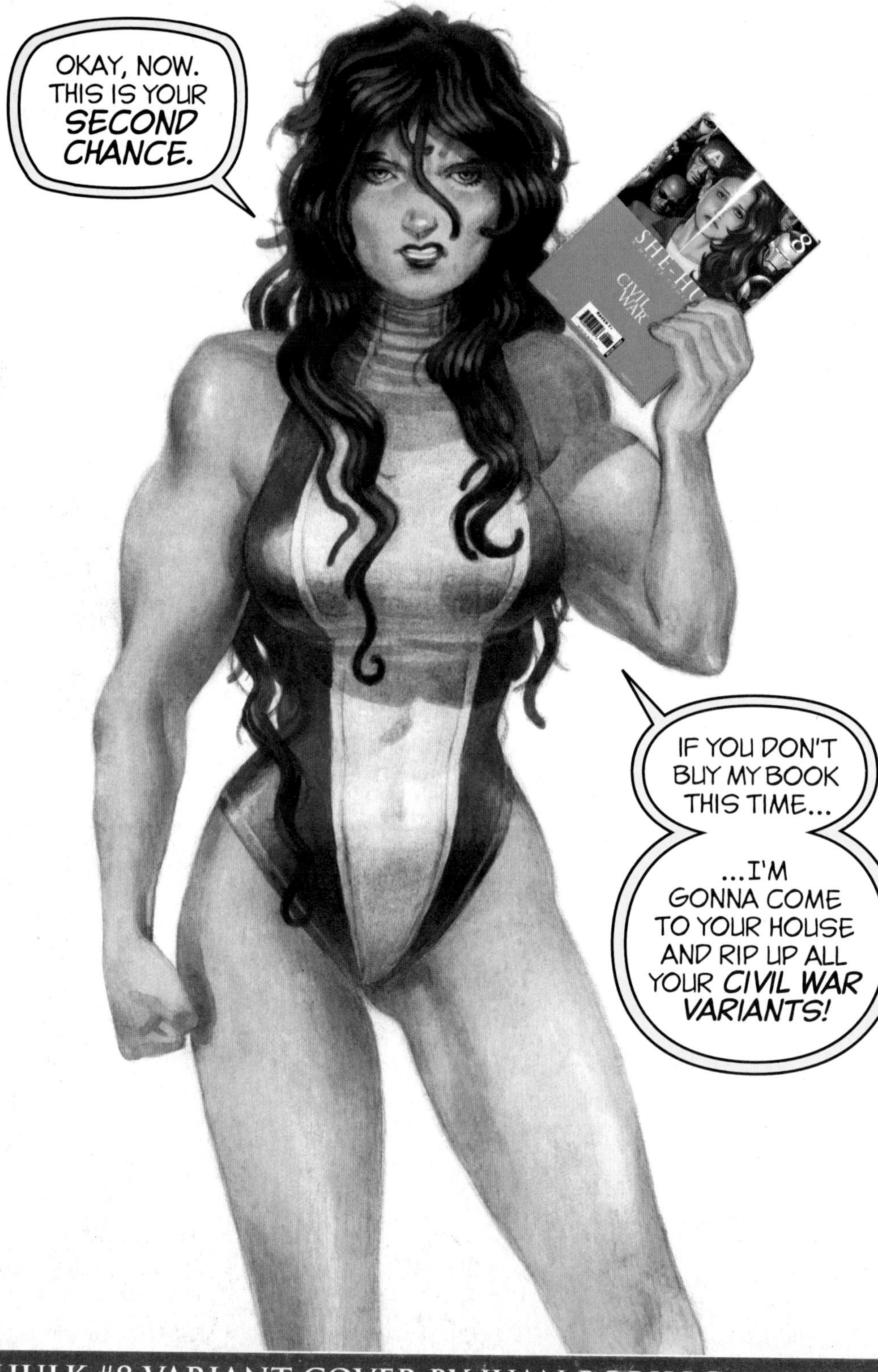
OKAY, NOW. THIS IS YOUR *SECOND CHANCE.*
IF YOU DON'T BUY MY BOOK THIS TIME...
...I'M GONNA COME TO YOUR HOUSE AND RIP UP ALL YOUR *CIVIL WAR VARIANTS!*

SHE-HULK #8 VARIANT COVER BY JUAN BOBILLO

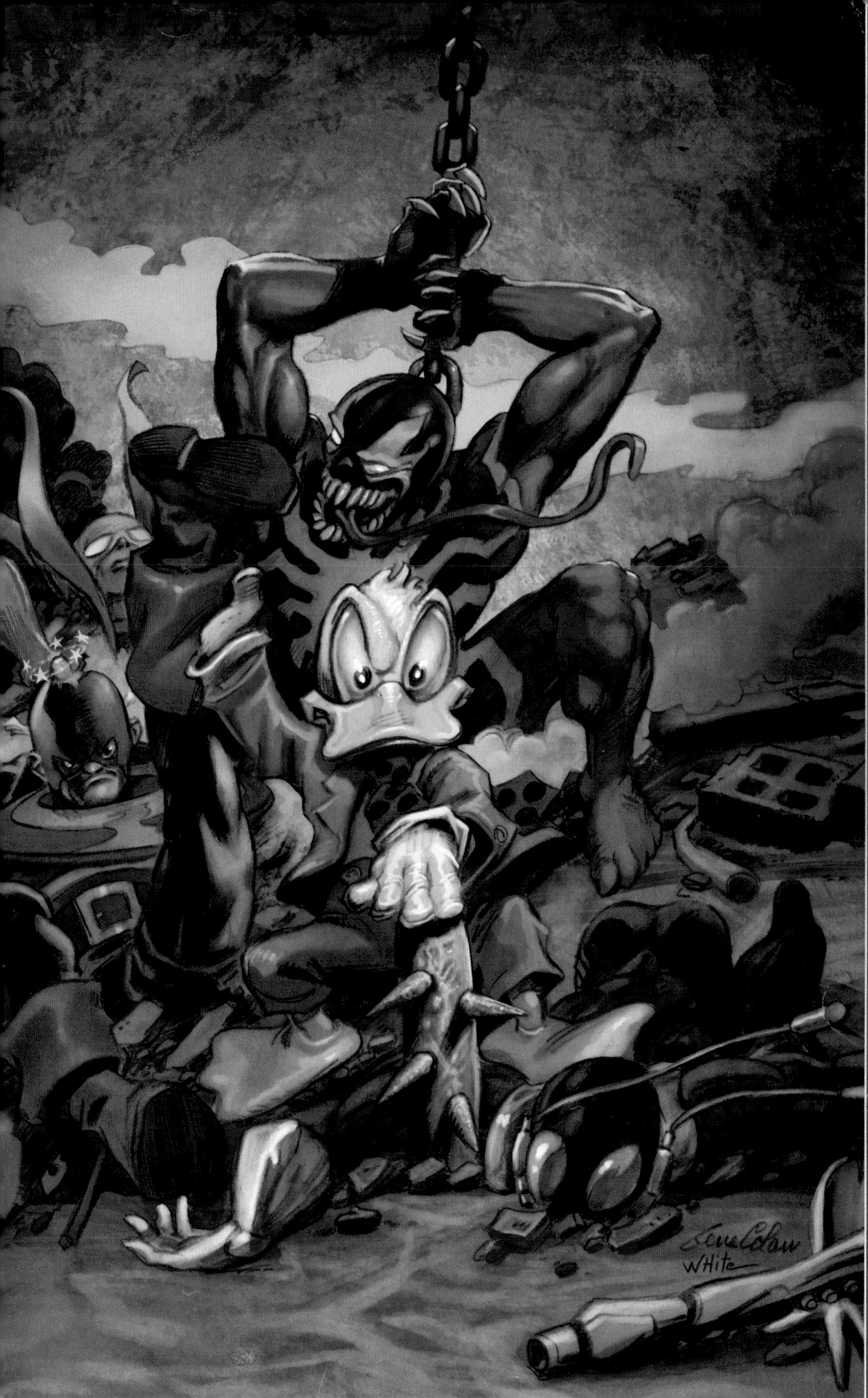
Gene Colan
WHite

IL WAR: CHOOSING SIDES VARIANT COVER BY GENE COLAN

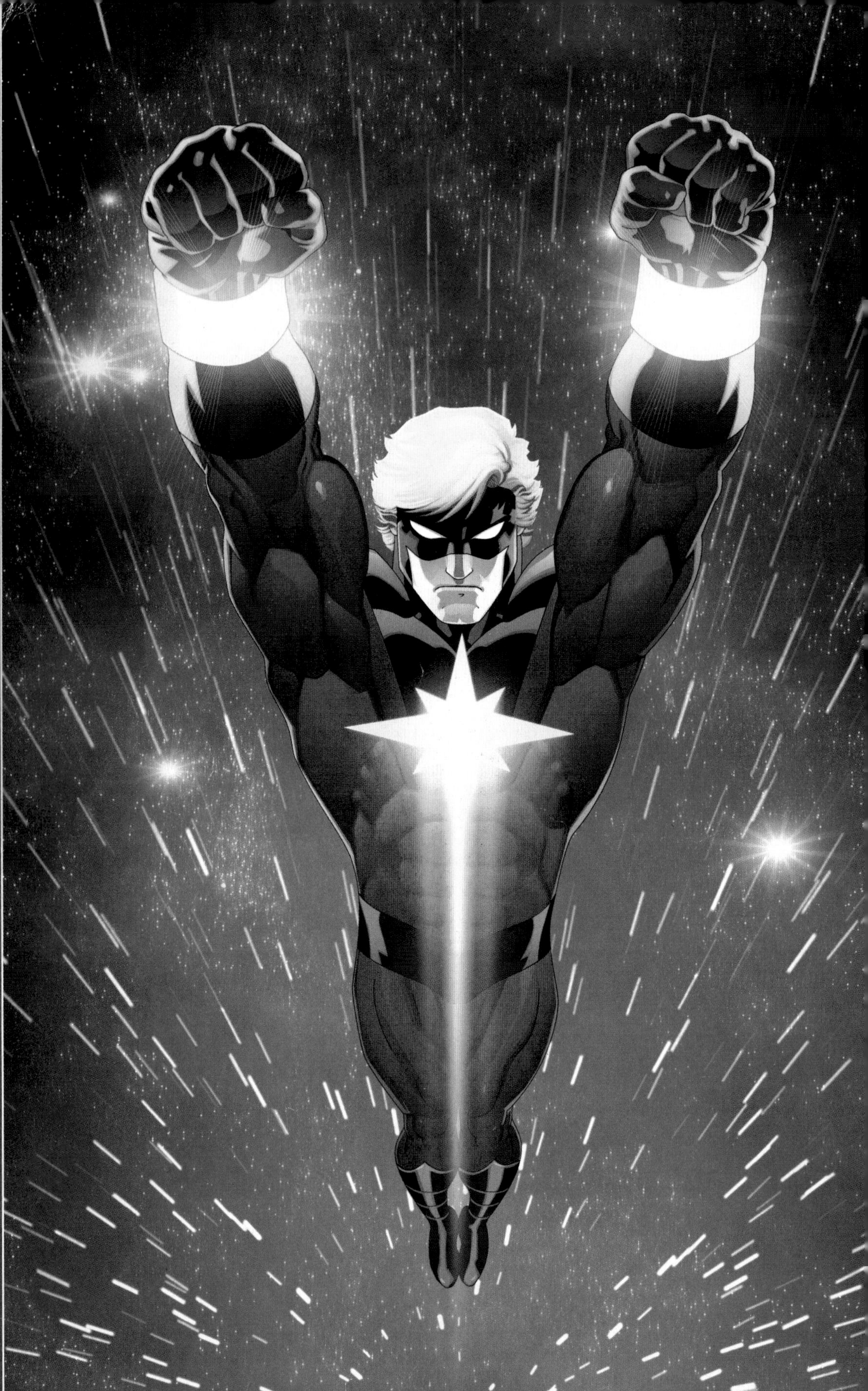

CIVIL WAR: THE RETURN VARIANT COVER BY ED MCGUINNE

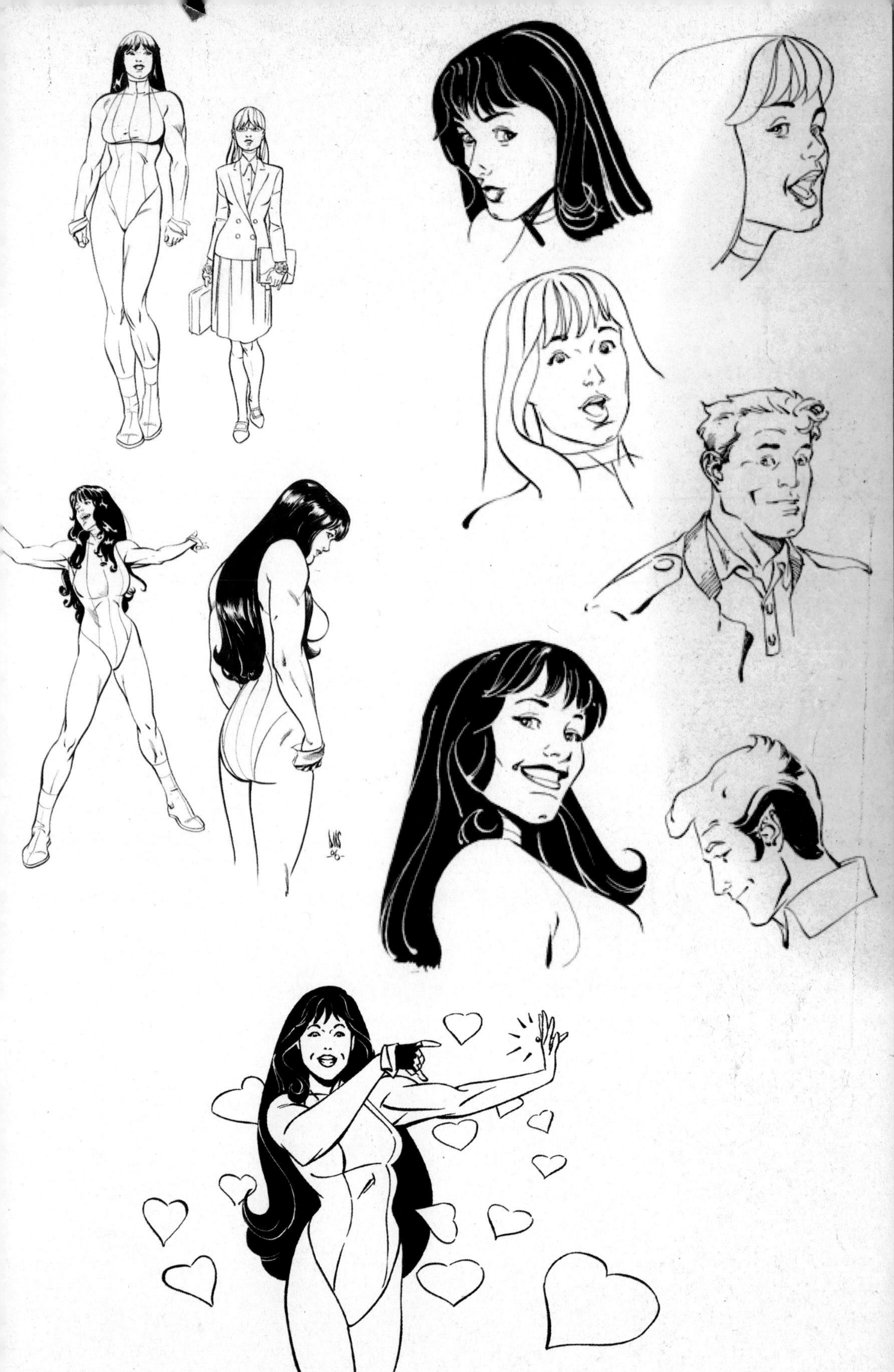

PWS
-96-

SHE-HULK SKETCHES BY PAUL SMITH